Transatlantic Transformations of Romanticism

Transatlantic Transformations of Romanticism

*Aesthetics, Subjectivity and
the Environment*

Mark Sandy

EDINBURGH
University Press

Edinburgh University Press is one of the leading university presses in the UK. We publish academic books and journals in our selected subject areas across the humanities and social sciences, combining cutting-edge scholarship with high editorial and production values to produce academic works of lasting importance. For more information visit our website: edinburghuniversitypress.com

Edinburgh University Press Ltd
The Tun – Holyrood Road, 12(2f) Jackson's Entry, Edinburgh EH8 8PJ

First published in hardback by Edinburgh University Press 2021

Typeset in 11/13 Adobe Sabon by
IDSUK (DataConnection) Ltd,
printed and bound by CPI Group (UK) Ltd
Croydon, CR0 4YY

A CIP record for this book is available from the British Library

ISBN 978 1 4744 2148 5 (hardback)
ISBN 978 1 3995 0836 0 (paperback)
ISBN 978 1 4744 2149 2 (webready PDF)
ISBN 978 1 4744 2150 8 (epub)

Contents

Acknowledgements

I first caught a glimmer of the idea for what became this book when I gave a lecture on reading forms of Romanticism in the fiction of Saul Bellow in a lecture series in 2006. This lecture series was the first of several similar events that I co-organised with Michael O'Neill and Sarah Wootton at Durham University under the auspices of the 'Romantic Dialogues and Legacies' Research Group, supported by additional funding from the Institute of Advanced Study and the Department of English Studies. Such an encouraging intellectual environment helped me to develop further my thinking about questions of Romantic dialogue and inheritance, more generally, and how these issues were, more specifically, a vital part of transatlantic literary and cultural encounters. I have been extremely fortunate to count both Michael and Sarah as colleagues and friends. A great deal of my thinking about this project has been usefully shaped and sharpened through the many insightful and stimulating discussions that I have shared with them.

I am also immensely indebted to many other people who have, over the time that it has taken to fashion this book into its final form, contributed in innumerable and varied ways to its completion: Alex Abichou, William Bainbridge, Audrey Bowron, Kostas Boyiopolous, Frederick Burwick, Madeleine Callaghan, Yoonjoung Choi, Stefano Cracolici, Richard Cronin, Sofia Hofkosh, Simon J. James, Greg Kucich, Edward Larrissy, Beth Lau, Helen Leatherland, Yimon Lo, Michael Mack, Charles Mahoney, Vincent Newey, Daniel Norman, Stephen Olsen-Smith, Catherine Paine, Seamus Perry, Stephen Regan, Fiona Robertson, Nicholas Roe, Robert Sharkie, Jonathon Shears, Michael Sinatra, Andrew Stauffer, Barbara and Ray Storr, Sharon Tai, Jenny Terry, Samuel Thomas, Heidi Thomson, Paige Tovey, Lisa Vargo, J. R. Watson and Duncan Wu.

In the last ten years or so, I have been fortunate enough to discuss some, if not all, of my ideas about the complexity of Romanticism and its transatlantic legacies at international conferences or events, including a recent conference on 'Keats Reading / Reading

Keats' hosted by the University of Notre Dame in London (2018), the annual 'Keats Foundation Conference' (2015), 'Performance in American Fiction' (2011) and 'Toni Morrison: New Directions' (2009). I am grateful, too, to have had the opportunity to give papers on authors and topics related to this study at the University of Sheffield, Dundee University and the University of Oxford.

Over the past fifteen years or more, I have been delighted to share my ideas and thoughts about transatlantic Romantic inheritance and disinheritance discussed in the pages that follow with my taught postgraduate and undergraduate students in Jewish American Fiction seminars, as well as with those undergraduates studying modules in American Poetry and American Fiction. I hope that these students found our deliberations, reflections and discussions as helpful and illuminating as I certainly have.

I am extremely grateful to Vicky Penn, whose methodical attention to detail and care proved invaluable as a research assistant in the preparation of the finalised typescript of this book for press, as well as the bibliography, index and other critical apparatus. Many thanks are owed to Michelle Houston at Edinburgh University Press for her initial interest in, and support of, this project from an early stage, as well as for her continued support of my research related to this book. Thanks to Ersev Ersoy for all her kindness and patience over the time it took for me to submit the finalised version of the typescript to the press. I am also grateful to Cathy Falconer for all her acuity, sensitivity and skill in preparing the text of my book for publication. I am also appreciative of the encouraging and insightful advice I received from the two anonymous readers when I first proposed this book to Edinburgh University Press.

I am grateful to Durham University for the award in 2018 of two terms of Research Leave (including an additional term of leave in Michaelmas), which significantly assisted with the completion of my research for this book. I equally appreciate the Faculty of Arts and Humanities at Durham funding my research trip to the Special Collections Center, University of Chicago, so that I could consult their holding of Saul Bellow Papers. I am indebted to the courtesy, helpfulness and expertise of all of the librarians at the Special Collections Center, but I would, especially, like to extend my heartfelt thanks to Barbara Gilbert, Ashley Locke Gosselar and Daniel Meyer, who helped make my research visit in January 2019 as pleasurable and as productive as possible. I acknowledge the Special Collections Center at the University of Chicago for their permission to quote from unpublished material held in the Saul

Bellow Papers in Chapter 5, which explores Bellow's response to Romanticism. Much of the research for Chapter 2 on Emerson and Thoreau was conducted with the support of a one-month Visiting Library Fellowship at the Armstrong Browning Library, Baylor University, Texas, during late August and early September 2017. For their warmth, generosity, guidance and expertise I am grateful to Jennifer Borderud, Joshua King, Christi Klempnauer and Melvin Scheutz at the Armstrong Browning Library.

Completed during the United Kingdom's Covid-19 lockdown of 2020, the finishing of this book may have tested more than usual the enduring patience, understanding, friendship, humour and love of my partner, Hazel, and my son, Michael. Without their love and encouragement, and so much more that they have given me, this book, like others before it, would not have been completed. Hazel's incisive judgement and editorial interventions have without doubt made this a better book than it would otherwise have been. Any obfuscations, lapses or inaccuracies that remain are of my own making.

Many thanks also to Nicholas Roe, editor of *Romanticism*, for permission to draw on material, reworked in Chapter 5, which originally appeared as '"Webbed with Golden Lines": Reading Saul Bellow's Romanticism', *Romanticism* 14.1 (2008): 57–67; and Jenny Terry and Kathryn Nicol, co-editors of *MELUS: Toni Morrison: New Directions*, for permission to recast in Chapter 6 my article '"Cut by Rainbow": Tales, Tellers, and Reimagining Wordsworth's Pastoral Poetics in Toni Morrison's *Beloved* and *A Mercy*', *MELUS* 36.2 (2011): 35–51. For permission to reproduce revised matter in Chapter 3 and the coda that originally appeared, respectively, in *Romantic Presences in the Twentieth Century* (2012), ed. Mark Sandy, and *The Persistence of Beauty: Victorians to Moderns* (2015), ed. Michael O'Neill, Mark Sandy and Sarah Wootton, I acknowledge the editors of these collections.

Writing these acknowledgements presses home to me even more keenly the fact that Michael O'Neill is no longer with us, having passed away just over seventeen months ago on 21 December 2018. It was my honour and privilege to be supervised by Michael as a doctoral student, to have worked with him for over twenty years and to have been his friend over those years until his untimely death. This book is dedicated to Michael's memory.

Mark Sandy
22 May 2020

Abbreviations

Select List of Frequently Cited Editions and Critical Studies

ASA   Michael O'Neill. *The All-Sustaining Air: Romantic Legacies and Renewals in British, American, and Irish Poetry since 1900*. Oxford: Oxford University Press, 2007.

'ATM'   Saul Bellow. 'A World Too Much with Us'. *Critical Inquiry* 2 (1975): 1–9.

BD   F. Scott Fitzgerald. *The Beautiful and Damned*. Intro. Geoff Dyer. 1922; Harmondsworth: Penguin, 2004.

'BER'   Allan Chavkin. 'Bellow and English Romanticism'. In *Saul Bellow in the 1980s: A Collection of Critical Essays*. Ed. Gloria L. Cronin and L. H. Goldman. East Lansing: Michigan State University Press, 1989, pp. 67–79.

BL   Toni Morrison. *Beloved*. London: Picador-Pan, 1988.

CCWF   A. Nicholas Fargnoli, Michael Golay and W. Hamblin. *A Critical Companion to William Faulkner: A Literary Reference to his Life and Work*. New York: Infobase, 2008.

CH   George Gordon Byron. *Childe Harold's Pilgrimage*. In *Lord Byron: The Major Works*. Ed. Jerome J. McGann. Oxford: Oxford University Press, 2008.

CSB   Victoria Aarons. Ed. *The Cambridge Companion to Saul Bellow*. Cambridge: Cambridge University Press, 2017.

CSF   F. Scott Fitzgerald. *The Cambridge Companion to F. Scott Fitzgerald*. Ed. Ruth Prigozy. Cambridge: Cambridge University Press, 2002.

CU   F. Scott Fitzgerald. *The Stories of F. Scott Fitzgerald: The Crack-Up with Other Pieces and Stories*. Vol. 2. Harmondsworth: Penguin, 1965.

CWE   Ralph Waldo Emerson. *The Collected Works of Ralph Waldo Emerson: Nature, Addresses, and Lectures*. Vol. 1. Ed. Alfred Riggs Ferguson, Joseph Slater and Joseph

Ferguson Carr. Intro. Robert E. Spiller. Cambridge, MA: Belknap-Harvard, 1971.

CWES   Ralph Waldo Emerson. *The Collected Works of Ralph Waldo Emerson: Society and Solitude.* Vol. 8. Ed. Douglas Emory Wilson. Intro. Ronald A. Bosco. Cambridge, MA: Harvard University Press, 2010.

DRI   Joanne Feit Diehl. *Dickinson and the Romantic Imagination.* Princeton: Princeton University Press, 1981.

EDL   Emily Dickinson. *The Letters of Emily Dickinson.* Ed. Thomas H. Johnson and Theodora W. Ward. Cambridge, MA: Belknap, 1958.

ET   Timothy Morton. *The Ecological Thought.* Cambridge, MA: Harvard University Press, 2010.

EWN   Timothy Morton. *Ecology without Nature: Rethinking Environmental Aesthetics.* Cambridge, MA: Harvard University Press, 2007.

FU   Frederick Landis Gwynn and Joseph Leo Blotner. Eds. *Faulkner in the University.* Charlottesville: University of Virginia Press, 1959.

'FVR'   Martin Bidney. 'Faulkner's Variations on Romantic Themes: Blake, Wordsworth, Byron, and Shelley in *Light in August*'. *The Mississippi Quarterly* 38.3 (1985): 277–86.

GG   F. Scott Fitzgerald. *The Great Gatsby.* 1925; Harmondsworth: Penguin, 2006.

GM   Milton R. Stern. *The Golden Moment: The Novels of F. Scott Fitzgerald.* 1970; Chicago: University of Illinois Press, 1971.

H   Toni Morrison. *Home.* London: Vintage, 2012.

HH   Friedrich Nietzsche. *Human All-Too Human: A Book for Free Spirits.* Trans. R. J. Hollingdale. Intro. Richard Schacht. Cambridge: Cambridge University Press, 1996.

HZ   Saul Bellow. *Herzog.* Harmondsworth: Penguin, 1965.

IWF   Theresa M. Towner. *The Cambridge Introduction to William Faulkner.* Cambridge: Cambridge University Press, 2008.

JKL   John Keats. *The Letters of John Keats 1814–1821.* 2 vols. Ed. Hyder Rollins. Cambridge, MA: Harvard University Press, 1958.

LA   William Faulkner. *Light in August.* 1932; London: Picador, 1991.

LSB   Zachary Leader. *The Life of Saul Bellow: Love and Strife 1965–2005.* London: Cape, 2019.

LSF   F. Scott Fitzgerald. *The Letters of F. Scott Fitzgerald.* Ed. Andrew Turnbull. Harmondsworth: Penguin, 1968.

M	Toni Morrison. *A Mercy*. London: Chatto, 2008.
MR	Morris Dickstein. *A Mirror in the Roadway: Literature and the Real World*. Princeton: Princeton University Press, 2005.
MSP	Saul Bellow. *Mr Sammler's Planet*. 1970; Harmondsworth: Penguin, 1972.
NA	Wallace Stevens. *The Necessary Angel: Essays on Reality and Imagination*. New York: Knopf, 1951.
'NPS'	Michael Fredrickson. 'A Note on "The Idiot Boy" as a Possible Source for *The Sound and the Fury*'. *Minnesota Review* 6 (1966): 368–70.
OEW	Helen Vendler. *On Extended Wings: Wallace Stevens' Longer Poems*. Cambridge, MA: Harvard University Press, 1969.
OMC	Rebecca Rio-Jelliffe. *Obscurity's Myriad Components: The Theory and Practice of William Faulkner*. Lewisburg: Bucknell University Press, 2001.
PD	Toni Morrison. *Playing in the Dark: Whiteness and the Literary Imagination*. Cambridge, MA: Harvard University Press, 1992.
PWF	William Faulkner. *The Portable William Faulkner*. Ed. Malcolm Cowley. 1948; London: Penguin-Viking, 1977.
R	Saul Bellow. *Ravelstein*. Harmondsworth: Penguin, 2000.
'RIB'	Allan Chavkin. 'The Romantic Imagination of Saul Bellow'. In *English Romanticism and Modern Fiction*. Ed. Allan Chavkin. New York: AMS, 1993, pp. 113–38.
RPT	Mark Sandy. Ed. *Romantic Presences in the Twentieth Century*. Farnham: Ashgate, 2012.
RS	Max F. Schulz. *Radical Sophistication: Studies in Contemporary Jewish-American Novelists*. Athens: Ohio University Press, 1969.
SB	Tony Tanner. *Saul Bellow*. London and Edinburgh: Boyd, 1965.
SBL	Saul Bellow. *Saul Bellow: Letters*. Ed. Benjamin Taylor. Harmondsworth: Viking-Penguin, 2010.
SBVR	Daniel Fuchs. *Saul Bellow: Vision and Revision*. Madison: University of Wisconsin Press, 1974.
SD	Saul Bellow. *Seize the Day*. 1956; Harmondsworth: Penguin, 1988.
SFTF	Jackson R. Bryer, Ruth Prigozy and Milton R. Stern. Eds. *F. Scott Fitzgerald in the Twenty-First Century*. Tuscaloosa: University of Alabama Press, 2003.
SNSM	Tony Tanner. *Scenes of Nature, Signs of Men*. Cambridge: Cambridge University Press, 1987.

SPP   Percy Bysshe Shelley. *Shelley's Poetry and Prose*. Ed. Donald H. Reiman and Neil Fraistat. 1977; New York: Norton, 2002.

SSF   John Kuehl. *F. Scott Fitzgerald: A Study of the Short Fiction*. Twayne's Studies in Short Fiction. Series 22. Boston: Hall, 1991.

TN   F. Scott Fitzgerald. *Tender is the Night*. 1934; Harmondsworth: Penguin, 1986.

TOO   Toni Morrison. *The Origin of Others*. The Charles Eliot Norton Lecture. 2016. Foreword Ta-Neshisi Coates. Cambridge, MA: Harvard University Press, 2017.

TPE   Ralph Waldo Emerson. *The Portable Emerson*. Ed. Carl Bode and Malcolm Cowley. Harmondsworth: Viking-Penguin, 1981.

TPT   Henry David Thoreau. *The Portable Thoreau*. Ed. Carl Bode. 1965; Harmondsworth: Viking-Penguin, 1987.

TSF   William Faulkner. *The Sound and the Fury*. 1929; London: Picador, 1993.

TWCI   David L. Minter. Ed. *Twentieth-Century Interpretations of 'Light in August'*. Englewood Cliffs, NJ: Prentice Hall, 1969.

TYB   Cleanth Brooks. *William Faulkner: Toward Yoknapatawpha and Beyond*. Baton Rouge: Louisiana State University Press, 1990.

TYC   Cleanth Brooks. *William Faulkner: The Yoknapatawpha Country*. Baton Rouge: Louisiana State University Press, 1991.

WMW   William Wordsworth. *William Wordsworth: The Major Works*. Ed. Stephen Gill. Oxford: Oxford University Press, 2008.

WP   Friedrich Nietzsche. *The Will to Power*. Trans. Walter Kaufmann and R. J. Hollingdale. 3 vols. New York: Vintage, 1968.

For Michael O'Neill (1953–2018),
your generosity, wisdom, wit, and insight are much missed.

'To love, and bear; to hope, till Hope creates
From its own wreck the thing it contemplates . . .'

(P. B. Shelley, *Prometheus Unbound*)

Part I

Imagining Nature

Chapter 1

Introduction: Reflections on Transatlantic Exchanges, Subjectivity and Nature

Here nature opens her broad lap to receive the perpetual accession of new comers, and to supply them with food. I am sure I cannot be called a partial American when I say, that the spectacle afforded by these pleasing scenes must be more entertaining, and more philosophical than that which arises from beholding the musty ruins of Rome.

J. Hector St John Crèvecoeur, *Letters from an American Farmer*, 1782

the greatest single fact about our modern American writing is our writers' absorption in every last detail of their American world together with their deep and subtle alienation from it.

Alfred Kazin, *On Native Grounds*, 1942

The need to establish difference stemmed not only from the Old World but from the difference in the New.

Toni Morrison, 'Romancing the Shadow', *Playing in the Dark*, 1992

Writing nearly fifty years before the recently deceased African American novelist Toni Morrison, the Jewish American autobiographer and literary critic Alfred Kazin identifies difference as the complexly contradictory defining feature of American letters. For Morrison, it is racial difference in particular that haunts the material and cultural economies of transatlantic transactions between the Old and the New World. Her tracing of American Romanticism's abiding fascination with the genre of romance (long after its form had become less favoured by European culture) recognises, too, other kinds of differences that helped to both shape and define the nature of these transatlantic exchanges. Some of these differences, such as the founding of a new individual and national identity, are bound up with the question of race, but others have more to do with settlers coming to terms with the initial absence of civic codes and institutions, as well as the unknown geography of the New World, the unprecedented vastness of the land- and sky-scape.

For Morrison, these significant social, cultural, natural and geographical differences generated a utopian belief that, in her words, 'The new setting would provide new raiments of self'[1] for the nascent American nation. Such a utopian aspiration is encapsulated by the French settler J. Hector St John Crèvecoeur, who, writing two hundred years earlier in 1782, identifies the land as a nourishing and maternal source of sustenance on a biblical scale and recognises that this nurturing process is integral to being reborn as an American. American identity and the fecundity of the female soil are as inextricably bound to one another – as Crèvecoeur's comparison with 'the musty ruins of Rome' implies – as are myth and history in the national character of the United States. Yet even when enraptured by the euphoric promise of freedom afforded by the New World, Crèvecoeur's vision cannot entirely banish the spectre of the Old World of Europe.

Whether embedded within a particular historical period or from a transhistorical perspective, temporal, spatial and cultural difference at once enables the fledgling American literary imagination to soar and clips its wings. No matter how hopeful these 'noble impulses' (*PD*, p. 35) were, they were equally countered by feelings of fear, anxiety and impotency, which found an outlet in the form of romance where early American writers could, as Morrison observes, 'imagine their demons' (*PD*, p. 36). On the one hand, the American literary imagination struggled to extricate itself from the demons of its European past, and, on the other, it populated the unknown spaces of its new found land with demons of their own.

Old, New and American Romanticism

Rejecting the self-concentration of its European Romantic forebears, the American literary imagination found itself compelled centrifugally towards, as Tony Tanner observes, 'a dilation of self, which can become an abandoning of self, into the surrounding vastness'. The idiosyncrasies of American poetic and prose styles become not a means, Tanner claims, 'to explore self or environment so much as to fill in the spaces between self and environment'.[2] These two distinct but interconnected American imaginative impulses (one positive and the other negative) are anticipated by Kazin's sense of how American writers are, simultaneously, diffused in their new 'American World' and subtly 'alienated from it'. As Gavin Cologne-Brookes remarks of the American literary imagination, 'one key to the links between the writing, the culture and the geographic land mass is the unity and the diversity.'[3] This vexatious mode of difference that permits affinity and alienation is partly a response to and embodies America's sense of itself and its people as a uniform and yet diversified entity. Such a concatenation of the real, the land and the people and their culture may suggest something of a distinct and emergent form of American Romanticism that finally breaks with its British and European ancestry. Equally, though, these emerging, what Mark S. Cladis terms 'storied landscapes' of the American imagination make explicit an imaginative attachment latently present in Wordsworth, especially in *Michael* and *The Ruined Cottage*, concerned with local environs, their diverse peoples, customs, lifestyles and things.[4] American Romanticism's diversification and unification of its land and its people differs in scale rather than kind from the Wordsworthian moral and social vision of the landscape and its inhabitants.

Crucially, difference emerges in the economy of transatlantic literary and cultural exchange as, paradoxically, a marker of deviation, resistance and disinheritance and a sign of affinity, acceptance and inheritance. A recent collection of critical essays, *Transatlantic Romanticism: British and American Art and Literature, 1790–1860* (2015), co-edited by Andrew Hemingway and Allan Wallach, explores the literary and visual culture of the period to resist the notion that these transatlantic exchanges are exclusively entrenched in nationalism and to recognise that the founding of both British and American Romanticism was an inclusive, international and global phenomenon.[5]

One overarching concern here is a transatlantic transmission and transformation of British Romanticism as an important imaginative exchange within world Romanticism – the extent, that is, to which Ralph Waldo Emerson and Henry David Thoreau responded (positively or negatively) to patterns of thought and modes of being found in the writings of British Romantics. Such an approach reassesses our understanding of culture and nature by focusing on literary and cultural dialogues between Britain and the United States about aesthetics, subjectivity, nature and the wider environment. It does so through innovative readings of literary works of British Romanticism and twentieth- and twenty-first-century American literary culture and thought (and the interactions between them). By drawing on aesthetic models and modes of thought prevalent in British Romanticism, my study offers fresh accounts of transatlantic transactions and transformations of aesthetics and subjectivity in relation to the natural world.

Culturally diverse and historically distinctive, each of my chosen epigrams reflects on the formation of American literary culture and character. Both collectively and individually, they attest to the three diverse but interrelated preoccupations central to this transatlantic study: aesthetics, subjectivity and nature. All three of these terms are difficult to disentangle and to define without recourse to enigmatic elusiveness, ineffability or paradox.

Even in the late eighteenth century, the sublimity or persuasiveness of powerful writing has to be measured, for the Irish writer and thinker Edmund Burke, in comparison with 'the passion caused by the great and sublime in *nature*' (original emphasis). When we encounter the truly sublime in the natural world we experience a sense of 'astonishment' which, as Burke observes with religious sensibility, 'is that state of the soul, in which all its motions are suspended, with some degree of horror'.[6] This overwhelming excess of the sublime produces in the observing subject a new awareness of subjectivity. By contrast, Burke hoped to show beauty was of a lesser and more tempered order than that of the sublime. Such a distinction between the sublime and the beautiful Burke found to be untenable, as the strong feelings and passions these two supposed contraries evoked suggested more affinities than decisive differences between them.

Much, then, of the power of the sublime and beautiful is derived, as Burke discovered, from the mysteriousness, uncertainty and often terrifying incomprehension they engender in the observer. Anticipating Freudian modes of psychology, Friedrich Nietzsche, by the end of the nineteenth century, questions our belief in the singularity and purpose of human agency or 'ego'. Responding to the claim that 'Everything is subjective', Nietzsche writes, 'even this is interpretation. The "subject" is not something given, it is something added and invented and projected behind what there is.' For Nietzsche, then, the idea of the subject is not the originator of an action or interpretation, but an afterthought after the fact, act or observation. In this sense, the world is only 'knowable' in that it is, according to Nietzsche, '*interpretable* otherwise, it has no meaning behind it, but countless meanings' (original emphasis).[7]

The endless interpretability of our environs and the natural world has led to the haunting of current ecological thought by the falsified idyllic image of a 'Nature' that pre-dates technological innovation. 'In the ghost of Nature', as Timothy Morton observes, 'modern humans were looking in a mirror . . . they saw the reflected, inverted image of their own age.'[8] Morton's striking claim finds an accord with Nietzsche's equally bold assertion that 'It is our needs that interpret the world' (*WP*, 3, III [481], p. 267). For Morton, our misconception of 'Nature' – even in its wildest forms – has rendered the natural world a sanitised ideal that exists out there beyond our reach and a private possession (which can be owned and sold) locked away in a crystal cabinet for its own protection and preservation. 'Nature', Morton recognises, 'defines itself through extreme contrasts' (*ET*, p. 81) and contradiction.

Transatlantic Exchanges and Critical Ideas

This extreme contradiction is no less true of the transatlantic exchanges between both British and European strands of Romanticism and America. In nineteenth-century America, the haunting presence of Romanticism can be detected in the lesser known literary productions of Mary Austin and John Muir, as well as the instantly recognisable works of Ralph Waldo Emerson and Henry David Thoreau. For all of his self-proclaimed anti-Romantic stance, Nietzsche acknowledged Emerson as one of those 'worthy of being called masters of prose' and borrowed Emerson's words on the sanctity of 'all things' as the epigraph to *The Gay Science*.[9] In such a curiously circuitous manner British Romanticism, refracted through the lens of American Transcendentalism and Nietzsche's writings, found a way back to its European roots. More tellingly, too, Nietzsche's self-styled brand of (anti-)Romanticism sired two of the, arguably, last great twentieth-century Romantic enterprises: on one side of the Atlantic the late lyrics of W. B. Yeats and, on the other, the Romantic brio of Wallace Stevens's poetry.[10] A brief sketch of this reception of British and European Romanticism in American writing illuminates how these inventive acts of self-discovery (and rediscovery) within transatlantic Romantic exchanges and Romanticism itself coloured, unavoidably, any later post-Romantic position and poetics.

Versions of Romanticism abound and proliferate within its transatlantic transmission and return. Such a proliferation of this already complexly elusive and slippery term necessitates a broader conception of the poetic for the purposes of my study. This capacious definition of the poetic, derived from an obsolete mode of the word meaning 'ficti-tious' or 'imaginary' (*OED*, adj. a.1), is intended to operate, like the very transatlantic transactions to which it contributes, across those traditional generic boundaries of prose and poetry, as well as national borders. Identifying the defining characteristic of the poetic as an abil-ity to carry over or move between both literary genres and geo-politi-cal limits shares certain assumptions with Susan Manning's *Poetics of Character: Transatlantic Encounters 1700–1900* (2013). The mobil-ity that Manning attributes the poetic (due to its capacity for analogy) enables her to remap Romanticism in ways that cut across established temporal, generic, cultural and national restrictions.[11]

My own measure of these transatlantic transactions and transfor-mations depends, too, on the operations of the poetic at the level of 'allusion' or 'echo'. These poetic or literary 'allusions' can take the form of a precise verbal allusion to another writer, but they can also occur as accidental (or incidental) repetitions or 'echoes', which occur within and across literary works. Similarly, as John Hollander argues, 'echo' has a double meaning which, in the strict literary sense, operates at the level of deliberate allusion and, in a less restricted sense, is an accidental (conscious or unconscious) repetition by a writer. In this latter sense, the tracing of these echoes as evidence of literary influence (and indebt-edness) is, as Harold Bloom concludes in *The Anxiety of Influence*, 'the art of knowing the hidden roads that go' from text to text.[12]

The mobility afforded here to the play of poetics within a given text and the poetical interplay between texts means that what fol-lows is not in any strict sense (nor is it intended to be so) a source study. My approach is more closely aligned with Roland Barthes's theorisation of intertextuality in which all texts exist as a complex multi-layered and tonal 'chamber of echoes' comprising conscious, unconscious and incidental allusions created in and through the processes of writing and reading alike.[13] Whether direct or indirect, explicitly signalled or fully absorbed into a text, all poetic echoes (or allusions) remain dormant awaiting cross-pollination from an attentive (or even casual) reader. The limitless transhistorical mobil-ity that this process might theoretically permit of a poetics of allusion is curtailed by the focus of the present study. Its ambit is defined by an alertness to the literary transactions (in the form of echoes or bor-rowings) between Romanticism and American writers, as well as a sensitivity to their ability to transform Romantic concepts of nature, aesthetics and subjectivity in their work.

My own sense of the mobile nature of the poetic finds some affinities with Stephen Shapiro's *The Culture and Commerce of the*

Early American Novel: Reading the Trans-Atlantic World System (2008),[14] which conceives of a global web of transatlantic intertextuality, exchange and interconnection. Focusing on the late eighteenth century and early nineteenth century, Shapiro's book offers refreshing ways of rethinking the rise of the early American novel and reconfiguring the dynamics (cultural and commercial) of early-nineteenth-century transatlantic exchanges. Differing from the studies by Manning and Shapiro, the historical compass of my own project points to twentieth- and twenty-first-century American writers and specifically focuses on their cultural and imaginative transatlantic transactions with British Romanticism about aesthetics, subjectivity and nature. This shift in chronological emphasis aligns my project in intellectual spirit and historical focus to Paige Tovey's *The Transatlantic Eco-Romanticism of Gary Snyder* (2013).[15] Tovey persuasively identifies the British Romantic Eco-Poetic tradition (comprising, in addition to Blake, Coleridge and Wordsworth, the legacies of Keats and Shelley) as a vital and originating source for later American Eco-Romanticism and earlier American Transcendentalism. Our separate endeavours do share a common interest in the multiplicities of Romanticism(s), selfhood, poetics and the natural world. Both our discrete approaches provide a renewed sense of the place of second-generation British Romantic writers within the web of transatlantic transactions, encounters and transformations.

Rather, then, like the banner, or banners, of Romanticism (whether American or British) under which they are made to serve in my book's subtitle, definitions of the aesthetic, self and environment may aspire towards singularity but are often at their most successful when they spawn contradictory, multiple and polyvalent meanings. Consequently, the complications, contradictions and possibilities that attend any definition of aesthetics, subjectivity and environment (encompassing the human and natural world) can be better appreciated by thinking about them in relation to one another. Such an approach also enhances our appreciation of the multifaceted aspects that attend to each one of these three terms, as well as the varying manifestations of Romanticism that championed them. The effect is one of a phantasmagoria in which we witness illumination and obfuscation; an interplay of dark and light, the shadow-play of a self haunted by itself and others, of simultaneity and difference.

The complex patterns of these imaginative and cultural exchanges between American Romanticism and British Romanticism, between the Old and New World, about aesthetics, subjectivity and nature have been the object of much recent critical investigation. It has been shown how multifaceted responses to Romanticism's legacy evident in fictional models of environmentalism are revealing, at a communal and national level, about socio-political identities. Wordsworth's pastoral poetry of the uncultivated landscape is distinct from Emerson's brand of American pastoral fiction which, as Tony Tanner argues, celebrates rural industriousness and naturalising technological innovation in response to the natural environment.[16]

Unlike Wordsworth's 'storied landscapes', within the American literary tradition the site of pastoral fiction is rarely aligned with the ideals and the power of the imagination and more often with the realities of aggressive colonial ownership of the land and its people. By contrast, James C. McKusick suggests, Wordsworth resists the extension of the railways (and the urban human pollution they would bring) into the natural environs of the Lake District.[17] McKusick's important study, *Green Writing: Romanticism and Ecology* (2000), extends the seminal work of Lawrence Buell's ecocritical readings of Thoreau's literary imagination in *The Environmental Imagination: Thoreau, Nature Writing, and the Formation of American Culture* (1995).[18] McKusick focuses on the writings of Blake, Coleridge and Wordsworth as protoecological and the legacies that these British Romantic writers bestowed to Emerson, Thoreau and the late-nineteenth-century American novelist John Muir.

The historical scope of McKusick's book focuses on the long nineteenth century. My own work recognises the importance of these nineteenth-century transatlantic cultural and imaginative transactions and concerns itself more with the modes of thought and sensibilities that British Romanticism bequeathed to twentieth- and twenty-first-century American writers and thinkers. Both Buell and McKusick also rightly recognise the transatlantic imaginative influence of Wordsworth and Coleridge on the writings of Emerson and Thoreau. My account does not deny the significance of Wordsworth (a recurrent figure in the chapters that follow) and Coleridge to Emerson and Thoreau, but instead offers a reconfiguration of this transatlantic imaginative exchange by giving a much greater emphasis to second-generation British Romantics.

Critical Directions: Transatlantic Transactions and Transformations

It is not the purpose of my study to make a critical intervention into the fields of environmental aesthetics and ethics. The environment of my subtitle refers, as does one etymological meaning of the word (*environnement; OED*, etym. d.1487), to the encompassing natural and urban surroundings of a thing or entity. In the broadest sense, then, it is within and through both these physical human and non-human environs that differing notions of identity and concepts of nature are forged.[19] My own thinking, however, about the inter-actions of Romantic and post-Romantic subjectivities with nature has been shaped by Morton's deconstructive approach in *Ecology without Nature: Rethinking Environmental Aesthetics* (2007). Morton conveys how certain environmental aesthetics, especially those which purport a position of critical distance between human activities and the natural sphere, turn out only to be a fictional delusion that fails to recognise the self as an inexorable part of nature and its processes.[20] Morton shows how 'Post-Romantic writing is obsessed with space and place' (*EWN*, p. 4) and, as my subsequent chapters touch upon, with how identities (individual and communal) of those who dwell within specific environs are shaped according to their own fictions of the self. Within the constructions of these original worldviews 'aesthetics . . . performs a crucial role, establishing new ways of experiencing and feeling a place' (*EWN*, p. 2), as well as disclosing our ideas and assumptions about subjectivity. Ultimately, such fictions are more telling about the subject that created them than they are revealing about the nature (or a subject's experience) of those objects within a given environment.

Attentive to a series of literary transactions and imaginative transformations, I explore the reoccurrence of Romantic motifs and concepts of aesthetics, subjectivity and nature in American Romanticism and post-Romantic American poetics. This aspect of my critical endeavour is indebted to, and finds affinities with, the seminal exploration of George Bornstein's *Romantic and the Modern: Revaluations of Literary Tradition* (1977), Carlos Baker's groundbreaking study *The Echoing Green: Romanticism, Modernism, and the Phenomena of Transference Poetry* (1984) and Michael O'Neill's subtly astute readings of lines of poetic influence in *The All-Sustaining Air: Romantic Legacies and Renewals in British, American, and Irish Poetry since 1900* (2007).[21] For my own part, I trace closely, especially in the coda of this study, the transatlantic exchanges of British Romantic modes and patterns of thought within the writings of Emerson, Emily Dickinson and Walt Whitman, as well as the post-Romantic poetry of Stevens.

In the first instance, my approach re-evaluates the influence that the thought and writings of Lord Byron, John Keats and P. B. Shelley exerted on the thought and poetics of Emerson and Thoreau about subjectivity, aesthetics and nature. A more fine-grained appreciation of the influence of Byron, Keats and Shelley on the writings of Emerson and Thoreau (the subject of Chapter 2) points to important touchstones between them and departs from those critical readings and their distinctions that so decisively separate the poetics of self and nature advocated by Emerson and Thoreau. Secondly, discrete hermeneutic interpretations of literary transactions and imaginative transformations in the writings of other American writers provide, more broadly, a new understanding of the relations between American and British Romanticism and their aesthetic treatment of self and nature, as well as a fresh sense of the fate of Romantic legacies in the twentieth-century and contemporary American literary imagination.

Divided across two parts, each of the subsequent four chapters read prominent twentieth- and twenty-first-century American novelists as actively involved in imaginative transactions and transformations of vital motifs, concepts and poetics bequeathed by British Romanticism. This part of my critical endeavour finds sympathies with, and builds upon, those critical enterprises undertaken by Martin Bidney, Allan Chavkin and Morris Dickstein.[22] My own critical readings of a selection of American novelists are attentive to those forms of Romantic bequest that are embodied in names of characters, epiphanic moments, episodic interludes and motifs, but extend these terms of reference to include a consideration of both the narrative frames and the poetic textures of these writers' prose styles as a hallmark of Romantic influence.

Through a select series of critical readings of American writers, the force of these significant engagements with Romantic and post-Romantic ideas about the aesthetic, subjectivity and the environment is accumulative in effect. The following chapters are not exhaustive in their coverage of American literature but serve, effectively, as provocative case studies that signal fresh configurations of the relations between American writers and their Romantic forebears. Chapter 2 alongside these introductory reflections form the first section of this book, 'Imagining Nature'. A reassessment of British Romantic influence on Emerson and Thoreau in Chapter 2, 'Romantic Influence and Nature Reconsidered: Ralph Waldo Emerson and Henry David Thoreau', reads their thought and writing as exhibiting a knowing self-consciousness about their treatment of self and nature and its use of allusion to the literary and cultural tradition of British Romanticism. This transatlantic context for critical reassessments of American Transcendentalism has been the focus of critical attention in Lisa M. Steinman's *Masters of Repetition: Poetry, Culture, and Work in Thomson, Wordsworth, Shelley, and Emerson* (1998), Kerry McSweeney's *The Language of the Senses: Sensory-Perceptual Dynamics in Wordsworth, Coleridge, Thoreau, Whitman, and Dickinson* (1998) and, more recently, David Greenham's *Emerson's Transatlantic Romanticism* (2012).[23] My own account offers a fresh awareness of the intellectual and imaginative engagement of the thought of Emerson and Thoreau with the works of Byron, Shelley and Keats.

Chapters 3 and 4 form the second section, 'Romantic Transactions: Subjects in Nature', which attends to the close textual engagement of F. Scott Fitzgerald and William Faulkner with the poetic thoughts, imagery and temporal modes of British Romanticism. These two chapters take up many of the concerns outlined in Chapter 2 about Romantic inheritance, influence and aesthetics to explore the varying representations of subjectivity and nature in the fiction of Fitzgerald and Faulkner. Chapter 3, 'Dissolving Subjectivities: Imagined Selves in F. Scott Fitzgerald and John Keats', focuses on the lyrical fiction of Fitzgerald and his life-long critical and creative engagement with Keats's biographical and poetic presence. Critics have configured Fitzgerald's portrayal of gender relations through Keats's sense of the self-contained idealising and pastoral world of romance tainted by a darker reality from without and populated by alluring *femmes fatales* and tragic heroines. Such critical views often claim that Keats's poetry is the template for the sympathetic ambivalence displayed by Fitzgerald's narrators toward their female characters.

This sympathetic ambivalence, my chapter suggests, need not necessarily be confined to gender relations and is an essential part of Fitzgerald's mode of narration (for instance, exemplified in *The Great Gatsby* (1925) by Nick Carraway's curious ambivalence towards the subject of his narration, Jay Gatsby). Paradoxically, Fitzgerald portrays subjectivity as involved in both an intimate immediacy from within and an incisive viewpoint marshalled from without. Fitzgerald's narrative technique – one of empathetic engagement and critical distance – constitutes a form of Keats's negatively capable poetics. Fitzgerald's negatively capable poetics depict a process of self-dissolution which reconfigures the relationship between inner and outer identities, as well as the dynamics between self and world. Such fictions of the self, for Fitzgerald, are paradoxically a release from and an imposition on subjectivities (as played out through Dick Diver's dilemma in *Tender is the Night* (1934)) and the environs they occupy.

For all of its celebration of nature's environs and vitality through an evocative language of presence, Chapter 4, 'Ghostly Selves, Light and Nature in William Faulkner: Wordsworthian Shadows and Byronic Shades', suggests that Romanticism bequeaths to Faulkner a legacy of haunts and hauntings: Romantic poetry is populated with Wordsworthian 'strange half-absence[s]',[24] spectral forms and ghostly figures. For example, Wordsworth's poetry centres on liminal figures (the Idiot Boy, Lucy Gray, the Discharged Soldier and Michael to name only a few) as revenants. Wordsworth's poetics are haunted by these spectral presences which, invariably, point to the limitations of both Romantic communion with nature and imaginative vision, as well as those inadequacies inscribed within poetic language and form.

Faulkner's fiction, especially *The Sound and the Fury* (1929) and *Light in August* (1932), shares a similar elegiac attachment to both the past and place in its representation of nature and natural haunts. In *The Sound and the Fury*, for instance, Benjy's experience of the past (in particular his attachment to the absent Caddy) is a kind of haunting in which figures glide in and out of his narration like ghostly forms.

Nature, for Faulkner, emerges as a ghostly presence within his fiction which points up the secrets that haunt, but are often concealed (or delayed) by, his own narrative structures. These figurations of the ghostly and nature's spectral presence are refracted through Byron's poetic motifs of light and water in *Light in August*. Nietzsche's reflection that 'A truly "historical" rendition would be ghostly speech before ghosts'[25] usefully characterises Faulkner's literary transactions and encounters with Wordsworthian shadows and Byronic shades in his very real imaginings of Yoknapatawpha.

The final section, 'Romantic Transformations: Fictional Selves and Nature', concentrates on the writings of Saul Bellow and Toni Morrison. The two chapters that comprise this section foreground conceptual encounters, in the respective writings of these authors, with Romantic ideas about the self and nature and how they are refracted through American Romanticism and post-Romantic poetics. Chapter 5, 'Fictions of the Self and Nature: Reading Romanticism in Saul Bellow', examines how Bellow advocates an intuitive Romantic knowledge in *Herzog* (1964), *Mr Sammler's Planet* (1970) and *Ravelstein* (1999) that recognises that the sacrosanct resides in the ordinary nature of things and teaches us that we have wider communal obligations to one another as fellow human beings. Such obligations in Bellow's fiction, especially *Herzog*, recall William Blake's emphasis on the divine within the human breast and the possibility of a Wordsworthian communion with nature. British and American Romanticism were decisive in shaping his aesthetic vision of the relations between the self and the urban and rural environment. Bellow's brand of Romanticism is read as indebted to Emersonian and Wordsworthian reflections on the interconnection between the visionary and the natural world, as well as moving towards a darker, sceptical, even Shelleyan sensibility.

My final chapter, 'Reimagined Pastoral Poetics: Narrative Structures and the Environment in Toni Morrison, Thoreau and Wordsworth', focuses on Toni Morrison's *Beloved* (1987), *A Mercy* (2008) and *Home* (2012). Central to these novels is the question of what constitutes a homely domestic and natural space, the relationship between environs and memory and the marginalisation of individual and communal voices. *A Mercy*, for example, challenges Thoreau's claim that we 'consider every spot as the possible site of a house',[26] as the unfinished colonial house is reclaimed by the forces of a nature indifferent to architectural design or fictional models of improvement and control. Drawing on Emerson's urbanised pastoral modes, Morrison translates the darker features of Wordsworth's rural poetics into her own version of the American pastoral to speak of those unassailable issues of identity, property and ownership.

Frequently, these nineteenth-century British and American attitudes assume a controlling influence over their respective environments and the subjectivities of their inhabitants. Reflecting on the accounts of aesthetics, subjectivity and nature in the previous chapters, my coda, 'Nature without Self: Beauty, Death and Subjectivity in the Poetics of Walt Whitman, Emily Dickinson and Wallace Stevens', explores how post-Romantic poetics avow and disavow Romantic ideas about beauty, nature and the self in a bid to come to terms with life in all its ordinariness; with what Stevens plainly identifies as the state of things merely as they are. Ironically, those necessary fictions of the self and environment (the world of the human and non-human things) find themselves contradictorily embedded both in and beyond the fictive. Imaginative acts of self-dissolution signal an aesthetic critical distance between the self and nature to be illusory and the extent to which the self is inescapably mired in the fragility of natural process and perpetually aware of its own terminus in death. Accordingly, my coda evinces the British Romantic entanglements in the poetic thought of Emerson, Dickinson and Whitman, as well as Stevens's complicated, and complicating, post-Romantic responses to those British and American Romantic models of self and nature that Stevens both imaginatively inherits and transforms.

This transatlantic transformative inheritance of later poetics provides proof that, as Lisa Steinman observes of contemporary poetics, 'both Romantic practice and the caricatured ghosts of Romanticism continue to haunt'.[27] Instructive here, too, is Derrida's claim that 'Everyone reads, acts, writes with . . . their own ghosts, even when we seek out the ghosts of others'.[28] Such a dual spectre haunts transatlantic, Romantic and post-Romantic ideas about aesthetics, subjectivity and nature. Fictions of the self and nature are a necessary and inescapable aspect of these transatlantic, Romantic and post-Romantic transactions with the natural world. Transatlantic exchanges and transformations of British Romantic concepts of the aesthetic, subjectivity and the environment make us feel all the more keenly the darker plight and fate of a self acutely aware of its own precarious existence and inevitable demise occasioned by a realisation of a vital disconnect between observing subject and observed nature.

Seeking to curtail (if not entirely vanquish) the ghost of British Romanticism, the transatlantic imagination fashioned out of its inheritance of Romantic ideas an apparently independent and more existentially charged aesthetic of self and nature. Yet this transatlantic exorcism of a haunting by British Romanticism only, ironically, summoned up those spectres of alienation, disconnection and solipsism that already stalked, and were latent within, earlier Romantic concepts of the aesthetic, subjectivity and nature. The site of these transatlantic transactions and transformations turns out to be doubly haunted by both the ghostly presence of the Romantic and Romanticism's self-reflexive sense of its own spectral otherness.

Notes

1. Toni Morrison, *Playing in the Dark: Whiteness and the Literary Imagination* (Cambridge, MA: Harvard University Press, 1992), p. 34. Hereafter *PD*.
2. Tony Tanner, 'Notes for a Comparison between American and European Romanticism', *Journal of American Studies* 2.1 (1968): 87; 83–103.
3. Gavin Cologne-Brookes, 'Writing and America: An Introduction', in *Writing and America*, ed. Gavin Cologne-Brookes, Neil Sammells and David Timms (London: Longman, 1996), p. 17.
4. Mark S. Cladis, 'Radical Romanticism: Democracy, Religion, and the Environmental Imagination', *Soundings: An Interdisciplinary Journal* 97.1 (2014): 38; 21–49.
5. See Andrew Hemingway and Allan Wallach, eds, *Transatlantic Romanticism: British and American Art and Literature, 1790–1860* (Amherst: University of Massachusetts Press, 2015), pp. 1–28.

6. Edmund Burke, *A Philosophical Enquiry into the Origin of our Ideas of the Sublime and Beautiful*, ed. Adam Phillips (Oxford: Oxford University Press, 1992), p. 53.

7. Friedrich Nietzsche, *The Will to Power*, trans. Walter Kaufmann and R. J. Hollingdale (New York: Vintage, 1968), 3, III [481], p. 267. Hereafter *WP*.

8. Timothy Morton, *The Ecological Thought* (Cambridge, MA: Harvard University Press, 2010), p. 5. Hereafter *ET*.

9. See Friedrich Nietzsche, *The Gay Science*, trans. and intro. Walter Kaufmann (New York: Vintage-Random, 1974), p. 146 [72], p. 8, and Mark Sandy, ed., *Romantic Presences in the Twentieth Century* (Farnham: Ashgate, 2012), pp. 4–5. Hereafter *RPT*.

10. See pp. 6 and 15, respectively, of Patrick Bridgwater, *Nietzsche in Anglosaxony* (Leicester: Leicester University Press, 1972).

11. See Susan Manning, *Poetics of Character: Transatlantic Encounters 1700–1900* (Cambridge: Cambridge University Press, 2013), pp. 3–53.

12. See John Hollander, *The Figure of Echo: A Mode of Allusion in Milton and After* (Berkeley: University of California Press, 1981), pp. ix–x. See also Harold Bloom, *The Anxiety of Influence: A Theory of Poetry* (1973; Oxford: Oxford University Press, 1975), p. 96.

13. Roland Barthes, *Roland Barthes by Roland Barthes* (Berkeley: University of California Press, 1994), p. 76. Drawing on Michael Riffaterre, Foteini Lika discriminates between studies that are genuinely intertextual in approach and those whose focus are really that of 'imitation or influence'. See Lika, *Roidis and the Borrowed Muse: British Historiography, Fiction and Satire in Pope Joan* (Newcastle: Cambridge Scholars, 2018), p. 15.

14. See Stephen Shapiro, *The Culture and Commerce of the Early American Novel: Reading the Trans-Atlantic World System* (Chicago: University of Chicago Press, 2008).

15. Paige Tovey, *The Transatlantic Eco-Romanticism of Gary Snyder* (London: Palgrave Macmillan, 2013).

16. Tony Tanner, *Scenes of Nature, Signs of Men* (Cambridge: Cambridge University Press, 1987), p. 32. Hereafter *SNSM*.

17. James C. McKusick, *Green Writing: Romanticism and Ecology* (New York: St. Martin's, 2000), p. 74.

18. Lawrence Buell, *The Environmental Imagination: Thoreau, Nature Writing, and the Formation of American Culture* (Cambridge, MA: Belknap-Harvard University Press, 1995).

19. For a sense of how enmeshed ideas of identity and nature have become with ideas about and responses to the environment see Timothy Clark, *Cambridge Introduction to Literature and the Environment* (Cambridge: Cambridge University Press, 2011), pp. 87–9.

20. See Timothy Morton, *Ecology without Nature: Rethinking Environmental Aesthetics* (Cambridge, MA: Harvard University Press, 2009); see especially chapter 3 (pp. 140–205) and Morton's sense that 'When we

drag [nature] front and center, against our ideological interests, it stops being a world we can immerse ourselves in' (p. 204). Hereafter *EWN*.

21. See George Bornstein, *Romantic and the Modern: Revaluations of Literary Tradition* (Pittsburgh: University of Pittsburgh Press, 1977); Carlos Baker, *The Echoing Green: Romanticism, Modernism, and the Phenomena of Transference Poetry* (Princeton: Princeton University Press, 1984); and Michael O'Neill, *The All-Sustaining Air: Romantic Legacies and Renewals in British, American, and Irish Poetry since 1900* (Oxford: Oxford University Press, 2007).

22. See Martin Bidney, *Patterns of Epiphany: From Wordsworth to Tolstoy, Pater, and Barrett Browning* (Carbondale: Southern Illinois University Press, 1997); Allan Chavkin, *The Secular Imagination: The Continuity of the Romantic Tradition in Wordsworth and Keats in Stevens, Faulkner, Roethke, and Bellow*, dissertation, University of Illinois, Urbana-Champaign, 1977; and Morris Dickstein, *A Mirror in the Roadway: Literature and the Real World* (Princeton: Princeton University Press, 2005).

23. Lisa M. Steinman, *Masters of Repetition: Poetry, Culture, and Work in Thomson, Wordsworth, Shelley, and Emerson* (New York: St. Martin's, 1998); Kerry McSweeney, *The Language of the Senses: Sensory-Perceptual Dynamics in Wordsworth, Coleridge, Thoreau, Whitman, and Dickinson* (Liverpool: Liverpool University Press, 1998); David Greenham, *Emerson's Transatlantic Romanticism* (London: Palgrave Macmillan, 2012). See also Patrick J. Keane, *Emerson, Romanticism, and Intuitive Reason: The Transatlantic 'Light of All Our Day'* (Columbia: University of Missouri Press, 2005).

24. Quotation modified from William Wordsworth, 'The Discharged Soldier', in *William Wordsworth: The Major Works*, ed. Stephen Gill (Oxford: Oxford University Press, 2008), p. 48, l. 143. Hereafter *WMW*. Unless otherwise stated all Wordsworth quotations are from this edition.

25. Friedrich Nietzsche, *Human All-Too Human: A Book for Free Spirits*, trans. R. J. Hollingdale, intro. Richard Schacht (Cambridge: Cambridge University Press, 1996), [126], p. 242. Numbers in square brackets refer to section numbers. Hereafter *HH*.

26. Henry David Thoreau, *Walden; or Life in the Woods*, in *The Portable Thoreau*, ed. Carl Bode (1965; Harmondsworth: Viking-Penguin, 1987), p. 334. Hereafter *TPT*. Unless otherwise stated all Thoreau quotations are from this edition.

27. Lisa M. Steinman, 'Introduction to Romanticism and Contemporary Poetry and Poetics', July 2003, <https://romantic-circles.org/praxis/poetics/steinman/steinman.html> (date of access: 20 May 2020).

28. Jacques Derrida, *Spectres of Marx: The State of the Debt, the Work of Mourning, and the New International*, trans. Peggy Kamuf, intro. Bernard Magnus and Stephen Cullenberg (New York: Routledge, 1994), p. 139.

Chapter 2

Romantic Influence and Nature Reconsidered: Ralph Waldo Emerson and Henry David Thoreau

Transatlantic Transmissions and Reception

With their brand of American Romanticism often characterised as the inheritance of William Wordsworth and Samuel Taylor Coleridge, Ralph Waldo Emerson and Henry David Thoreau are equally responsive to the cadences, rhythms and modulations of the English poetic tradition in general, and the poetical thought and practice of Lord Byron, John Keats and P. B. Shelley in particular. Emerson praised 'certain lines' in Keats's *Hyperion* for their poetic 'inward skill'[1] and Thoreau had read a range of the poetry of Shelley and Keats, most likely in *The Poetical Works of Coleridge, Shelley, and Keats in One Volume. Stereotyped by John Howe. Philadelphia [J. Grieg], 1832*. The single 1832 Grieg volume in question consists of a biographical memoir of each of the three poets and a widely varied selection of their poetry, including the poems of Coleridge's *Sibylline Leaves* and a range of Shelley's significant works, including but not limited to *Alastor, Mont Blanc, Epipsychidion, Prometheus Unbound* and *Adonais*. Grieg's volume also contains a representative coverage of Keats's shorter lyrics, the Spring Odes, as well as conveying a sense of Keats as a narrative poet through the inclusion of *Endymion, The Eve of St Agnes* and *Hyperion: A Fragment*.

Additionally, Thoreau almost certainly possessed a separate and unidentified edition of P. B. Shelley's lyrical drama *Prometheus Unbound*.[2] Amongst Emerson's frequent borrowings of the writings of William Wordsworth and Coleridge from the Boston Athenaeum and Harvard College Library, we also find Emerson loaning an 1840 London edition of Shelley's *Letters from Abroad, Translations, and*

Fragments, edited by Mary Shelley in two volumes. Although Emerson and Thoreau desired a 'poetry and philosophy of insight and not of [English] tradition', Emerson was a keen reader of Thomas Campbell's *Specimens of the British Poets* (London, 1819) in seven volumes. Volume six of this edition is of particular note for its gathering together of a selection of writings by key proto-Romantic figures such as Edward Young, Mark Akenside, Thomas Gray, Thomas Chatterton and Oliver Goldsmith. For his part, Thoreau eagerly devoured Alexander Chalmer's 1810 edition (in twenty-one volumes) of *The Works of the English Poets: From Chaucer to Cowper*. Thoreau was also well-acquainted with Lord Byron's writing through an American edition of *The Works of Lord Byron, in verse and prose, including letters, journals, etc. With a sketch of his life*, published in New York by George Dearborn in 1836. It is likely, too, that Emerson would have been familiar with this edition of Byron's writing, as his notebooks demonstrate an engagement with, and response to, a plethora of Byronic poetic modes. Along with Wordsworth, Byron is listed as a favourite amongst Emerson's 'Modern Poets', and elsewhere Byron is praised as one of those poets who possesses an 'uncontrollable inward impulse'.[3]

Emerson, Byron, Shelley and Keats

What Emerson identifies as this Byronic 'uncontrollable inward impulse' characterises much of Cantos III and IV – originally published, respectively, in 1816 and 1818 – of *Childe Harold's Pilgrimage* and reprinted in the 1836 New York edition. Lines blur between the actual and the imaginary, between biographical and fictional persona, as Byron, at the start of Canto III, celebrates 'The wandering outlaw of his own dark mind'.[4] Childe Harold as a figure is, at once, a separate figment of Byron's own 'dark mind' and an inextricable embodiment of the madness that Byron hoped that, at best, poetic creation could exorcise. Later in the same Canto, this notion of madness as a contagion of fire that 'once kindled' remains 'quenchless evermore' (*CH*, III, 43, l. 375) and fully takes hold of Byron's portrait of the troubled Rousseau:

> His love was Passion's essence – as a tree
> On fire by lightning; with ethereal flame
> Kindled he was, and blasted; for to be
> Thus, and enamoured, were in him the same.

> But his was not the love of living dame,
> Nor of the dead who rise upon our dreams,
> But of ideal Beauty, which became
> In him existence, and o'erflowing teems
> Along his burning page, distempered though it seems.
> (*CH*, III, stanza 78)

Byron's deliberate verbal slippage allows a mobility of self that oscillates between observing subject and observed objects (the lone tree and the lightning strike) and fuses together the interior and the exterior worlds in the stanza, which are immersed in, and felt through, those outer and inner spaces of 'ideal Beauty'. This fusion creates an inner or emotional landscape, which conflates the isolated watcher (whether Rousseau, Childe Harold or Byron himself) with the fire-stricken 'tree' wounded by the lightning. Such emotional intensity prepares the reader for the description of the 'burning page' as subjectively charged ('In him existence') with – and objectively observed as – the creative-destructive energy of the mobile poetic artistry of these selves turning mad. This enables the 'dark mind[s]' of Byron and Rousseau to be both imaginatively kindled into the life of the 'ethereal flame' and forever tormented ('blasted') by the self-same destructive fire that can never be quenched.

For all Byron indulges an 'uncontrollable inward impulse' through an immersion in his own subjectivity and that of others, he remains sympathetic to and yet wary of a negatively capable poetics of subjectivity and knew the perils of seeking out what Keats understood as the treacherous 'fog-born elf' of selfhood:

> But my Soul wanders; I demand it back
> To meditate amongst decay, and stand
> A ruin amidst ruins . . . (*CH*, IV, 25, ll. 217–19)

Byron realises a self-consciously staged moment, which objectively seeks to circumscribe an endlessly mobile, meandering subjectivity and, subjectively, borders on a solipsistic collapse into a fractured and fracturing self. This splintered yet unified Byronic self is as much 'absorb'd' in as it is reflective of all the life's myriad goings-on: even as a broken mirror, which the 'glass / In every fragment multiplies; and makes / A thousand images as of one that was' (*CH*, III, 33, ll. 1–3). This instance, like many others in Cantos III and IV, encapsulates the perspectival, contradictory, self-conscious poetic performance of shifting subjectivities that is vital to the dynamism of Byron's mobile poetics of self. A poetics of self that, in spite of the risks of self-annihilation, we can 'in creating live / A being more intense' (*CH*, III, 6, ll. 46–7). Revelatory moments of self and world are contingent upon one another and only realisable through acts of poetic creation that embody or 'endow / With form our fancy, gaining as we give / The life we imagine . . .' (*CH*, III, 6, ll. 47–9). By seeing creatively – ''Tis to create, and in creating live' (*CH*, III, 6, l. 46) – with and through the poetic eye of selfhood we come closer to the 'intense' mystery of ourselves and the surrounding world.

In a core passage from *Nature* we catch flickers of Byron's brand of 'a being more intense', as well as elements of Keats's negative capability, when Emerson insists on seeing through, and with, a creative, active, eye:

> Standing on the bare ground, – my head bathed by the blithe air, and uplifted into infinite space, – all mean egotism vanishes. I become a transparent eyeball. I am nothing; I see all; the currents of Universal Being circulate through me; I am part or parcel of God.[5]

Here Emerson is attuned to Keats's conception of what it is for the 'I [to] live in the eye; and my imagination, surpassed, is at rest'.[6] Alert to Keats's account of the 'poetical Character' (*JKL*, 1, p. 387) as negatively capable and self-annihilating, Emerson stresses a moment of selflessness when 'all mean egotism vanishes'. The negatively capable mode of sympathy Byron swerved away from is embraced by Emerson. Emerson's formulation echoes Keats's empathetic ability to enter, unobtrusively, into other states of being and feel those inner psychic and physical spaces beyond ourselves 'upon our pulses' (*JKL*, 1, p. 279). Keats's negatively capable imagination permits the mind to 'take part in [the] existince' (*JKL*, 1, p. 186) of another being's inner spaces, solidity and life. It is unlikely, though not impossible, that Emerson or Thoreau would have read extracts of Keats's letters in the *Life, Letters, and Literary Remains of John Keats* in two volumes (1848), edited by Richard Monckton Milnes, who helped introduce Emerson to Britain (where the American writer visited Wordsworth on 28 August 1833). Thoreau may have, however, been aware of Keats's remarks on Milton's poetic genius through a letter on the subject of Keats's 'American Brother and Remarks on Milton by Keats' written by James Freeman Clarke to the editor (by this time Emerson) of *The Dial*, where it was published in April 1843.[7]

Emerson's central idea of self-reliance, like Keats's definition of poetical character, opposes 'consequitive reasoning' (*JKL*, 1, p. 185) to advocate a rejection of rationalised thought and habitual thinking in favour of a revelatory state achieved through embracing 'uncertainties, Mysteries, doubts' (*JKL*, 1, p. 193). Such an intuitive disclosure of being as presence, for Emerson, transforms the personal into the impersonal, dissolving habitual frictions between individual and society, subject and object, mind and body, spirit and matter. Recognising the importance of the imaginative capacity to transcend the boundaries of individual selfhood, Emerson succinctly endorses what is, essentially, a mode of Keatsian negative capability when he writes, 'We are not strong by our power to penetrate, but by our relatedness' ('Success', *CWES*, p. 153).

Notions of 'relatedness' are central to how Emerson and Keats, as well as Shelley, conceived of the interaction between the human subject and the natural world. Keats conveys his sense of the mazy, circuitous and bewildering voyage of selfhood when he writes:

Now it appears to me that almost any Man may like the spider spin from his own inwards his own airy Citadel – the points of leaves and twigs on which the spider begins her work are few, and she fills the air with a beautiful circuiting. Man should be content with as few points to tip with the fine Web of his Soul, and weave a tapestry empyrean full of symbols for his spiritual eye, of softness for his spiritual touch, of space for his wandering, of distinctness for his luxury. But the Minds of Mortals are so different and bent on such diverse journeys that it may at first appear impossible for any common taste and fellowship to exist between two or three under these suppositions. It is however quite the contrary. Minds would leave each other in contrary directions, traverse each other in numberless points, and at last greet each other at the journey's end. (*JKL*, 1, pp. 231–2, Keats to John Hamilton Reynolds, 19 February 1818)

Keats's use of imagery haunts Emerson's notion of the 'creative eye' and the cosmos in *Nature*, especially in Emerson's account of how technological innovation is as easily subsumed into the poet's view of nature's vast design as is the 'spider's geometrical web':

Readers of poetry see the factory-village, and the railway, and fancy that the poetry of the landscape is broken up by these, – for these works of art are not yet consecrated in their reading; but the poet sees them fall within the great order not less than the bee-hive, or the spider's geometrical web. Nature adopts them very fast into her vital circles, and the gliding train of cars she loves like her own.[8]

Nature, for Emerson, recognises and adopts the intricate and, by implication, those beautiful objects that are a product of industrial and human endeavour into her 'vital circles'. For Emerson, it is only by the individual's soul being in touch with this 'universal self' (or what he also calls the 'Over-Soul') that the chaos of experience can be made sense of:

> Let man then learn the revelation of all nature and all thought to his heart; this, namely; that the Highest dwells with him; that the sources of nature are his own mind, if the sentiment of duty is there.[9]

For Emerson, at least, the only point of anchorage in the endless ebb and flow of a continually expanding and contracting, fluidly dynamic universe is the fixity of the soul. The soul achieves its moorings through (as Emerson terms it) a 'subtile spiritual connection' with the divine over-soul within the material universe. It is through, Emerson claims, this revelatory power of an active imagination and 'creative reading' that 'we come to look at the world with new eyes' (*Nature*, CWE, p. 44). It is only then that we will recognise the invisible handicraft of the north wind, on wintry nights, as nature's 'fierce artificer' who bequeaths to the day 'Astonished Art / To mimic in slow structures, stone by stone, / Built in an age, the mad wind's night-work, / The frolic architecture of the snow'.[10] Nature's design and purpose may be discrete and mysterious to us, but her imprint is everywhere and there, even within ourselves, to be discovered and disclose the relatedness of everything in existence.

Emerson's note strikes an accord with Shelley's speculations (included in a London 1840 edition of Shelley's *Letters from Abroad, Translations, and Fragments* known to Emerson) about the relationship between perceiving self and observed world in 'On Life':

> Nothing exists but as it is perceived. The difference is merely nominal between those two classes of thought which are vulgarly distinguished by the names of ideas and external objects. Pursuing the same thread of reasoning, the existence of distinct individual minds similar to that which is employed in now questioning its own nature, is likewise founded to be a delusion. The words, *I, you, they* are not signs of any actual difference subsisting between the assemblages of thoughts thus indicated, but are merely markers employed to denote the different modifications of the one mind. Let it not be supposed that this doctrine conducts to the monstrous presumption that I, the person who now write and think, am that one mind. I am but a portion of it.[11]

Shelley's insistence on the importance of perception and the limitations of language as a grammatical device is remarkably prescient of Nietzsche's emphasis on the subject as merely a necessary fiction whereby 'We set up a word at the point at which our ignorance begins at which we can see no further, e.g., the word "I", the word "do" . . .' (*WP*, 3, III [482], p. 267). As Shelley concludes, we are brought to the 'verge where words abandon us, and what wonder if we grow dizzy to look down the dark abyss of – how little we know' (*SPP*, p. 508).

In distinctly Shelleyan vein, Thoreau is suspicious of conventional 'Knowledge' and believes in a higher form of wisdom comprising 'Sympathy with intelligence' (*Walking*, TPT, p. 623). 'I do not know that this higher knowledge', Thoreau continues, 'amounts to anything more definite than a sudden . . . revelation of the insufficiency of all that we called Knowledge before . . .' (*Walking*, TPT, p. 623). Such a revelatory moment for Thoreau is arrived at by 'the lighting up of the mist by the sun' (*Walking*, TPT, p. 623). Thoreau's comment, along with his emphasis on intelligence tempered by sympathy, recalls Keats's own sense of 'when we feel the "Burden of the Mystery"' as being as if 'We are in Mist' (*JKL*, 1, pp. 277, 281).[12]

For Emerson, too, the true, mysterious relatedness and right proportion of the self to the world is hampered by our tendency to construe our experience of reality through empirical and conceptual categories that 'freeze their subject under the wintry light of the understanding' (*Nature*, CWE, pp. 48–9). Such modes of thought and understanding blind us to the mystery and the beauty of the quotidian by providing us with a reassuring, comforting sense of 'understanding' when instead, as Emerson urges, 'The invariable mark of wisdom is to see the miraculous in the common' (*Nature*, CWE, p. 49). On Emerson's account, to see otherwise reveals to us that 'Nature is full of a sublime family likeness' and her delight 'in startling us with resemblances in the most unexpected quarters' (*History*, TPE, p. 122). Emerson's advocacy of a renewed encounter with self and world that strips away our misperceptions of existence reworks Shelley's own claim, in *A Defence of Poetry*, that poetry 'purges from our inward sight the film of familiarity which obscures from us the wonder of our being' and enables us to 'feel what we perceive and to imagine that which we know' (*SPP*, p. 533).

Thoreau, Shelley and Keats

Thoreau's own sense of imaginative disclosure shares to a certain degree Shelley's notion of the 'different modifications of the one mind'. Other aspects of Thoreau's notion of imaginative revelation test Keats's suspension of 'a fine isolated verisimilitude caught from the Penetralium of mystery' and, alternatively, delight in the revelation of 'verisimilitude' (*JKL*, 1, p. 194) that flows from the world once mystery has been restored to it. When Thoreau writes of echoes as part of the 'universal lyre' (*Walden*, 'Sounds', *TPT*, p. 375), he does so in a mode that captures Keats's claim that the 'Mind may have its rewards in the repeti[ti]on of its own silent Working' (*JKL*, 1, p. 185):

> The echo is to some extent, an original sound, and therein is the magic and the charm of it. It is not merely a repetition of what was worth repeating in the bell, but partly the voice of the wood, the same trivial words and notes sung by a wood-nymph. (*Walden*, 'Sounds', *TPT*, p. 375)

In a swerve away from Keats, Thoreau's own sense of negative capability does not dissipate difference and division or realise a synaesthetic blurring of the senses, but instead recaptures a dual poetic vision in which a renewed experience of each sense is felt doubly keenly. Thoreau's sharpened double-sense requires that the act of perception (feeling, hearing, seeing and smelling) becomes itself perceptive and speaks of what it is to be caught in a given moment of sensation or experience of feeling, seeing, smelling, tasting or (as with the 'echo') hearing.

Thoreau is again closer to Keats than he may himself have recognised. His echoes of the woods and song of the 'wood nymph' are haunted by Keats's 'leaf-fring'd legend' of 'the dales of Arcady'.[13] Thoreau's meditation on quietness, silence and sound attempts to resolve itself in the contradictory 'ditties of no tone' ('Ode on a Grecian Urn', l. 14) and to approximate those Keatsian repetitions in 'a finer tone' (*JKL*, 1, p. 185). Thoreau's alertness to 'what was worth repeating in the bell' reimagines Keats's own insistence that 'the very word is like a bell' ('Ode to a Nightingale', l. 71). Thoreau presses us not to hear the 'repetition' of the repeating sound of the bell, but within that repetition to listen for a new (and yet continually) heard and unheard sound of the 'notes' of the Dryad and the 'voice of the wood' itself.[14]

Unheard sounds, those Keatsian 'ditties of no tone' of the Grecian Urn, form a silently working and shaping force in the movement of the concluding section to Thoreau's *A Week on the Concord and the Merrimack Rivers* (1849):

> Silence is audible to all men, at all times, and in all places. She is when we hear inwardly, sound when we hear outwardly. Creation has not displaced her, but is her visible framework and foil. All sounds are her servants, and purveyors, proclaiming not only that their mistress is, but is a rare mistress, and earnestly to be sought after. They are so far akin to Silence that they are but bubbles on her surface, which straightaway burst, as evidence of the strength and prolificness of the undercurrent; a faint utterance of Silence, and then only agreeable to our auditory nerves when they contrast themselves with and relieve the former. In proportion as they do this, and are heighteners and intensifies of the Silence, they are harmony and purest harmony. (*TPT*, p. 228)

For Thoreau, silence is a palpable yet elusive presence; a desirable and prized 'mistress' made all the more dear by her rarity. Silence here is the 'undercurrent' of all sounds, but it equally frustrates the possibility of verbal or musical expression by threatening, as does the reticent eloquence of Keats's Grecian Urn, to 'tease us out of thought' (l. 44). Thoreau imaginatively reshapes Keats's 'bride of quietness and foster-child of silence and slow time' (l. 1) into a no less beguiling but equally silent female figure, who courts the eloquence of writers only to deny them their linguistic mastery over her. Thoreau's passage, like Keats's speaker at the end of the Grecian Urn ode, exhibits linguistic control in the face of silence only to relinquish that control ('It were vain for me to endeavour to interpret the Silence' (*TPT*, p. 227)). Such a recognition on Thoreau's part is a means to both open up his own text to interpretation and retain authorial control over those possible (presently silent) meanings that the artefact of his own writing may generate.

Exquisitely typified in 'To Autumn', Thoreau is fascinated with Keats's sense of the 'silent Working[s]' of poetic thought. The temporal, spatial and imagistic architecture of Keats's pastoral elegy and existential meditation is central to Thoreau's revelatory closing scene of *Walking*:

> We had a remarkable sunset one day last November . . . When we reflected that this was not a solitary phenomenon, never to happen again, but that it would happen forever and ever, an infinite number of evenings, and cheer and reassure the latest child that walked there, it was more glorious still.
>
>   . . .

> We walked in so pure and bright a light, gilding the withered grass and leaves, so softly and serenely bright. I thought that I had never bathed in such a golden flood, without a ripple or a murmur in it. The west side of every wood and rising ground gleamed like the boundary of Elysium, and the sun on our backs seemed like a gentle herdsman driving us home at evening.
>
> So we saunter toward the Holy Land, till one day the sun shall shine more brightly than ever he has done, shall perchance shine into our minds and hearts, and light up our whole lives with a great awakening light, as warm and serene and golden as on a bankside in autumn. (*TPT*, pp. 629–30)

Thoreau reflects on a 'remarkable sunset' to discover an 'infinite number of evenings' so, as in Keats's autumnal ode, one single present, transitory, temporal moment encapsulates eternity. The panoramic glance of Thoreau's poetic eye from the particular to the universal, from the material to the spiritual, also marks out a spatial movement from the defined boundaries of woods and meadow to the boundless fields of Elysium. Similarly, within the seasonal and metrical rhythms of Keats's 'To Autumn', human existence ebbs towards its own natural demise and non-existence, coming into being and expiring as naturally as the 'light wind that lives or dies' (l. 29). That Thoreau's revelatory and reassuring 'great awakening light' is described 'as warm and serene and golden as a bankside in autumn' explicitly recalls the setting for much of the funereal autumnal music in Keats's ode.[15]

Thoreau's final sentence in *Walking* alludes to Keats's autumnal ode, as much as it self-consciously recalls an earlier river bank scene in Thoreau's own life and writing:

> But here on the stream of the Concord, where we have all the while been bodily, Nature, who is superior to all styles and ages, is now, with pensive face, composing her poem Autumn, with which no work of man will bear to be compared.
>
> In summer we live out of doors, and have only impulse and feelings, which are all for action, and must wait commonly for the stillness and longer nights of winter before any thought will subside; we are sensible that behind the rustling leaves, and the stacks of grain, and the bare clusters of the grape, there is a field of a wholly new life, which no man has lived; that even this earth was made for more mysterious and nobler inhabitants than men and women. In the hues of October sunsets, we see the portals to other mansions than those we occupy, not far off geographically . . . (*A Week*, *TPT*, pp. 221–2)

By commingling transience with eternity, action with inaction, the corporeal with the incorporeal, Thoreau creates a kaleidoscopic effect of temporal modes, as realised in Keats's own 'To Autumn', which dissolves harvesting activities into the eternity of nature and the annual cycle of the seasons into the passage of a single day. Thoreau's depiction of nature with 'pensive face' engaged in the composition of 'her poem Autumn' remodels Keats's figure of autumn who, with 'patient look', watches 'the last oozings hours by hours' of both the 'cyder-press' ('To Autumn', ll. 20–1) and those last drops of human existence.

Emerson, Thoreau and Subjectivity Revisited

Tracing the poetic presences of Byron, Shelley and Keats in the writings of Emerson and Thoreau identifies important touchstones between how the American writers engaged with, and represented, interactions between the self and world. These centre on questions of process and final end state, of existence and non-existence, of the transcendental and the material, of subjectivity as a continual flux of becoming or subjectivity as a revelatory state of being. Such questions both shape and (supposedly) segregate Emerson's metaphorical treatment of nature as an extension of the observing mind from Thoreau's later writings, which present nature as a separate material entity, a being in its own right, disentangled from a coterminous contract with the human. Both Emerson and Thoreau share in the power of nature to disclose the beauty of existence in all its varied forms but, deviating from Emerson's claim that 'The beauty of nature reforms itself in the mind' for the purposes of 'new creation' (*Nature*, CWE, p. 16), Thoreau has been read as investing in a materiality of the interconnectedness of nature that denies human perception a creative function and questions the grounding (whether as a presence of being or becoming) of selfhood:

> No wonder the earth expresses itself outwardly in leaves, it so labors with the idea inwardly. The atoms have already learned this law, and are pregnant by it. The overhanging leaf sees here its prototype . . . The very globe continually transcends and translates itself, and becomes winged in its orbit . . . The whole tree itself is but one leaf, and rivers are still vaster leaves whose pulp is intervening earth, and towns and cities are the ova of insects in their anvils. (*Walden*, 'Spring', *TPT*, pp. 546–7)

Thoreau's description may recall Keats's axiom that 'if Poetry does not come as naturally as the Leaves to a tree it had better not come at all' (*JKL*, 1, pp. 238–9). Keats's remark, more obviously perhaps than Thoreau's account, operates at the level of analogy. Thoreau's language of analogy elides the distance between the spheres of human and natural activity by presenting us not with poetry as organic life (as Keats does), but with the poetry of the material processes of nature – its rhythms, cadences and patterns – imagined 'inwardly'. Where Thoreau finds in material process an analogy to voice the inner workings of nature, Emerson, by contrast, like Keats's dictum, finds in the outward signs of nature an analogy for human creativity and the workings of the human mind.[16] If this distinction holds true, we might, then, claim that Emerson avows a self that is perpetually caught in a vital process of becoming and Thoreau advocates a sense of self grounded in the metaphysics of being as presence.

Such a distinction proves untenable when we consider that elsewhere Emerson hopes that 'we are not built like a ship to be tossed, but like a house to stand' (*Nature*, *CWE*, p. 30) for a metaphysical anchorage for a self that would otherwise be totally at sea in a continual process of becoming. At key moments, Emerson is also much closer to a conception of being as a mode of revelatory disclosure when, for instance, in analogy with Keatsian overtures, he claims that the Over-Soul or 'the Supreme Being, does not build up nature around us, but puts it forth through us, as the life of the tree puts forth new branches and leaves through the pores of the old' (*Nature*, *CWE*, p. 38). It is only with this realisation that, for Emerson, 'man has access to the entire mind of the Creator, is himself the creator in the finite' (*Nature*, *CWE*, p. 38). Emerson's formulation is as much indebted to Coleridge's theory of the primary imagination, which permits 'a repetition in the finite mind of the eternal act of creation in the infinite I AM',[17] as it is to Shelley's sense of individual minds as 'different modifications of the one mind' (*SPP*, p. 508).

As in Emerson, nature and selfhood for Thoreau often emerge as inseparably melded together and as indivisible as the natural and cultural spheres are from one another. Observed world and observing self dissolve into one another with Keatsian negatively capable ease when Thoreau's own thoughts possess the ability to 'flit by quickly on their migrations'[18] like a flock of sparrows or become multi-varied and strewn like the fallen leaves of autumn. Marked by watery reflections and reflective thoughts, an autumnal boat voyage undertaken by Thoreau reaches a quiet cove, where I unexpectedly find myself surrounded by myriads of leaves, like fellow voyagers, which have the same purpose, or want of purpose, with myself. See this great fleet of scattered leaf-boats, which we paddle amid, in the smooth river bay, each one curled up on every side by the sun's skill, each nerve a stiff Spruce-knee – like boats of hide, and all patterns, Charon's boat probably among the rest, and some with lofty prows and poops, like the stately vessels of the ancients, scarcely moving in the sluggish current . . .[19]

Nature's outward patterns, design and a sense of purpose ('sun's skill') is an extension of the purposeful voyage undertaken in the boat and now accompanied by the fallen leaves as 'fellow voyagers'. But this sense of a chartered voyage with a clear destination is set against a 'want of purpose' in which the 'scattered leaf-boats' and the aimlessly drifting thoughts of the observer have no defined end point in mind. Meandering in 'the sluggish current', neither the 'leaf-boats' (remarkable for their timeless antiquity) nor the scattered leaves of the observer's thoughts (alert to their transience) are eager to hasten the passage of their voyage or time itself. Yet the probable presence of 'Charon's boat' among Thoreau's flotilla of leaves signals the finality of death, the end terminus of all voyages, whether physical or spiritual, even if for now that final crossing of the rivers Styx and Acheron is substituted by a 'scarcely moving' scene that is itself a product of a purposeful indecision in both the natural and mental spheres.

By reimagining the temporal, spatial and figural patterns of Keats's 'To Autumn' and 'Grecian Urn' odes, Thoreau's prose occupies and traverses time (memory, history and myth), place and space to 'tease us out of thought' ('Ode on a Grecian Urn', l. 44). Similarly, Emerson as a writer sought to revisit and revise aspects of Keats's poetics, reworking the dictum 'Beauty is truth, truth Beauty' ('Ode on a Grecian Urn', l. 49) into 'Beauty is its own excuse for being' ('The Rhodora'). For Emerson, the presence of beauty in the ordinary was its own self-justification without, as he may have felt in Keats, the need for any otherworldly or metaphysical underpinnings. Such a yearning for the otherworldly in Keats chimed with Thoreau's own conviction that golden fields of Elysium existed just beyond the boundaries of the known. In spite of these differences and (re)negotiations, the poetic practices and theories of Emerson and Thoreau are indebted to Keats's Spring Odes and their distinctive self-conscious artistry which, as does so much of American Romanticism in their wake, ponder the status of poetry and the role of the poet.

Whitman, Dickinson and Keatsian Influence

Keats had thought seriously about visiting the United States and harboured 'hopes' that 'such a stay in America' (*JKL*, 1, p. 343) would benefit his family and his health. Although his brother and sister-in-law did emigrate, Keats never went to America. This did not deter him from speculating that one of the 'Children' of George and Georgina Keats 'should be the first American Poet' (*JKL*, 1, p. 398). Nor did it prevent him from recreating the supposed moment when Cortez first espied the mountainous isthmus of 'Darien' ('On First Looking into Chapman's Homer', l. 14), which conjoins North and South America. The fact that Keats was confined only to imagining as present the vastness of the American coast has not curtailed the variety and array of responses, as we have already seen, to Keats's own imaginative presence in American letters from the early nineteenth century onwards.[20]

How the poetry of Walt Whitman and Emily Dickinson engages with Keats's poetic bequest is evident from the following brief sketch of their poetic concerns and practice. Two poems in Whitman's *Sea-Drift* are concerned with tragic poetic consciousness. Both poems traverse the threshold of Keats's 'magic casements' to focus on, and distance us from, 'perilous seas, in faery lands forlorn' ('Ode to a Nightingale', ll. 69–70) and their attendant states of confused consciousness. Whitman writes large Keats's 'perilous seas' on the vast canvas of the seascape of America's Eastern Seaboard.

In 'Out of the Cradle Endlessly Rocking', the action of singing recalls Keats's nightingale and serves as a retrospective 'reminiscence' of the decisive event in time and space that fashioned the youthful Whitman into the poet (the 'out-setting bard').[21] Here poetic selfhood is forged into a continual state of becoming through the unending 'self-same song' ('Ode to a Nightingale', l. 65) of a forlorn bird. The song of Whitman's dark songster, recalling Keats's sensuously existential sense in the words 'Darkling I listen' ('Ode to a Nightingale', l. 51), grieves for its lost mate: '*O night! Do I not see my love fluttering out among the breakers? / What is that little black thing I see there in the white?*' ('Out of the Cradle Endlessly Rocking', ll. 79–80, original emphasis). The Whitmanesque imagination transmutes Keats's Miltonic inflected 'Darkling' into the desperately hoped for sighting of the 'little black thing' of the missing (or deceased) she-mate somewhere out there on the horizon.

This unfolding tragic love affair of the two birds sets in motion two contradictory ideas: one, that the sea finally gives up its dark secret to both poet and bird, and the other, that a change within the observing consciousness of the boy would-be-poet grants him access to the tragic secret that the sea has always been whispering. In actuality, this change in the boy's consciousness occurs, simultaneously, within the instance (the moment of perception) that the sea surrenders its 'clew':

> Whereto answering, the sea,
> Delaying not, hurrying not,
> Whisper'd me through the night, and very plainly before daybreak,
> Lisp'd to me the low and delicious word death,
> And again death, death, death, death.
> ('Out of the Cradle Endlessly Rocking', ll. 165–9)

Recalling Keats's 'eternal whisperings' ('On the Sea', l. 1) of the sea, Whitman's contracted phrase 'Whisper'd me' ('Out of the Cradle Endlessly Rocking', l. 167) breathes the poet into existence out of the womb-like 'embalmed [nocturnal] darkness' ('Ode to a Nightingale', l. 43). This verbal contraction both registers the vital birth, albeit tragic, of the would-be poet into an existential poetic consciousness and completes the 'destiny of me', as the poet's subjectivity is that which is whispered into a continual state of becoming (and, by implication, singing) as the 'chanter of pains and joys, uniter of here and hereafter' ('Out of the Cradle Endlessly Rocking', l. 20).

In another of Whitman's twilight coastal poems, 'As I Ebb'd with the Ocean of Life', the specific singularity of purpose and action of a version of Keatsian 'quiet breathing' (*Endymion*, 1. 5) – 'I inhale' ('As I Ebb'd with the Ocean of Life, l. 20) – dramatises an illusory sense of an autonomous self-enclosed state of withdrawn isolation. But in the same breath, Whitman's poem also suggests such introspection is susceptible to (if not akin with) an outer landscape of fractured and fragmenting 'wash'd up drift', 'dead leaves' and breaking billows of the mysterious 'ocean' ('As I Ebb'd with the Ocean of Life', ll. 23, 24, 21).

Instantaneously, Whitman endeavours to preserve the boundaries between self – 'the real Me' ('As I Ebb'd with the Ocean of Life', l. 28) or the Keatsian 'sole self' ('Ode to a Nightingale', l. 72) – and world, while he stages a self decentred by the centripetal force of the ocean's gathering power. The merging of Whitman's 'myself' with 'part of the sands and drift' ('As I Ebb'd with the Ocean of Life', l. 24) is both a wilful enactment of agency and an enforced (by the outer power of the ocean) merger and fracturing of the self. Whitman's perilous romance of the sea, as it does for Keats, encapsulates all elements of life, no matter how painful. Whitman shared in Keats's conviction that the intensity of poetic art is 'capable of making all disagreeables evaporate' (*JKL*, 1, p. 192).

This Keatsian negatively capable poetic intensity is felt through and questioned by the self-reflexivity of Emily Dickinson's poetry. A series of tropes questioning what is visible or invisible culminate in the final stanza of 'From Cocoon forth a Butterfly':

> Till Sundown crept – a steady Tide –
> And Men that made the Hay –
> And Afternoon – and Butterfly –
> Extinguished – in the Sea – [22]

In this poem, light, life and the ability to see, whether with visionary or mundane eyes, is called into doubt. After all, the elusive, enigmatic flight of the butterfly tracks a passage across the sky that marks out its own ephemeral journey from life (emergence from the cocoon) to death as its colourful seen or unseen existence is 'Extinguished' by an implied 'Sea' of darkness.

Dickinson's use of diction and reluctant commitment to certainties in 'From Cocoon forth a Butterfly' captures something of Keats's hope that 'The poetry of earth is never ceasing' ('On the Grasshopper and Cricket', l. 9). Her speakers, like many of Keats's, often reflect on the transient nature of existence.[23] In a late poem, 'The Earth Has Many Keys', Dickinson contemplates further her own mortality and claims 'The cricket is utmost / Of elegy to me' (l. 13). Dickinson is again attuned to both Keats's hopeful claim for the cricket's melody and the funereal song of 'To Autumn'. Nature's music, for Dickinson and Keats, mourns our passing and promises the possibility of an afterlife seemingly secured by the eternal rebound of seasonal change. But Dickinson, after Keats, remains sceptical about the restorative powers of nature. Dickinson's butterfly is a focal centre which absents itself from the visual field and the poem itself. Sensitive to the shifting shades, hues and tones of Keats's 'camelion Poet' (*JKL*, 1, p. 387), Dickinson declares, 'I Dwell in Possibility – / A fairer House than Prose – / More numerous of Windows' ('I Dwell in Possibility'). She reminds us, as Keats understood, that the 'Mansion' of poetic fiction-making consists of 'Many Apartments' (*JKL*, 1, p. 280) and is capacious enough to accommodate numerous 'Windows' – possibilities and perspectives (apertures of vision) – which, paradoxically, can also incorporate impossibilities and ways of not seeing.

Dickinson follows Keats in understanding poetic vision as the imagining of what cannot be seen or felt; an immersion in the Keatsian sensation of 'The feel of not to feel' ('In drear nighted December', l. 21). Conscious also of Keats's weighing-up of beauty, art and truth against our mortal realm in 'Ode on a Grecian Urn', Dickinson's poetry tests whether nature and artistic vision are able to compensate us for our transient and contingent existences. These subtle entanglements of questions of beauty, natural process, selfhood and death in the poetics of Dickinson and Whitman anticipate Wallace Stevens's keen post-Romantic though very Romantic formulation, that 'Death is the mother of all beauty, mystical / Within whose burning bosom we devise / Our earthly mothers waiting, sleeplessly'.[24] This enigmatic entanglement of beauty, nature, death and subjectivity in Romantic and post-Romantic British and American poetics forms the focus of this study's coda.

Notes

1. Ralph Waldo Emerson, *The Collected Works of Ralph Waldo Emerson: Society and Solitude*, vol. 8, ed. Douglas Emory Wilson, intro. Ronald A. Bosco (Cambridge, MA: Harvard University Press, 2010), p. 30. Hereafter *CWES*.
2. Robert Sattlemeyer, *Thoreau's Reading: An Intellectual Life with Bibliographical Catalogue* (Princeton: Princeton University Press, 1988), pp. 155, 168.
3. Ralph Waldo Emerson, *The Topical Notebooks of Ralph Waldo Emerson*, vol. 2, ed. Ronald A. Bosco, intro. Ralph H. Orth (Columbia: University of Missouri Press, 1993), pp. 234, 291. For an account of the influence of Thomson, Gray, Wordsworth and Shelley on Emerson's earlier work see Lisa M. Steinman, *Masters of Repetition: Poetry, Culture, and Work in Thomson, Wordsworth, Shelley, and Emerson* (New York: St. Martin's, 1998), pp. 160–5.
4. George Gordon Byron, *Childe Harold's Pilgrimage*, in *Lord Byron: The Major Works*, ed. Jerome J. McGann (Oxford: Oxford University Press, 2008), III, 3, l. 20. Hereafter *CH*. All Byron quotations are from this volume.
5. Ralph Waldo Emerson, *The Collected Works of Ralph Waldo Emerson: Nature, Addresses, and Lectures*, vol. 1, ed. Alfred Riggs Ferguson, Joseph Slater and Joseph Ferguson Carr, intro. Robert E. Spiller (Cambridge, MA: Belknap-Harvard, 1971), p. 10. Hereafter *CWE*. All Emerson quotations are from this edition unless otherwise stated.
6. John Keats, *The Letters of John Keats 1814–1821*, 2 vols, ed. Hyder Rollins (Cambridge, MA: Harvard University Press, 1958), 1, p. 301. Hereafter *JKL*. All quotations are from this edition.

7. Branka Arsić, *Bird Relics: Grief and Vitalism in Thoreau* (Cambridge, MA: Harvard University Press, 2016), n. 4 (On Keats), p. 401. Keats writes of Milton's genius being 'Some Sort of thing that operated with in him escaping his control – breaking out into otherness'.

8. Ralph Waldo Emerson, *The Complete Works of Ralph Waldo Emerson: Essays Second Series*, vol. 3, ed. Alfred R. Ferguson and Jean Ferguson Carr, historical intro. Joseph Slater and textual intro. Jean Ferguson Carr (Cambridge, MA: Belknap Press, 1983), p. 11. Compare with Thoreau, *TPT*, p. 367.

9. Ralph Waldo Emerson, 'The Over-Soul', in *The Complete Works of Ralph Waldo Emerson: Essays First Series*, vol. 2, ed. Alfred R. Ferguson and Jean Ferguson Carr, historical intro. Joseph Slater and textual intro. Jean Ferguson Carr (Cambridge, MA: Belknap Press, 1979), p. 174.

10. Ralph Waldo Emerson, 'The Snow-Storm', in *The Portable Emerson*, ed. Carl Bode and Malcolm Cowley (Harmondsworth: Viking-Penguin, 1981), p. 681. Hereafter *TPE*.

11. Percy Bysshe Shelley, *Shelley's Poetry and Prose*, ed. Donald H. Reiman and Neil Fraistat (1977; New York: Norton, 2002), p. 508, original emphasis. Hereafter *SPP*. All Shelley quotations are from this edition unless otherwise stated.

12. For a detailed discussion of Keats's latent modernity and anticipatory poetics see Emily Rohbach, *Modernity's Mist: British Romanticism and the Poetics of Anticipation*, Lit Z Series (New York: Fordham University Press, 2016).

13. John Keats, 'Ode on a Grecian Urn', in *The Poems of John Keats*, ed. Jack Stillinger (1978; Cambridge, MA: Harvard University Press, 1979), p. 282, ll. 7, 5. All quotations of Keats's poetry are from this edition.

14. For a discussion of the importance of the sense of sound for Thoreau see Kerry McSweeney, *The Language of the Senses: Sensory-Perceptual Dynamics in Wordsworth, Coleridge, Thoreau, Whitman, and Dickinson* (Liverpool: Liverpool University Press, 1998), pp. 101–3.

15. Compare with Lorrie Smith, '"Walking" from England to America: Re-Viewing Thoreau's Romanticism', *The New England Quarterly* 58 (1985): 221–41.

16. See Sean Ross Meehan, 'Ecology and Imagination: Emerson, Thoreau, and the Nature Metonymy', *Criticism*, 55.2 (2013): 314; 299–329. For a sense of Emerson's more 'earthly' mode of thinking in contrast with Thoreau's 'embodied thinking' see David Robinson, *Natural Life: Thoreau's Worldly Transcendentalism* (Ithaca: Cornell University Press, 2004), pp. 110–14.

17. Samuel Taylor Coleridge, *Biographia Literaria; or Biographical Sketches of my Life and Work*, 2 parts, vol. 7, in *The Collected Works of Samuel Taylor Coleridge*, ed. James Engell and Walter Jackson Bate (London: Routledge & Kegan Paul, 1983), p. 304.

18. Henry David Thoreau, *Notes on Birds of New England*, ed. Francis H. Allen, illus. John James Audubon (New York: Dover, 2019), p. 223.

19. Henry David Thoreau, *Autumnal Tints* (Bedford, MA: Applewood, 1996), p. 32.

20. This and the following account draw on my 'American Writing', in *Keats in Context*, ed. Michael O'Neill (Cambridge: Cambridge University Press, 2017), pp. 300–9.

21. Walt Whitman, 'Out of the Cradle Endlessly Rocking', in *The Complete Poems*, ed. Francis Murphy (Harmondsworth: Penguin, 1996), p. 275, l. 144. All quotations of Whitman's poetry are from this edition.

22. Emily Dickinson, *Emily Dickinson: The Complete Poems*, 2nd edn, ed. Thomas H. Johnson (London: Faber, 1975), p. 168. All quotations of Dickinson's poetry are from this edition.

23. Compare with Richard Gravil, *Romantic Dialogues: Anglo-American Continuities, 1776–1862* (New York: St. Martin's, 2000), pp. 187–212.

24. Wallace Stevens, 'Sunday Morning', in *Wallace Stevens: Collected Poems* (London: Faber, 1984), VI, p. 61. Unless otherwise stated all Stevens quotations are from this edition.

Part II

Romantic Transactions:
Subjects in Nature

Dissolving Subjectivities: Imagined Selves in F. Scott Fitzgerald and John Keats

Undoubtedly John Keats was a persistent presence in the creative life of F. Scott Fitzgerald who found in the poet's work some of 'the richest most sensuous imagery in English, not excepting Shakespeare'.[1] Numerous critics have traced Fitzgerald's fascination with Keats's Odes and narrative poems in *The Beautiful and Damned* (1922), *The Great Gatsby* (1925) and *Tender is the Night* (1934).[2] There is a critical tendency to reduce the influence of Keats's poetry to a treasure-trove of images that Fitzgerald plundered for his own prose passages or, alternatively, to read Fitzgerald through Keats's idealising worlds of self-contained romance populated by alluring *femmes fatales* and forlorn heroines.[3] More significantly, Keats's poetry provides the template for the ambivalence of sympathy exhibited in Fitzgerald's fiction. Identifying this sympathetic ambivalence recognises an essential aspect of Fitzgerald's writing, which maps subjectivity from the immediacy of within and often marshals an incisive judgement from without. Fitzgerald's fictive mode – one of empathy and critical distance – is itself an exercise in Keats's negatively capable poetics in which the artistic self, in Keats's words, 'is every thing and nothing – It has no character – it enjoys light and shade; it lives in gusto be it foul or fair . . . It has as much delight in conceiving an Iago as an Imogen' (*JKL*, 1, p. 387). This critical and creative engagement with the ever-present 'Fiery Particle'[4] of Keats's poetic presence is central to Fitzgerald's fictional spaces of feeling and memory.

Writing in 1936, Fitzgerald does not – ironically, given 'The Romantic Egoist' was the title of his first abandoned novel[5] – appreciate Keats's distinction between the 'camelion Poet' and 'the Wordsworthian or egotistical sublime' (*JKL*, 1, p. 387). In *The Crack-Up* Fitzgerald worried '*he had become identified with the objects of my horror or compassion*' (original emphasis) and found in William Wordsworth and Keats a resistance to that over-identification which 'spells the death of accomplishment':

> It was dangerous mist. When Wordsworth decided that 'there had passed away a glory from the earth', he felt no compulsion to pass away with it, and the Fiery Particle Keats never ceased his struggle against t.b. nor in his last moments relinquished his hope of being among the English poets. (*CU*, p. 52)

Fitzgerald identifies his own weakness as an over-engagement with his subject – or what he describes as 'a melancholy attitude towards melancholy' – to distinguish himself from the resistant self-interest of a Wordsworthian or Keatsian aesthetic. But, in the same breath, Fitzgerald recognises his own condition as 'distinctly not modern' and likens his own 'self-immolation' to 'something sodden-dark' (*CU*, p. 52). Fitzgerald's choice of compound adjective echoes the 'sod' ('Ode to a Nightingale', l. 60) of Keats's Ode to the darkling songster which, as Fitzgerald confessed to his daughter, Scottie, 'I can never read through without tears in my eyes' (*LSF*, p. 104). Even when Fitzgerald distances himself from Keats's Romantic poetic self, he affirms Keats's notion of self-dissolution (recast as a flaming sacrificial act of 'self-immolation'[6]) as that moment the observing self is overwhelmed by the entirety of existence which extended, in Keats's view, to the sublime 'setting-sun' and the insignificant sparrow picking 'about the Gravel' (*JKL*, 1, p. 186). For Fitzgerald, his own aesthetic success was, paradoxically, dependent on the hope that the trajectory of 'the ego would continue as an arrow shot from nothingness to nothingness with such force that only gravity would bring it to the earth at last' (*CU*, p. 40).

Keats, Fitzgerald and Inwardly Felt Poetics

Four years later Fitzgerald, reflecting on his own style and the artistry of his contemporaries Ernest Hemingway and Thomas Wolfe, perceives with uncanny Keatsian precision the differences between Wordsworth and Keats:

> What family resemblance there is between we three as writers is the attempt that crops up in our fiction from time to time to recapture the exact feel of a moment in time and space, exemplified by people rather

than by things – that is, an attempt at what Wordsworth was trying to do rather than what Keats did with such magnificent ease, an attempt at a mature memory of a deep experience. (*LSF*, p. 270)

That Fitzgerald, eventually, sided with Keats is in itself unsurprising.[7] 'Poetry', Fitzgerald once observed, 'is either something that lives like fire inside you . . . or else it is nothing, an empty . . . formalised bore' (*LSF*, p. 104). Such a declaration about poetry as an elemental – the fiery quality Fitzgerald associated with Keats's character and poetic temperament[8] – and natural force is tinged by the sentiment of Keats's own maxim that 'if Poetry comes not as naturally as Leaves to a tree it had better not come at all' (*JKL*, 1, pp. 238–9). Fitzgerald had, even before the publication of *The Crack-Up*, speculated that the indelible 'nostalgic sadness' which marked his own work was a consequence of reading 'Keats a lot' (*LSF*, p. 547) in his youth. This view was maintained by Fitzgerald in an earlier letter to Morton Kroll, dated 9 August 1939, where he concurred 'that one's first influences are largely literary but the point where the personal note emerges *can* come very young (*vidé* Keats)' (*LSF*, p. 613, original emphasis).

What is more remarkable is how Fitzgerald conceives of a distilled 'memory of a deep experience' as comprising a precise imaginative recollection of 'the exact feel of a moment in time and place'. Embodying Keats's 'trembling delicate' sense of 'snail-horn perception' (*JKL*, 1, p. 265), poetic writing, for Fitzgerald, exhibits 'the most concentrated form of style' which is sensitively attuned to the inward and outward, visible and invisible, emotional, psychic and physical pressures on an entity in a given temporal and spatial instance.[9] As the definition of 'tremble' is for the body 'to shake involuntarily as with fear or some other emotion' (*OED*), Keats lights upon the perfect verb to describe both his and Fitzgerald's artistic purposes. Fitzgerald's emphasis on the ability of the imagination to 'recapture' what inwardly and outwardly is acutely felt in a particular 'moment of time and space' is indebted to, and resembles, the transformative capacity of Keats's 'camelion Poet' to enter into another being's life-force, trembling delicately with every pulse of its existence.

For Fitzgerald, Keats was the assured exponent of the compressed verbal phrase capable of lending an exterior solidity and interior sensation to his chosen poetic subject. In the opening of *The Eve of St. Agnes*, a narrative poem in Spenserian stanzas admired by Fitzgerald as 'probably the finest technical poem in English', he found one of many such instances to justify his admiration for Keats's poetic accomplishments:

> A line like 'The hare limped trembling through the frozen grass,' is so alive that you race through it, scarcely noticing it, yet it has colored the whole poem with its movement – the limping, trembling and freezing is going on before your eyes. (*LSF*, p. 44)

As these observations of Fitzgerald imply, Keats's use of the verb 'trembling' on this occasion concretises the principle of Keatsian 'snail-horn perception' in practice, forging an intimacy between exterior physical effect and interior felt emotion. In spite of the vibrancy Keats breathes into this third line of *The Eve of St. Agnes*, the outward 'frozen grass' slows the pace of the line and the description of those living things, touching an inward nerve with the hare's hampered, fearful and presumably painful struggle through these wintry environs. It is precisely this empathetic ability to dissolve into these momentary inward spaces of feeling which Fitzgerald identified with Keats's negatively capable poetics and used as a model for his own artistry.

Keats's Poetic Signature in *The Beautiful and Damned*

Keats's 'signature' is one of many ghostly presences which abide with the past that haunts the tragic and debilitating decline of the disastrous marriage of Anthony Patch to Gloria Gilbert in Fitzgerald's second novel. In a crucial passage from *The Beautiful and Damned*,[10] Fitzgerald's poetics of transient intimacy and inner feeling self-consciously reveal the spectral Romantic presence of Keats's poetic 'signature'. Fitzgerald's narrator glances wistfully back to bygone times and anticipates the emotional waste yet to come:

> Halcyon days like boats drifting along slow-moving rivers; spring evenings full of a plaintive melancholy that made the past beautiful and bitter, bidding them look back and see that the loves of other summers long gone were dead with the forgotten waltzes of their years. Always the most poignant moments were when some artificial barrier kept them apart: in the theatre their hands would steal together, join, give, and return gentle pressures through the long dark; in the crowded rooms they would form words with their lips for each other's eyes – not knowing that they were following in the footsteps of dusty generations but comprehending dimly that if truth is the end of life happiness is a mode of it, to be cherished in its brief and tremulous moment. (*BD*, p. 116)

The touch of Keats's hand is felt in the delicacy of Fitzgerald's prose which, attuned to the transitory nature of love and beauty, is tinged with a 'plaintive melancholy' and an awareness of those passing 'dusty generations' that recollects the phrasing of Keats's Spring Odes. Fitzgerald's 'plaintive melancholy' and 'forgotten waltzes' reimagine the fading 'plaintive anthem' (l. 75) of Keats's birdsong at the close of 'Ode to a Nightingale' just as Fitzgerald's lost 'dusty generations' borrows from the transient 'hungry generations' (l. 62) Keats depicts in the previous stanza of the same poem. Through allusions to Keats's Ode, replete with its Nightingale's 'happiness' (l. 5), summers of 'dance, Provençal song, and sunburnt mirth' (l. 15), and alluring 'embalmed darkness' (l. 43), Fitzgerald recreates 'the loves of other summers long gone' as a poignant and wakeful vision of past and future disappointed love, failed connection and broken dreams. Anthony and Gloria are as oblivious to the emotional and physical devastation that awaits them as they are to their own incompatibility as a couple because – as Fitzgerald writes in a sentence that recalls the circumstances in which Keats is said to have composed 'Ode to a Nightingale'[11] – 'both were walking alone in a dispassionate garden with a ghost found in a dream' (*BD*, p. 116).

That Fitzgerald was intrigued by Keats's adjectival use of 'plaintive' is evident in the final scene of a short story published by Scribner in the autumn of 1922. 'Winter Dreams' was a transitional work, later collected in *All the Sad Young Men* (1926), which, consolidating an essential theme of his past and next major work, meditates in its closing pages on the loss of dreams, youth and love – all of 'these things were no longer in the world' – without ever fully realising the mythic grandeur of the final sentiment of *The Great Gatsby*. Yet stylistically, Fitzgerald's description of when 'the dream was gone' – and Dexter Green's efforts to rekindle his pure vision of Judy Jones (a prototype for Daisy Fay in *The Great Gatsby*) – achieves a tighter Keatsian precision in the felt, vernal sensuality of 'her mouth damp with his kisses and her *eyes plaintive with melancholy* and her freshness like new fine linen in the morning' (emphasis added).[12] Fitzgerald's fiction frequently inhabits, as does Keats's speaker at the close of 'Ode to a Nightingale', a bewildering world of fled vision and lost dreams.

Allusions to Keats may abound in this passage and elsewhere, but the genuine measure of his influence on Fitzgerald's writing resides with Keats's negatively capable poetics. Fitzgerald shares with Keats a fascination with those almost imperceptible inward spaces of feeling contained within the 'brief and tremulous moment' (*BD*, p. 116) of blossoming tragic romance between Anthony and Gloria. As Keats's speaker, enclosed in seductive darkness in the fifth stanza of 'Ode to a Nightingale', imagines with vivid tactility – achieved through the coalescence of taste, smell and sight – the intimacy of the visual scene hidden from view, so Fitzgerald's narrator empathetically penetrates the 'long dark' to recapture the inner life of 'gentle pressures', comprising those stolen 'poignant moments' when the lovers' hands commingle. Lips and eyes, sight and taste combine to synaesthetic effect in Fitzgerald's rendering of those intimate instances when Anthony and Gloria 'would form words with their lips for each other's eyes'.

For all Fitzgerald imaginatively dissolves the narrator's self into these 'tremulous moments' that form these private engagements between the lovers, the reference to the 'artificial barrier' – with its attendant sense of artifice – highlights an ironic distancing and curtailing of empathy, which pulls back from a complete self-dissolution in the inner, intimate life described. A life, in the case of Anthony and Gloria, composed of not so much feeling but 'artificial' unfeeling, as they play out their respective roles in the courtship game and subsequent marriage. Fitzgerald's depiction of these 'gentle pressures' of the inner life of *unfelt* feeling recalls the acute negation of feeling, which in itself becomes a positive sensation, that Keats records in those agonisingly anaesthetising opening lines of 'Ode to a Nightingale', dominated as they are by the poet's sense of a painful 'drowsy numbness' (l. 1). Keats understood such a felt negation of sensation as the negatively capable poet's ability to experience 'the feel of not to feel it' ('In drear nighted December', l. 21).

In *The Beautiful and Damned*, Keats's ever-present Romantic 'signature' acts as a cipher for those paradoxical tensions between authentic and inauthentic feeling. On a visit to General Lee's Arlington House, Virginia, Gloria objects to Anthony's desire to 'preserve old things' by posing the question, 'Would you value your Keats letter if the signature was traced over to make it last longer?' (*BD*, p. 140). Gloria yearns after an authentic feel of the past in terms which, ironically, prefigure her own physical demise into a 'sort of dyed and *unclean*' (*BD*, p. 361, original emphasis) woman, when she declares:

> 'It's just because I love the past that I want this house [General Lee's] to look back on its glamorous moment of youth and beauty, and I want its stairs to creak as if to the footsteps of women with hoop-skirts and men in boots and spurs. But they've made it into a blondined, rouged-up old woman of sixty.' (*BD*, p. 140)

Unwittingly, Gloria's words retrace those 'footsteps of dusty generations' of ill-fated lovers mired, for all the youthful optimism and expectations, in the brutally real world of disappointment and the unavoidable exigencies of mortality and death. Unlike Anthony's 'craving for romance' and impulsive preservation of beauty, Gloria contends that 'there's no beauty without poignancy and there's no poignancy without the feeling that it's going, men, names, books, houses – bound for dust – mortal' (*BD*, p. 140). Neither possesses empathy – as demonstrated, albeit in a limited manner, by the negatively capable sensitivity of Fitzgerald's narrator – for the antithetical aesthetic sensibility of the other. Therein unfolds the tragedy of their relationship. Anthony and Gloria lack the selfless empathy required for what Fitzgerald understood as the mark of 'a first-rate intelligence', which 'is the ability to hold two opposed ideas in the mind at the same time' (*CU*, p. 39). Fitzgerald's ideal is epitomised by Keats's negatively capable poet's capacity to live joyously in 'everything and nothing', 'light and shade' or 'gusto be it foul or fair' (*JKL*, 1, p. 387).

In terms still coloured by Keats's poetics, Fitzgerald reflected further about the 'romantic business' (*CU*, p. 39) of writing, whether it would ever be possible to reconcile the 'contradiction between the dead hand of the past and high intentions of the future' (*CU*, p. 40, emphasis added). Essentially, the novel's failed love affair is a failure of the imagination; a failure of the capacity for self-knowledge, mutual reciprocity of feeling and a sense of purpose. The Patches' disastrous marriage of ill-matched sensibilities, plagued by uncertainties over their vocation in life, discloses those tensions and dilemmas that the negatively capable artist encounters and endeavours to overcome. For Keats, poetic triumphs were typified by contradictory moments 'of being in uncertainties, Mysteries, doubts, without any irritable reaching after fact & reason' (*JKL*, 1, p. 193). Similarly, Fitzgerald felt most triumphant as an artist 'when the fulfilled future and the wistful past were mingled in a single gorgeous moment' (*CU*, p. 63).

Negatively Capable Perspectives and Romantic Identities in *The Great Gatsby*

Fitzgerald's richly impressionistic style, in *The Great Gatsby*, captures and obscures, reveals and romanticises the reality of a new fast-paced way of modern life in New York which, with the advent of technological developments (the telephone and the car dominate Fitzgerald's prose and determine individuals' personal relations), produces increased commercialisation, consumerism and the desire for individual success and material wealth (reflected in Fitzgerald's abundant references to newspaper adverts, neon lights and billboards). For all that *The Great Gatsby* seemingly revels in modern existence, Fitzgerald's novel equally diagnoses the spiritual, psychological and moral mores of 1920s America – a decline already identified by T. S. Eliot's arch-modernist poem *The Waste Land*, published in 1922, the same year that *The Great Gatsby's* narrative is set. Eliot's fragmented epic for the modern age is directly alluded to at the opening of chapter 2, where Fitzgerald captures the outer and inner existences of those who dwell in the 'desolation' that is the 'valley of ashes':

> About half-way between West Egg and New York the motor road hastily joins the railroad and runs beside it for a quarter of a mile, so as to shrink away from a certain desolate area of land. This is a valley of ashes – a fantastic farm where ashes grow like wheat into ridges and hills and grotesque gardens; where ashes take the forms of houses and chimneys and rising smoke and, finally, with a transcendent effort, of ash-grey men, who move dimly and already crumbling through the powdery air. Occasionally a line of grey cars crawls along an invisible track, gives out a ghastly creak, and comes to rest, and immediately the ash-grey men swarm up with leaden spades and stir up an impenetrable cloud, which screens their obscure operations from your sight. But above the grey land and the spasms of bleak dust which drift endlessly over it, you perceive, after a moment, the eyes of Doctor T. J. Eckleburg. The eyes of Doctor T. J. Eckleburg are blue and gigantic – their retinas are one yard high.[13]

Here we certainly feel the presence of Eliot's poetically realised spiritual vacuity of *The Waste Land*, but we also detect the influence of Joseph Conrad, as this desolate 'valley of ashes' is realised through Fitzgerald's incessant repetition of 'ashes', 'ash' and 'grey' to convey his sense of spiritual and moral loss, which is as inscrutable and as all-pervasive as the darkness of Conrad's *Heart of Darkness*.[14] Fitzgerald's reimagining of Eliot's spiritual waste land is subjected to the 'persistent stare' of those 'blue and gigantic' eyes of Doctor T. J. Eckleburg, whose billboard is an emblem of the consumerist desires of modern America and perhaps, as well, an indictment of the consumer culture and capitalism of which this newly erected god-like (godless) figure is an inevitable product. The 'motor road' and the 'line of grey cars' points up the rapid technological progress of the era and provides a counterpoint to Fitzgerald's sumptuous depiction of Jay Gatsby's parties and party-goers whose

> cars from New York are parked five deep in the drive, and already the halls and salons and verandas were gaudy with primary colours and hair shorn in strange new ways and shawls beyond the dream of Castile. (*GG*, p. 42)

On a cursory reading, this description of the latest fad, fashion and colours has a more seductive appeal than Fitzgerald's description of the 'valley of ashes', but the adjective 'gaudy' – as does the earlier phrase 'fantastic farm' – suggests that there is something preternatural, even against nature, about this modern way of life. Fitzgerald consciously conjures with the adjectives 'fantastic' and 'gaudy' to create an equally inwardly felt sense of how precarious such an unnatural existence might be. Such anxieties, Nick assures us, troubled Gatsby's fitful sleep, as 'The most grotesque and fantastic conceits haunted him in his bed at night. A universe of ineffable gaudiness spun itself out in his brain while the clock ticked on the washstand and the moon soaked with wet light his tangled clothes upon the floor' (*GG*, p. 95). This sense of the 'unreality of reality' (*GG*, p. 95), divorced from clock time, represents the extent to which Gatsby is out of step with the present moment and that modern life has lost touch with the natural order of things.

This increasing rootlessness of modern life provides a clue as to one way that we might respond to Gatsby. It is possible amongst all of the fragmented stories that we hear about Gatsby to read him through a prism of partial perspectives, as one of the last great Romantics who clings to the belief that the 'world was securely founded on a fairy's wing' (*GG*, p. 96). Gatsby's numerous reinventions of himself (eventually as Major Gatsby) are Romantic reimaginings of his identity, what Nick understands early in the novel as Gatsby's 'romantic readiness' (*GG*, p. 8) or later as Gatsby's 'Platonic conception of himself' (*GG*, p. 95). If Gatsby is a latter-day Romantic out of step with his own time (symbolised by Gatsby's precarious catching 'with trembling fingers' (*GG*, p. 84) the clock that he nearly knocks off the mantelpiece), then he finds his end indirectly at the hands of the modern technology of an aggressively progressive society that masks beneath its gaudy veneer a 'violent confusion' (*GG*, p. 54).

Nick Carraway's efforts to record the story or biography of Gatsby, presumably in a bid to obtain a clearer sense of Gatsby's personality and qualities, only further intensify the opacity, imprecision and confusion surrounding Gatsby's real nature. This tension is evident in Nick's curious final judgement (given at the outset of the narrative) that Gatsby represents 'everything for which I have an unaffected scorn' and possessed 'something gorgeous about him, some heightened sensitivity to the promises of life' (*GG*, p. 8). Nick's recollection of Gatsby turns out to be as much about trying to record clearly his biography as it is about mythologising the figure of Jay Gatsby.

Nick's double-edged response to Gatsby's personality mirrors Fitzgerald's response to American society in the 1920s that his novel both mythologises and demythologises. Nick's ambivalent attitude is explained partially by his sympathy for what Gatsby has done as he, too, aspires to a certain degree of 'romantic readiness' and reinvention of himself as the American ideal of the self-made man. Nick's desire for hard-working, honest success is at odds with the duplicitous society in which he finds himself implicated and which he comes to despise. Duplicity is the common currency in a society where Jordan Baker is a professional golfer and cheat, Myrtle Wilson is a wife and a mistress, Meyer Wolfsheim is a respectable business-man and a shady gangster, and Gatsby is a gentleman and bootleg-ger. Such a society is dominated by the nouveau riche of Tom and Daisy Buchanan, whose surface sophistication so often readily erupts into violence because, as Nick testifies, the Buchanans were 'careless people, they smashed things up and then retreated back into their money or their vast carelessness' (*GG*, p. 170).

Frequently, technology (especially in the form of the automobile) and violence carelessly collide in *The Great Gatsby*. One such col-lision dispels the Romantic enchantment of one of Gatsby's music-filled 'summer nights', where 'in his blue gardens men and girls came and went like moths among the whisperings and the champagne and the stars' (*GG*, p. 39). Nick informs us as the party draws to a close:

> But as I walked down the steps I saw that the evening was not quite over. Fifty feet from the door a dozen headlights illuminated a bizarre and tumultuous scene. In the ditch beside the road, right side up, but violently shorn of one wheel, rested a new coupé which had left Gatsby's drive not two minutes before. The sharp jut of a wall accounted for the detachment of the wheel, which was now getting considerable attention from half a dozen curious chauffeurs. However, as they had left their cars blocking the road, a harsh, discordant din from those in the rear had been audible for some time, and added to the already violent confu-sion of the scene. (*GG*, p. 54)

This is one of many such incidents in Fitzgerald's novel that associate the automobile with violence and even death. In the drive across New York City, 'Gatsby's splendid car' is caught up in the 'sombre holi-day' of a funeral cortege and its occupants witness 'a dead man . . . in a hearse heaped with blooms' (*GG*, p. 67). These references to the automobile, death and acts of violence both prefigure and culminate in (figuratively, at least) Daisy's killing of Myrtle Wilson whilst behind the wheel of Gatsby's distinctive (and readily identifiable) Rolls-Royce and Gatsby's death at the hands of Myrtle's husband. Moments before the occupants of Gatsby's car witness the procession of funeral cars, Fitzgerald presents us with a description of New York that renders her as a city of magnificent, dream-like – if not child-like – possibilities; a place of enormous promise that anticipates the novel's final description of the promise that America, as the 'fresh, green breast of the new world' (*GG*, p. 171), must have held out to its first settlers:

> Over the great bridge, with the sunlight through the girders making a constant flicker upon the moving cars, with the city rising up across the river in white heaps and sugar lumps all built with a wish out of non-olfactory money. The city seen from the Queensboro Bridge is always the city seen for the first time, in its wild promise of all the mystery and the beauty in the world. (*GG*, p. 67)

From this description, New York as the stuff of dreams at least on the surface appears to be an antidote to those soulless grey heaps of the 'valley of ashes', but it is, as Nick gradually realises, complicit in the spiritual and moral vacuity that lurks beneath its alluring, shiny, sun-lit surfaces. Such 'mystery' and 'beauty' Daisy might term 'romantic' but, for all that we are told of the mellifluous quality of her voice, it is apparent that she is not at all articulate and has a tendency to repeat phrases or words. One instance of this occurs when Daisy insists, on hearing a nightingale (Keats's poetic bird) singing in a garden, that it is 'romantic' – repeating the word until it is emptied of all meaning and only dully repeated by Tom (*GG*, p. 20),[15] who has no connection or empathy with such Romantic notions or old world sentiment.

Fitzgerald's *The Great Gatsby* is haunted by sumptuously visual sequences of, among other things, alluring twilights, Gatsby's golden parties, the luminescence of brightly lit modern New York's sidewalks and vibrant city-life. Fitzgerald's lyrical descriptions consist of one beautifully compressed 'single gorgeous moment' after another, which encapsulate the appealing present and seductive past. Like Keats's negatively capable poet, Nick's articulation of the inner meaning of the 'fragment of lost words' (*GG*, p. 112), which forms Gatsby's mythical biography, is caught delicately, often excruciatingly, between the fulfilment of a potential 'single gorgeous moment' and those elusive wasted 'poignant moments of night and life' (*GG*, p. 58), between empathetic Romantic immersion and a modern cold, ironic detachment. Such Romantic moments of communicating the 'uncommunicable' (*GG*, p. 112) circumscribe the inward space that is familiar terrain to the negatively capable poet and one which

Nick's mode of narration, in *The Great Gatsby*, often inhabits. Nick exhibits a remarkable imaginative empathy with those 'unbroken series of successful gestures', which might constitute Jay's 'personality', attributing to them 'something gorgeous' as well as a negatively capable 'heightened sensitivity to the promises of life' (*GG*, p. 2). As revealed through Gatsby's over-identification with an irrecoverable lost personal moment of 'unutterable visions' (*GG*, p. 112), embodied by Daisy and symbolised by her 'single green light' (*GG*, p. 22, p. 183), Nick exhibits a similar Keatsian capacity to live imaginatively in the private and intimate inner world of others. They may share this negatively capable ability and need to relive the past, but Nick, unlike Gatsby, does not think the past, in his case of his youth in the Midwest, is recoverable.[16] A social pariah and Westerner, like Gatsby himself, Nick possesses an unnervingly detached and intimate acquaintance with the lives of those he glimpses, voyeuristically, on the dark city-streets:

> I began to like New York, the racy, adventurous feel of it at night, and the satisfaction that the constant flicker of men and women and machines gives to the restless eye. I liked to walk up Fifth Avenue and pick out romantic women from the crowd and imagine that in a few minutes I was going to enter into their lives, and no one would ever know or disapprove. Sometimes, in my mind, I followed them to their apartments on the corners of hidden streets, and they turned and smiled back at me before they faded through a door into warm darkness. At an enchanted metropolitan twilight I felt a haunting loneliness sometimes, and felt it in others – poor young clerks who loitered in front of windows waiting until it was time for a solitary restaurant dinner – young clerks in the dusk, wasting the most poignant moments of night and life. (*GG*, pp. 57–8)

Tracing its geometric interstices of the human and mechanical, enchantment and cityscape, idealised romance and sexual passion, hoped-for fulfilment and disappointed desires, a yearning for attachment and desperate isolation, this passage has been responded to as a quintessentially modernist and abstract perception – with its 'constant flicker' and 'metropolitan twilight' – of the city and its spaces.[17] Nick's perspective, for all that it can be construed as modernist pastiche, exhibits a Keatsian subtlety through its palpable rounding out of those lost 'poignant moments of night and life', whether actual or imagined. Although, in part, a sexually charged fantasy, Nick's depiction of those fading 'romantic women' with their seductively alluring and enveloping 'warm darkness' – a phrase which itself erotically reconfigures the 'warm love' beckoned to by 'a casement ope at night' (ll. 66–7) in the closing lines of Keats's 'Ode to Psyche' – takes on an inwardly felt existence of its own.

This hoped for, but never realised, physical or emotional connection only intensifies the 'haunting loneliness' that Nick 'felt' within himself and 'in others'. Nick is at once the objectively modernist commentator on the fragmented and alienated lives experienced by the city's inhabitants and subjectively absorbed into their inwardly felt lives of wasted opportunities and loneliness. Like Keats's 'camelion Poet', Nick's empathetic self-dissolution equally permits him to share in the 'intimate excitement' of the city's theatre-goers conveyed through the sensual appeal of 'throbbing taxicabs' and the enigmatic dance of 'lighted cigarettes [which] made unintelligible circles inside' (*GG*, p. 58). This minutely observed insignificant detail of the 'unintelligible' patterns of the 'lighted cigarettes' anticipates the electric moment when Gatsby is reunited with his lover and 'he lit Daisy's cigarette from a trembling match, and sat down with her on a couch far across the room, where there was no light save what the gleaming floor bounced in from the hall' (*GG*, p. 96). Fitzgerald's description reinvents Keats's lines, 'But here there is no light, / Save what from the heaven is with the breezes blown' (ll. 39–40), from 'Ode to a Nightingale', to achieve a concentrated emotional intensity – a quality Fitzgerald much admired in Keats – in its use of what Scott Donaldson terms 'unexpected adjectives' to transfer intense inner feeling to the outer visible world of physical effect.[18]

Such an ability 'to enter into their lives' unobtrusively and make us feel these inner psychic and physical spaces of emotional existence and city-life 'upon our pulses' (*JKL*, 1, p. 279) is the poetic achievement of Fitzgerald's prose which, at its best, realises F. R. Leavis's praise for the ability of Keats's poetry to maintain, in every intricate detail, both a 'strong grasp upon actualities' and a 'sense of the solid world'.[19] Leavis's remark is instructive for its insight into Keats's ability to feel with each poetic nerve the most fantastical moments of myth, history and imagination. These dimly distant realms are glimpsed with a refreshingly tactile 'coolness to the eye', for instance, in Keats's rendering of the colossal suffering of Hyperion, who 'stretch'd himself in grief and radiance faint' (*Hyperion*, 1, ll. 210, 304); Cortez, espying the Pacific for the first time, 'silent, upon a peak in Darien' ('On First Looking into Chapman's Homer', l. 14); and those 'perilous seas, in faery lands forlorn' ('Ode to a Nightingale', l. 70).

Like Keats, Fitzgerald aspired to these intensely imaginative moments to realise the unrealisable, to fill the bodies and spaces of those imaginary realms with that pulse-felt solidity of the world of actualities. Nick's narrative culminates in one such exquisitely felt but tragically realised instance, with its hauntingly surreal description of the final event in Gatsby's story:

> No telephone message arrived, but the butler went without his sleep and waited for it until four o'clock – until long after there was anyone to give it to if it came. I have an idea that Gatsby himself didn't believe it would come, and perhaps he no longer cared. If that was true he must have felt that he had lost the old warm world, paid a high price for living too long with a single dream. He must have looked up at an unfamiliar sky through frightening leaves and shivered as he found what a grotesque thing a rose is and how raw the sunlight was upon the scarcely created grass. A new world, material without being real, where poor ghosts, breathing dreams like air, drifted fortuitously about . . . like that ashen, fantastic figure gliding toward him through the amorphous trees. (*GG*, p. 153)

From the opening, this description is poised with an expectancy which finds itself disappointed at the anticipated source of origin ('no telephone message ever arrived') and its anticipated recipient ('long after there was anyone to give it to if it came'). Such doubly disappointed expectation suggests the impossibility of the negatively capable space occupied by Nick's account of Gatsby's life as an expression of the inexpressible, a sudden disjuncture in the processes of communication, a rent in the fabric of narrative events or a short-circuit in the synapses of feeling and meaning. This sudden rapture permits the possibility, at least within Nick's consciousness, of tentative speculation – founded on 'perhaps' and 'if that was true' – about Gatsby's last thoughts. Gradually, Nick's faltering speculations about Gatsby's state of despair and emotional bankruptcy, brought on by the pursuit of a Romantic 'single dream', become a definite ('he *must* have felt', emphasis added) selfless identification with, and total immersion in, Gatsby's own intense perception of his forced abandonment of 'the old warm world'.

On the brink of disaster, Gatsby's and Nick's heightened sensitivities collide in a negatively capable natal instance, which witnesses the reluctant birth of Gatsby's consciousness from the womb-like 'old warm world' and Nick's narrating consciousness, born into the personal intensity of Gatsby's terrifyingly estranged world dominated by 'an unfamiliar sky' and 'frightening leaves'. It is the 'barely perceptible movement' (*GG*, p. 53) of this 'new world, material without being real' which Nick, because of his imaginative absorption into the synaptic gap of these last moments, feels with and through Gatsby. This negatively capable perspective urges the reader to experience the inwardly felt tangibility of a 'grotesque . . . rose' and the rawness of 'the sunlight . . . upon the scarcely created grass' within a scene that, visually and outwardly, dissipates, dissolves and re-forms into real and spectral presences, composed of 'those ghosts, breathing dreams like air' and the fatal approach of George Wilson's undetected 'fantastic figure'.

Fitzgerald's negatively capable spell of Gatsby's last feelings and thoughts before his murder is broken only by Nick's own second-hand relaying of the factual report of 'heard . . . shots' (*GG*, p. 163). This account produces the discovery of Gatsby's body, afloat on a 'mattress' in the pool, that replays the episode with the seeming neutrality of a camera lens, focusing on the externalities of the objects described, including the barely discernible 'fresh flow' of water and the mattress's 'accidental course with its accidental burden' driven by 'a small gust of wind' (*GG*, p. 164). With one final casual but symbolic cinematic flourish, Fitzgerald closes the initial aftermath of this tragic scene with – recalling the ominous autumnal 'yellowing trees' (*GG*, p. 163) alluded to before the carnage – 'the touch of a cluster of leaves . . . tracing . . . a thin red circle in the water' (*GG*, p. 164). Symbolically, the outline of 'a thin red circle' traces the cycles of birth, life and vitality, death, destruction and desire, which governed that 'transitory enchanted moment' when 'Dutch sailors' eyes' first saw 'a fresh green breast of the new world' as much as Gatsby's 'single dream' of his irretrievable past with Daisy.

For all that the 'thin red circle' demarcates those forces at work in the novel, Fitzgerald focuses on the feel, effect and representation of those invisible 'little ripples that were hardly the shadows of the waves' (*GG*, p. 164) circumscribed, but not wholly contained, by the visible bloody ring on the water. The negatively capable tendency of Nick's mode of narration articulates those events, instances and feelings which are not readily perceived and are themselves difficult to authenticate. That one of Nick's last acts is to erase the obscenity which 'stood out clearly in the moonlight', scrawled on the steps of Gatsby house with 'a piece of brick' (*GG*, p. 183), indicates his 'heightened sensitivity' (instrumental to Keats's imagined interiors of 'snail-horn perception') and questions the authenticity of Nick's narrative 'finer tone' (*JKL*, 1, p. 185) in *The Great Gatsby*.[20] 'Erasing' (*GG*, p. 183) the unarticulated although once highly legible piece of graffiti suggests that – in spite of his protests to the contrary – Nick deliberately obscures the origins and meanings of his own past and the past lives of others.[21] The preference Nick expresses for Gatsby has been understood as a successful merging of romantic vision with those lessons that Nick has learnt from the lives and events he narrates.[22] This imaginative union may endeavour to articulate the inner meaning of a 'fragment of lost words' (*GG*, p. 113) but, by Nick's own admission, not all those words are simply lost, because he has consciously erased some from memory and history. As Nick demonstrates in relation to Gatsby, 'romantic speculation' (*GG*, p. 44) is a negatively capable act which dimly illuminates, rather than authenticates, what lies out there 'beyond the city' and those 'fields of the republic' (*GG*, p. 183) obscured by memory and time in the historical darkness.[23]

Tragic Sensibility, Identity and Negative Capability in *Tender is the Night*

Fitzgerald's own anxieties over the conflicting identities between his career as a professional writer and his aspirations as a literary artist intensified in the mature vision of his fiction. Given very different financial and personal constraints, Keats and Fitzgerald were both uncertain of their vocation as writers. The inherent conflicts of the artistic self are, for Fitzgerald, played out in *Tender is the Night* – a title indebted to Keats's own visionary struggle of 'Ode to a Nightingale'[24] – and the novel's portrayal of Dick Diver, who as a psychiatrist embodies objective, scientific, rational detachment and subjective, empathetic, imaginative engagement. Ultimately, the self-division and duality of Dick's sympathies are 'paralyzing [to] his faculties'.[25] This is ironic, given that at the outset of *Tender is the Night* Dick possesses an 'extraordinary virtuosity with people' and is capable of admitting, and absorbing, individuals into his own psychological and emotional world through his 'power of arousing a fascinated and uncritical love' (*TN*, p. 36) in those around him. Those who gain admittance into Dick's inner sanctum of affectations are specifically not 'the tough-minded' and are required to exhibit an 'uncritical' empathy with his intense 'excitement about things' (*TN*, p. 36). To be a part of Dick's 'amusing world' necessitates a reciprocal act of negatively capable self-absorption through which, in return for another's uncritical identification with his own intensity of feelings, Dick unreservedly and selflessly invests in the 'proud uniqueness of their destinies' (*TN*, p. 37). Inclusion, as Fitzgerald's narrator elucidates, within Dick's charmed circle is powerful and transitory:

> But to be included in Dick Diver's world for a while was a remark-able experience: people believed he made special reservations about them, recognising the proud uniqueness of their destinies, buried under the compromises of how many years. He won everyone quickly with an exquisite consideration and a politeness that moved so fast and intuitively that it could be examined only in its effect. Then, without caution, lest the bloom of the relation wither, he opened the gate to his amusing world. So long as they subscribed to it completely, their happiness was his preoccupation, but at the first flicker of doubt as to its all-inclusiveness he evaporated before their eyes, leaving little com-municable memory of what he had said or done. (*TN*, p. 37)

This wonderful evocation of the insubstantial substance of 'Dick Diver's world' conceives of Dick's personality as constructed from a series of effects (as Nick does of Gatsby's own), which are a product of Dick's negatively capable capacity for an intuitive and 'exquisite consideration' for the finer feelings and psychological temperaments of others. Equally, Dick is an exemplum of Keats's own reservations about the empathetic and potentially transformative power of the 'camelion Poet' (*JKL*, 1, p. 387). 'Any flicker of doubt' (or cessation of the ability to remain in 'uncertainties, Mysteries, doubts') on the part of those participants and Dick's fragile social sphere and identity vaporises into the mere trace of memory which, again reminiscent of Gatsby's life, is barely 'communicable'.

Behind this 'remarkable experience', for Dick, as Nicole observes, lurks a darker 'form of melancholy' (*TN*, p. 36), perhaps born of the recognition that his polite world of gestures and decorum han-kers after an older nineteenth-century set of values, destroyed by the unprecedented violent trauma of the Great War.[26] Both profession-ally and personally, Dick's impulse is to redeem those around him even though he feels that the inhabitants of the post-war world are beyond psychological or spiritual redemption. Dick's uncertainty over previously held old world – or what he terms 'old romantic' (*TN*, p. 68) – assumptions about moral character, social values and gender roles precipitates his 'dying fall' (*LSF*, p. 529) in *Tender is the Night*. This calamity is traced through the disintegrating marriage of Nicole and Dick Diver, whose surname denotes his floundering and eventual immersion in modern mores.[27] What Dick fears the most is that the money-driven, superficial, rootless, promiscuous, amoral post-war world will destroy genuine sensibility, robbing individuals of their sense of integrity and interiority, reducing them to hollow 'broken shells' (*TN*, p. 195) in need of salvaging. Tragically, Dick knows that his own precarious world and identity gesture back to a bygone pre-war era for, as he bemoans, touring the First World War trenches in France, 'All my beautiful lovely safe world blew itself up here with a great gust of high explosive love' (*TN*, p. 68). The spectre of war permeates *Tender is the Night* to such an extent that Dick reflects upon 'the carnivals of affection he had given as a general might gaze upon a massacre he had ordered' (*TN*, pp. 36–7).

Fitzgerald's intermingling of the rhetoric of love, affection and military campaign[28] conjoins Dick's noble but ruined intentions of redeeming humanity and the tortured figure of the anonymous female artist afflicted by a severe 'nervous eczema' (*TN*, p. 202), who conceives of herself as a casualty of 'battle' (*TN*, p. 203). Dick's failed intentions and decline dramatise Keats's own misgivings over whether 'a poet is a sage; / a humanist, physician to all men' (*The Fall of Hyperion*, ll. 189–90). The only doctor able to calm the artist 'during spells of over-excitement' (*TN*, p. 202), Dick readily sympathises and identifies with her emotional, intellectual and physical suffering of imprisonment within the 'sarcophagus of her figure' (*TN*, p. 204). Such an agitated state echoes Dick's own tendency towards an 'excitement about things that reaches an intensity out of proportion to their importance' (*TN*, p. 36), implying that Dick and the female artist possess a 'heightened sensitivity' to their own existences and those of others. Like the eczema-plagued artist whose voice of 'subterranean melodies' (*TN*, p. 202) is indicative of beauty now tainted, Dick's magnanimity is corrupted by modern times and Nicole recovers only at the expense of her husband's equilibrium, reputation and self-control. In Fitzgerald's reworking of Keats's central motif in 'La Belle Dame sans Merci' and *Lamia*, Nicole vampirically drains to the dregs the intellectual, professional and emotional resources of Dick's personality.[29]

Both Dick and the artist have lost the worlds they once inhabited and with them they have lost their assured identities, as they struggle to recreate meaningful identities in a rapidly changing and uncertain world without depth, composed of sleek surfaces and 'refracting objects only half noticed' (*TN*, p. 122). Without the certainties of their former existences, Dick and the female artist are left to explore those terrifying '"frontiers of consciousness"' which, he believes, are 'the frontiers that artists must explore' but 'which were not for her, ever' (*TN*, p. 203). In the event, Dick is unable to survive the magnitude of these navigations of the self and he risks becoming, like the artist, an ambiguously undefined 'symbol of something' merely, as she says of herself, '"a ghostly echo from a broken wall"' (*TN*, p. 203).[30] Similar to Keats's negatively capable poet, Dick is anxious that, amidst his alcoholism and the modern chaos, '[h]e had lost himself – he could not tell the hour when, or the day or the week, the month or the year' (*TN*, p. 220).

Dick's divided self – as Nicole's partner and psychiatrist – replays Keats's dilemma, torn between the endless 'delights of the camelion Poet' and the unbearable realisations of the 'virtuous philosopher' (*JKL*, 1, p. 387). The effortless self-dissolution of the 'camelion Poet', attuned to the smallest fluctuations of some other being's essence, can be affirmative and instructive but, as Keats knew as well as Fitzgerald, there is an inherent risk that such imaginative empathy can leave the writer as the 'most unpoetical of any thing in existence; because he has no identity – he is continually in for – and filling some other Body' (*JKL*, 1, p. 387). Bereft of Romantic visions, all that is left to the negatively capable artist is, as Keats writes, 'the journey homeward to habitual self' (*Endymion*, 2, l. 276). Fitzgerald found in the texture of Keats's poetic language and thought the means to elegise his own actual and imaginary lost worlds, to depict their visionary moments as tantalisingly present and irrecoverably past. By the end Fitzgerald realised, as did Keats, that the negatively capable imagination can as easily destroy as create fictions of the self, stripping away our Romantic delusions until we experience the tragic reality of the contingent 'sole self' bound to time, change and circumstance.[31] Early-twentieth-century anxieties about an age that felt too much or did not feel enough, especially in the inter-war years, echo Keats's Romantic debate about rational detachment and imaginative engagement. As a modernist artist, Fitzgerald's wrench between Apollonian disciplined order and Dionysian destructive chaos finds its origin, beyond Nietzsche,[32] in an earlier struggle fought between sensations and thought by Keats's ideal Romantic poet.

Notes

1. Letter to Scottie, 3 August 1940, in *The Letters of F. Scott Fitzgerald*, ed. Andrew Turnbull (Harmondsworth: Penguin, 1968), p. 104. Hereafter *LSF*.
2. See R. L. Schoenwald, 'F. Scott Fitzgerald as Keats', *Boston University Studies in English* 3 (1957): 12–21; John Grube, '*Tender is the Night*:

Keats and Scott Fitzgerald', *Dalhousie Review* 45 (1964): 433–40; Richard D. Lehan, *F. Scott Fitzgerald and the Craft of Fiction* (Carbondale: Southern Illinois University Press, 1966); Dan Macall, '"The Self-Same Song that Found a Path": Keats and *The Great Gatsby*', *American Literature* 42 (1971): 521–30; Margaret Frances Loftus, 'John Keats in the Works of F. Scott Fitzgerald', *KIYO: Studies in English Literature* 7 (1972): 17–26; George Monterio, 'James Gatz and John Keats', *Fitzgerald/Hemingway Annual* (1972): 291–4. See more recently Barry J. Scherr, 'Lawrence, Keats, and *Tender is the Night*: Loss of Self and "Love Battler" Motifs', *Recovering Literature: A Journal of Contextualist Criticism* 14 (1986): 7–17; James W. Tuttleton, 'Vitality and Vampirism in *Tender is the Night*', in *Critical Essays on F. Scott Fitzgerald's 'Tender is the Night'*, ed. Milton R. Stern (Boston: Hall, 1986), pp. 238–46.

3. See Charles Swann, 'A Fitzgerald Debt to Keats? From "Isabella" into *Tender is the Night*', *Notes and Queries* 37 (1990): 437–8; Catherine B. Burroughs, 'Keats's Lamian Legacy: Romance and the Performance of Gender in *The Beautiful and Damned*', in *F. Scott Fitzgerald: New Perspectives*, ed. Jackson R. Bryer, Alan Margolies and Ruth Prigozy (Athens: University of Georgia Press, 2000), pp. 51–62.

4. F. Scott Fitzgerald, *The Stories of F. Scott Fitzgerald: The Crack-Up with Other Pieces and Stories*, vol. 2 (Harmondsworth: Penguin, 1965), p. 52. Hereafter *CU*.

5. Incorporated into *This Side of Paradise*, published in 1920. See F. Scott Fitzgerald, *This Side of Paradise*, ed. and intro. Patrick O'Donnell (Harmondsworth: Penguin, 2000).

6. John Kuehl notes that Fitzgerald and Keats fought a 'struggle between "objectivity" and "subjectivity"'. See Kuehl, *F. Scott Fitzgerald: A Study of the Short Fiction*, Twayne's Studies in Short Fiction, Series 22 (Boston: Hall, 1991), p. 152. Hereafter *SSF*.

7. Alternatively, Stanley Baldwin aligns Fitzgerald with Wordsworth. See Baldwin, 'F. Scott Fitzgerald and Willa Cather: A New Study', in *F. Scott Fitzgerald in the Twenty-First Century*, ed. Jackson R. Bryer, Ruth Prigozy and Milton R. Stern (Tuscaloosa: University of Alabama Press, 2003), p. 179. Hereafter *SFTF*.

8. Ronald Berman claims this association with fire surpasses Romanticism to 'Vergilian rather than Homeric' epic. See Berman, *The Great Gatsby and Fitzgerald's World of Ideas* (Tuscaloosa: University of Alabama Press, 1997), p. 111.

9. Ronald Berman reads Fitzgerald's fiction as centred on moments where 'place becomes space'. See Berman, *Modernity and Progress: Fitzgerald, Hemingway, Orwell* (Tuscaloosa: University of Alabama Press, 2005), p. 51.

10. F. Scott Fitzgerald, *The Beautiful and Damned*, intro. Geoff Dyer (1922; Harmondsworth: Penguin, 2004), p. 140. Hereafter *BD*. Michael

Nowlin notes Fitzgerald's working title for the novel was the Keatsian 'The Beautiful Lady without Mercy'. See Nowlin, 'Mencken's Defense of Women and the Marriage Plot of *The Beautiful and Damned*', *SFTF*, p. 104.

11. Charles Brown claimed that Keats composed 'Ode to a Nightingale' sitting one spring morning in the garden at Wentworth Place. See Robert Gittings, *John Keats* (1968; Harmondsworth: Penguin, 2001), p. 316.

12. F. Scott Fitzgerald, *The Collected Short Stories of F. Scott Fitzgerald* (Harmondsworth: Penguin, 1986), p. 383. See Kuehl, *SSF*, pp. 67–8.

13. F. Scott Fitzgerald, *The Great Gatsby* (1925; Harmondsworth: Penguin, 2006), p. 26. Hereafter *GG*.

14. Harold Bloom points to this imaginative configuration of Fitzgerald, Keats, Conrad and Eliot. Recognising commonality between Eliot's *The Hollow Men* (1925) and *The Great Gatsby* (published the same year), Bloom writes that Fitzgerald's achievement is 'to combine the lyrical sensibility of Keats and the fictive mode of Conrad' (p. 6). See Bloom, ed., *Modern Critical Views of F. Scott Fitzgerald*, Bloom's Modern Critical Views Series (New York: Chelsea, 2013).

15. See Ronald Berman, '*The Great Gatsby* and the Twenties', in *The Cambridge Companion to F. Scott Fitzgerald*, ed. Ruth Prigozy (Cambridge: Cambridge University Press, 2002), pp. 89–90; pp. 79–94. Hereafter *CSF*.

16. See Janet Giltrow and David Stouck, 'Pastoral Mode and Language in *The Great Gatsby*', *SFTF*, pp. 143–4; pp. 139–52.

17. See Ronald Berman's account in *The Great Gatsby and Modern Times* (Urbana and Chicago: Illinois University Press, 1996), pp. 88–91.

18. See Scott Donaldson, *Hemingway vs Fitzgerald: The Rise and Fall of a Literary Friendship* (London: Murray, 2000), p. 302.

19. F. R. Leavis, *Revaluation: Tradition and Development in English Poetry* (1936; Harmondsworth: Penguin, 1964), p. 261.

20. Morris Dickstein explores the 'authority of failure' in Fitzgerald's fiction. See Dickstein, *A Mirror in the Roadway: Literature and the Real World* (Princeton: Princeton University Press, 2005), pp. 77–88. Hereafter *MR*.

21. As Thomas H. Pauly observes, Nick's narration is ambiguous about whether Gatsby is 'one of the last great romantics' or 'a devious criminal mind'. See Pauly, 'Gatsby as Gangster', *Journal of American Fiction* 21.2 (1993): 225–6; 225–36.

22. See Milton R. Stern, *The Golden Moment: The Novels of F. Scott Fitzgerald* (1970; Chicago: University of Illinois Press, 1971), p. 176. Hereafter *GM*.

23. Ronald Berman notes 'what matters as much as the object perceived is the mist and darkness in which it is viewed' (p. 90) in *The Great Gatsby*. See Berman, '*The Great Gatsby* and the Twenties', *CSF*.

24. For a recent detailed account of the shared concerns of irresolution, resistance and mortality in Keats's Ode and Fitzgerald's *Tender is the*

Night see Philip McGowan, 'Reading Fitzgerald Reading Keats', in *Twenty-First-Century Readings of 'Tender is the Night'*, ed. William Blazek and Laura Rattray (Liverpool: Liverpool University Press, 2007), pp. 204–20.

25. F. Scott Fitzgerald, *Tender is the Night* (1934; Harmondsworth: Penguin, 1986), p. 207. Hereafter *TN*.

26. I am indebted to Milton R. Stern's account in *'Tender is the Night* and American History'. See *CSF*, pp. 103–4; pp. 95–117.

27. See Stanley Baldwin on Dick's decline and suspension between new and old worlds, *SFTF*, pp. 186–7.

28. See Milton R. Stern's discussion, *CSF*, pp. 103–9.

29. For a detailed discussion of Fitzgerald's reimagining of this Keatsian motif in *Tender is the Night* see James W. Tuttleton, *Vital Signs: Essays on American Literature and Criticism* (Chicago: Dee, 1996), pp. 263–7.

30. See Stern, *GM*, pp. 339–41.

31. Morris Dickstein understands this moment in Keats and Fitzgerald as 'the self without romantic illusions' (*MR*, p. 88). As Matthew J. Bruccoli comments on *Tender is the Night* and 'Ode to a Nightingale', 'the escape proves illusory, and the poet is called back to the despair of his situation'. See Bruccoli, *The Composition of 'Tender is the Night': A Study of the Manuscripts* (Pittsburgh: Pittsburgh University Press, 1963), pp. 35–40, 174. Milton R. Stern recognises in Fitzgerald a Keatsian 'dark, destructive reconnaissance' (*GM*, p. 462). Andrew Hook suggests 'realism and romanticism' combine as early as Fitzgerald's *The Beautiful and Damned*. See Hook, *F. Scott Fitzgerald: A Literary Life* (London: Palgrave Macmillan, 2002), p. 41.

32. Robert Roulston and Helen H. Roulston note Nietzsche's influence on Fitzgerald. See Roulston and Roulston, *'The Great Gatsby*: Fitzgerald's Opulent Synthesis (1925)', in *Critical Interpretations*, ed. Morris Dickstein (Pasadena: Salem, 2009), p. 141.

Chapter 4

Ghostly Selves, Light and Nature in William Faulkner: Wordsworthian Shadows and Byronic Shades

Romantic shades and presences haunt William Faulkner's literary imagination. 'The depth and quality of Faulkner's romanticism'[1] in his early poetry and verse are, for Cleanth Brooks, undeniable. Subsequent critics have been equally persuaded of the shaping presence of Romanticism in Faulkner's later fiction. Robert M. Slabey reads Faulkner as engaged with, and critical of, a 'Romantic sensibility' of transcendence, Martin Bidney draws on Faulkner's allusions to William Blake, William Wordsworth, Lord Byron, John Keats and P. B. Shelley to trace moments of continuity with Romantic epiphanic episodes, and Dieter Meindl detects a broader 'romantic impulse' in Faulkner that extends beyond healing the schism between subject and object.[2]

Subjectivity is one familiar concern of Faulkner's fiction which, along with those of memory, time, the inescapable past, seasonal change, ghostly presences and variations in light, is inflected through the Romantic and post-Romantic contours of his writing. Primarily focusing on *The Sound and the Fury* (1929) and *Light in August* (1932), this chapter reconsiders the influence of British Romantic poetry on Faulkner's treatment of ghostly figures and landscape, fragmentation and perspective and, lastly, shifting light and shade. These tropes constitute part of Romanticism's bequest to Faulkner, but the remainder of his Romantic inheritance is a legacy of haunts and hauntings.[3] Romanticism as a haunted and haunting site becomes, as Paul de Man comments on the poetry of Charles Baudelaire, 'the ghostly memory of mourned absences'.[4] Certainly, Friedrich Nietzsche (one spectre who haunts de Man's critical work)[5] is attuned to the familiarity and unfamiliarity of these haunted and haunting 'mourned absences' when he observes that 'If we greatly transform ourselves, those friends of ours who have not been transformed become ghosts of our past: their voice comes across to us like the voice of a shade' (*HH*, [242], p. 274). Implicit in Nietzsche's aphoristic comment on 'friends as ghosts' (*HH*, [242], p. 274) is a sense of the self perturbed by the 'voice' of its spectral other; a haunting sense of otherness that, anticipating a Freudian notion of the uncanny (*unheimlich*), renders the subject both estranged from itself and unhoused. In Bergsonian terms, such an estrangement has been conceived of as a haunting of those distorted, fractured entities of the subject, forged in mathematical or mechanical time, by the continuous, unified, real self of consciousness that exists in pure time or duration.[6]

Wordsworth and Faulkner: Ghostly Selves and Haunts of Memory

A haunting of a different kind occurs in the closing remarks of his Nobel Prize acceptance speech, where Faulkner ascribes a redemptive power to the role and purpose of the artist, whose task it is to testify to the prevailing human 'spirit capable of compassion and sacrifice and endurance'. Faulkner goes on to conclude triumphantly that 'The poet's voice need not merely be the record of man, it can be one of the props, the pillars to help him endure and prevail'.[7] The 'puny' yet 'inexhaustible voice' of the true poet, attuned to 'love' and the 'heart', will be the one sound that, Faulkner assures us, will withstand the apocalypse 'when the last ding-dong of doom has clanged and faded from the last red and dying evening' (*PWF*, p. 724). Refracted through A. E. Housman's poem 'The Immortal Part', as well as the darker turn of the final stanza of 'How Clear, How Lovely Bright',[8] Faulkner strikes a surprisingly Romantic tenor, as he also conjures with the imagery of Wordsworth's claim, in the 1798 Preface to *Lyrical Ballads*, that the poet is 'the rock of defence of human nature; an upholder and preserver, carrying everywhere with him relationship and love'.[9]

In *The Prelude*, Wordsworth imaginatively returns to a ghostly site of emotional impairment (the death of a father), as if 'to drink / at a fountain',[10] in the hope of spiritual restoration and consolation. Yet reimagining a traumatic event is never, for Wordsworth, an indisputable assurance of restoration or consolation. A familiar and hauntingly peculiar pattern of return (to the site of Margaret's ruined cottage or Michael's incomplete sheepfold, for instance) is one often enacted by Wordsworth's poetry only to call into question that 'chearful faith' (*The Ruined Cottage*, 1. 134), which hopes to create a harmonised 'dwelling-place' (*The Ruined Cottage*, ll. 141–2) for memory, avowed towards the close of *Tintern Abbey*. These consoling and disconcerting effects of nature constitute, in Canto 4 of *The Waggoner* (Wordsworth probably punning on haunts as places in nature and sites of ghostly happenings), a ghostly presence that 'haunts me with a familiar face, / Returning like a ghost unlaid' (ll. 213–14).[11] Wordsworth's imaginative return to nature's sights and sounds (positive and negative) ultimately reduces them to a series of ghostly presences by an erosion of the distinction between poetic representation and actual recollected events.[12] That these recalled events are obliterated to indeterminate spectral presences is apt enough given that the child's view, as the adult Wordsworth notes, was hampered by mist which reduced the 'sights and sounds' of the scene to 'indisputable shapes' (*Prelude*, IX, ll. 365–7). But Jonathan Wordsworth, one of the most attentive and astute readers and editors of Wordsworth's poetry, reminds us of another kind of ghostly presence – that of literary allusion or echo – which haunts those 'indisputable shapes' of Wordsworth's mist. The literary echo is that of Hamlet's address to the ghost of his murdered father, 'Thou camest in such a questionable shape / That I would speak to thee.'[13]

A textual echo in a similar vein, though perhaps more deliberate, occurs, Jonathan Wordsworth observes, in Wordsworth's thankfulness not for a simple and pure childhood in 'Ode: Intimations of Immortality':

> But for those obstinate questionings
> . . .
> Blank misgivings of a Creature
> Moving about in worlds not realized,
> High instincts, before which our mortal Nature
> Did tremble like a guilty Thing surprised (ll. 144–50)

The allusion here in the final line is once again to the ghost of Hamlet's father which, with the crowing of a cock, 'started like a guilty thing / Upon a fearful summons' (*Hamlet*, I, i, ll. 148–9). Why should these textual echoes (deliberate or accidental) haunt Wordsworth's recollections of childhood? Why is the spectre (or ghostly memory) of Wordsworth's father blurred with the ghost of Hamlet's murdered father? 'The answer', Jonathan Wordsworth writes, 'can only be that at some level the poet [Wordsworth] associated the "blank misgivings" and "high instincts" of childhood with his father's death, and with the guilt that has been taken over from the Ghost.'[14]

These spectres, along with the ghostly qualities of Wordsworth's poetry, continue to fascinate critics. Geoffrey Hartman's seminal account of *The Unremarkable Wordsworth* notes the 'feeling of ghostliness'[15] that haunts Wordsworth's poetics of the ordinary. With a focus on social concern and commodities, David Simpson offers a reading, refracted through Derrida's *Spectres of Marx*, of Wordsworth's poetry and 'the ghostliness of things'.[16] Other theoretically inclined perspectives conceive of Wordsworth and the Romantic lyric as encountering the import, weight (emotional, psychic or physical) and gravitation of those things real and spectral, sensible and insensible, material and immaterial. For Mary Jacobus, the Wordsworthian lyric recognises that 'Even breathing becomes breathing toward death, just as the gift of a poem becomes a form of conversing with the dead'.[17] Wordsworth emerges, for these critics and others, as an existential poet of encounters with mourning, loss, grief and the limitations of our fragile and spectral existences. These spectral encounters, echoes, doublings, relays and haunted wordplay define the palimpsest that is Romanticism, as well as the story of its own inception and reception.[18]

Wordsworth's sympathy for, and vision of, the tragedy of commonplace experience as expressed by those dispossessed, revenant-like figures of Lucy Gray, Martha Ray, the Discharged Soldier, Margaret and Michael is primarily shaped by a concatenation of allusion to Shakespeare's *Hamlet*, *King Lear* and *Macbeth*. Where Wordsworth assumes a familiarity among his readers with such a nexus of allusion, Faulkner openly announces his Shakespearean borrowings from *Macbeth* and their resonance for his own unfolding tragic tale of individual, familial and communal decline of the South in *The Sound and the Fury*. Faulkner's tale of the debilitation, ruined innocence and disappointed expectations (whether social or existential) of the Compson family finds its fullest, yet confusing and seemingly inchoate, expression through Benjy's narrative perspective.

Benjy's account is a physical and psychological embodiment of what Macbeth, wracked by despair and beyond hope, equates the wretchedness of life to: 'a tale / Told by an idiot, full of sound and fury / Signifying nothing'.[19] If Shakespeare has Macbeth frame life as an idiotic tale of brief, treacherous illumination that only throws into relief the futility of 'Life's ... walking shadow' (*Macbeth*, V, v, l. 24), then, Faulkner frames (and crystallises within that frame) the tragic events of *The Sound and the Fury* through the babbling idiocy of Benjy's voice. Benjy's fractured perspective, an undifferentiated collation of his own voice and others, in times present and past, on first reading may signify 'nothing' and yet that nothing, on a re-reading, constitutes the very something, the substance, of Faulkner's novel. Everything that we subsequently learn of the Compson household, including Caddy's sexual awakening and unfortunate marriage, Quentin's suicide and Jason's cruelty, is mutely recorded without judgement or discernment by, in spite of his thirty-three years, Benjy's (three-year-old) child-like mind.

Without condoning or condemning Faulkner's representation of Benjy's idiocy,[20] one of the ways in which Benjy's mute, closed-in world signifies a something out of its apparent 'nothing' emerges from those distinctly Romantic shades of Faulkner's rendition of Shakespeare's 'tale told by an idiot' – not least that the fateful day of Benjy's opening sequence marks to the day 158 years since Wordsworth's birth.[21] Concerned with the events of 7 April 1928, Faulkner's characterisation of Benjy's responsiveness to the immediacy of the sensory world recalls, more generally, a Wordsworthian mode of child-like engagement with the phenomenal world and, specifically, the consciousness of Wordsworth's Idiot Boy, whose experiences defy time and circumstance.

Much of Wordsworth's poem, first published in *Lyrical Ballads* in 1798, takes place one fretful night, the fraught passage of which is marked out partially by the actions of Betty Foy, the devoted mother of the Idiot Boy, Johnny, who reluctantly sends him out into the darkness to fetch the Doctor to attend to their ailing neighbour, Susan Gale. Betty's increasing anxiety about the whereabouts of her son and his failure to return home (with or without the Doctor) is underscored by the narrator's acute awareness of clock, mechanical or mathematical time as measured out by the persistent reference to the clock which, by warning and striking of eight, eleven, twelve, one and three, demarcates the timeframe of those nocturnal adventures of the Idiot Boy 'from eight o'clock till five' ('The Idiot Boy', ll. 456, 158, 162, 182, 281). Wordsworth's narrator's reckoning of the temporal as clock time is a far cry from how the temporal and experiential world is perceived and recorded by the Idiot Boy, whose suggestively enigmatic summary of his own 'travel's story' states 'The cocks did crow to-whoo, to-whoo / And the sun did shine so cold!' ('The Idiot Boy', ll. 463, 460–1). Johnny's confused and confusing final words unwittingly rail against the conventional measurements of time passing (reinforced by the narrator's frequent references to clock time and the natural operations of the moon and owls) by conflating sunshine with moonlight, the crowing of cocks with the hooting of owls, the break of day with the onset of evening. Wordsworth's Idiot Boy may fail to grasp the temporal as measured mechanically or mathematically, but Johnny's apparent failure enables him to reconfigure habitual notions of temporality and defy the defined, restrictive boundaries of clock time. By virtue of his idiocy, Johnny's conclusive statement transforms the fixities and definites of this mode of temporal experience and frees his consciousness from its conventional restrictions. By so doing, Wordsworth's Idiot Boy creates a seamless continuum between the markers of night and day that captures the atemporality of his mind; a perspective that transcends time and delights in its own sense of timelessness. Such an air of timelessness is hinted at by the twilight – 'the stars were almost gone' and 'the moon was setting' ('The Idiot Boy', ll. 412–13) – that presides over the closing action and final spoken words of Wordsworth's Idiot Boy.

Benjy, too, in Faulkner's *The Sound and the Fury*, expresses something resembling the last word as 'his voice mounted, with scarce interval for breath' to achieve an 'unbelievable crescendo'.[22] Benjy's loudening 'Bellow on bellow' (*TSF*, p. 277), at the close of the novel, is occasioned by Luster's decision to take the wagon to the left rather than to the right around the town square.[23] This episode permits a mute voice a place amidst the competing narratorial voices of Faulkner's novel which, in the form of Benjy's nihilistic cry, lies beyond the signifying power of language. Such a cry outrightly rejects any notion of metaphysical order and hopeful redemption implied by the Easter sermon attended by Dilsey.[24] In the event, Jason redirects the horse, Queenie, physically chastises Luster and rebukes him, 'Don't you know any better than to take him to the left?' (*TSF*, p. 277), before instructing him to take Benjy home. The redirection of the horse-drawn wagon averts near catastrophe and restores Benjy's own unique sense of relation to the world in which 'cornice and façade flowed smoothly once more from left to right; post and tree, window and doorway, and signboard, each its ordered place' (*TSF*, p. 278). This return to a sense of serenity, home and secure order, for Benjy one spring day, appears to be Faulkner's reimagining of the fortunes of Wordsworth's Idiot Boy who, at his mother's insistence, is competent enough at 'How to turn left, and how to turn right' (l. 66) and so, guiding his horse at the outset of his journey, 'turns right' at 'the guide post' (l. 104) to ensure both his safe moonlit wanderings and return home in a spring twilight.

Unexpectedly, then, Wordsworth's twilit scene resonates with Faulkner's working title, *Twilight*,[25] for *The Sound and the Fury* and its complex narrative mode of shifting timeframes which, ultimately, crystallise in the apparent nonsensical idiocy of Benjy's narration. His consciousness and experience of the world and time recalls 'Life's . . . walking shadow' (*Macbeth*, V, v, l. 24) and the 'tale told by an idiot' of Macbeth's soliloquy,[26] as much as it does the atemporality of mind enjoyed by Johnny in Wordsworth's 'The Idiot Boy'. Yet neither allusion cancels out the other, especially as one connotation of Macbeth's 'dusty death' to which 'our yesterdays have lighted fools' (*Macbeth*, V, v, ll. 22–3) is that of the twilight ('dusky') of existence in which we, as mere semblances of ourselves, misguided shadows, stumbling 'poor players' (*Macbeth*, V, v, l. 25), find our final end.[27] Twice Wordsworth's Idiot Boy is likened to an apparitional presence. The capacity of Wordsworth's central character to be in nocturnal 'wonder lost' is associated, through the narrator's speculation about Johnny's night time ventures, with the apparitional appearance of a 'silent horseman ghost' ('The Idiot Boy', ll. 334–5). The Idiot Boy's spectral presence is, simultaneously, disparaged and reinforced when the narrator urges Betty to embrace her missing son, because we are told ''tis no ghost / 'Tis he whom you so long have lost' ('The Idiot Boy', ll. 379–80). As embodied in Johnny's response and final word to his mother's question, Faulkner's Benjy sees everything in exactly the same way he relays events to the reader, that is to say, in a continual present, so that past and present episodes and voices move, ghost-like, in and out of his mind's eye.

Shifting shades, the interplay of shadow and light, symbolise the temporal spectrum of past and present that comprises Benjy's opening narrative section in Faulkner's *The Sound and the Fury*. Cutting 'along the fence . . . to the garden fence, where our shadows *were*' (*TSF*, p. 2, emphasis added) in the crisp sunny present of 7 April 1928 renders, through verbal slippage, the present selves of Benjy and Luster as shadowy representations of both their past selves as they are to become and as they have been. Teased by Luster about being '"snagged on that nail again"' (*TSF*, p. 2) and earlier taunted – prompted by the golfer's cry '"Here, caddie"' (*TSF*, p. 1) – about the absence of his sister, Caddy, Benjy's mind indistinguishably interpolates one time with shadowy recollections of another time when, for instance, 'The sun was cold and bright' (*TSF*, p. 3) and the comforting absently present 'Caddy smelled like leaves' (*TSF*, p. 4). Composed only of haunted absences and inexplicable loss, Benjy's mute articulacy hints at the failure of words to give adequate shape or expression to the haunting hollowness, which forms the almost entirely meaningful silence and coreless core of his tale that borders on 'signifying nothing'. Yet, ultimately, still beyond the spoken word, Benjy does realise the pure 'utter sound' of his 'unbelievable crescendo' (*TSF*, p. 277). Through a 'Bellow on bellow' (*TSF*, p. 277) rather than words, Benjy affirms the purposelessness and tragic existence of the Compson household, as well as vocalising their individual and his own, in Wordsworth's phrase, 'tale of silent suffering, hardly clothed / In bodily form' (*The Ruined Cottage*, ll. 233–4). Through

Benjy's speechless revelation and its 'tale of silent suffering', Faulkner's written literary form transcends the spoken word to imbue the silence of the unsaid with irrefutable significance.[28]

Faulkner's matter-of-fact tone in the Compson Appendix,[29] written twenty years or so after the publication of *The Sound and the Fury*, still manages to emphasise the ghostly 'timeless' and haunted nature of the peculiar mindset and particular circumstances that form Benjy:

> Who loved three things: the pasture which was sold to pay for Candace's wedding and to send Quentin to Harvard, his sister Candace, firelight. Who lost none of them, because he could not remember his sister but only the loss of her, and firelight was the same bright shape as going to sleep, and the pasture was even better than before, because now he and Luster could . . . follow timeless along the fence . . .[30]

Past cruelties, taunts, slights and indifferences towards Benjy, including his mother's shame and his eventual castration, serve as triggers for undifferentiated recollections of Caddy's tenderness, patience and affection towards her brother. His sister's gentler actions and offers of comfort rebuff those present, past and future taunts and cruelties of his caretakers, like Luster, his elder brother, Jason, and others, such as his mother, experienced by Benjy. Even after her departure from the Compson household, the affection Benjy felt (and still feels) from Caddy replays in his mind as a constant and fraught source of comfort, as well as a perpetually anguished reminder of the continual absence of Caddy's love. The closing scene of Benjy's narrative lends shape to Caddy's painfully present absence through patterns of light and dark:

> Then the dark came back, and [Father] stood black in the door, and then the dark turned black again. Caddy held me and I could hear us all, and the darkness, and something I could smell. And I could see the windows, where the trees were buzzing. Then the dark began to go in smooth, bright shapes, like it always does, even when Caddy says that I have been asleep. (*TSF*, p. 64)

The silhouetted figure of their father symbolises the encroaching degrees of darkness that obscure past points of origin and usher in those ominous shadows of futurity. Such darkness is offset by the comforting scent of Caddy and the light of 'windows' (both of which put Benjy in mind of the smell of leaves and the sound of trees), which smoothes the 'dark' into the dreamt 'bright shapes' of sleep. Adumbrated by Caddy's fall into sexuality and marriage, Benjy's consciousness exists in a temporal continuum, but Faulkner's commingled imagery of light, darkness and shadow implies a maturing and awakening marked out by a trajectory from light into darkness. Such a symbolic trajectory offers a reimagining of the subject matter and elegiac tone of Wordsworth's 'Ode: Intimations of Immortality' that registers a psychological, emotional and temporal falling away from the 'celestial light' (l. 67) of nurturing infancy into the maturity and tragic 'light of common day' (l. 76).

In our fallen condition, Wordsworth attests, all that is left to us are 'those shadowy recollections' ('Ode: Intimations of Immortality', l. 153) of what had once been 'the fountain light of all our day' (l. 154) and 'the master light of all our seeing' (l. 55). Such faint remnants of a 'radiance which once was so bright' (l. 178) both remind us of our present mortal condition and intimate the immortality we once enjoyed and as such become a source of 'Strength in what remains behind' (l. 183). Glimpsed in the 'sobering colouring' of 'the setting sun' (ll. 199–200), or 'the innocent brightness of a new-born Day' (l. 198), 'what remains behind' reminds us, paradoxically, that these intimations of immortality originate in the breast of 'human suffering' (l. 187).[31] Wordsworth's final image in the Ode, of 'those thoughts that do *often* lie too deep for tears' (l. 206, emphasis added), is an affirmation that triumphant poetic vision originates in the 'meanest flower' (l. 205). The extent of Faulkner's imaginative response to Wordsworth's Ode can be measured from the wider celestial significance ascribed to Benjy's final bellow, recounted by Dilsey as 'Just sound. It might have been all time and injustice and sorrow become vocal for an instant by a conjunction of the planets' (*TSF*, p. 249).

Surprisingly, it is through Dilsey's more objectively factual description of how Benjy 'bellowed slowly, abjectly, without tears; the grave hopeless sound of all voiceless misery under the sun' (*TSF*, p. 274) that the poignancy and relevance of Wordsworth's Ode is felt. Like Wordsworth's speaker of the Ode Benjy feels, from the particularity of his daily experience of the universal human plight, what it is to be exposed to all of the sufferings 'under the sun' (Wordsworth's 'light of common day') and to clutch, perpetually, at the residual 'shadowy recollections' of the 'celestial light' of Caddy's loss. Such profundity of grief, as Wordsworth's close of the Ode suggests, is 'often' but not always entirely beyond outward show or sign and, for Faulkner, is fully rounded out in the meaningless meaning that comprises, at least in Dilsey's eyes, the 'nothing' (*TSF*, p. 274) of Benjy's final revelatory cry. Without ever knowing it, Benjy hankers after a time irrecoverably lost in his past, acutely absent from his present and inaccessible in his future. Benjy's inability to differentiate between temporal modes distinguishes him from Wordsworth's speaker in the Ode, who is aware that 'There was a time' ('Ode: Intimations of Immortality', l. 1) of 'celestial light' and primordial oneness before the fall into the quotidian comprising rational categories, logical taxonomies and the habitual 'Shades of the prison-house' (l. 67). For Benjy, there is no single reality, but only an indivisible series of competing realities whereby there can be no reconciliation between his acknowledgement of '*There was a fire*' in his mother's room and '*another fire in the mirror*' (*TSF*, p. 52). As is the case with Wordsworth's Idiot Boy, Benjy's state of consciousness is both a curse and a blessing, which affords him his mute articulacy and blind insight, and his narrative the fragmentary wholeness of the truth it conveys.

If Benjy, as Faulkner's reimagining of Wordsworth's Idiot Boy, figures unconventional modes of comprehension and expression, his brother Quentin embodies a tragic over-awareness of the mechanical and mathematical reckoning of clock time that Benjy's mode of consciousness and mute narrative defies. Quentin's sense of demarcated time, divided and subdivided into units, serves as a counterbalance to Benjy's perception of time as a continuum. Quentin, as an intelligent and articulate Harvard freshman, represents the flipside of Benjy's mode of consciousness and being. Quentin is bound fatally by clock time and the need to render his existence, actions and words as meaningful. Other ostensible differences are evident between Benjy's narratorial fixity on the absence of his sister's kindnesses and comforting presence and Quentin's obsession with her purity, honour and virginity (which, paradoxically, extends to his fantasy of incest with her). Yet Caddy and her fall remain the gravitational centre of both their narratives.

Shadows, shadowy remembrances and twilight are woven together in Quentin's fateful account of the final day of his life, 2 June 1910. Seasonal fragrances of spring (past and present), rain and the light on the Charles River interfuse with one another so Quentin 'could feel water beyond the twilight, smell' (*TSF*, p. 146). Through a 'draft in the door', the smell of water is also felt as 'a damp steady breath' perfumed with 'honeysuckle' which, for Quentin, comes to 'symbolize night and unrest' (*TSF*, p. 147). Infused with the odour of water and scent of honeysuckle, twilight binds Quentin to his past, present and inexorable future suicide. His first suicide attempt with Caddy was marked by 'the water gurgling among the willows in the dark and waves of honeysuckle' (*TSF*, p. 131). Faulkner overlays another allusion to Wordsworth with an echo of Keats in the description of Quentin's nightly 'unrest' that follows: 'I seemed to be lying neither asleep nor awake looking down a long corridor of grey half-light where all stable things had become shadowy paradoxical all I had done shadows . . . I was I was not who was not was not who' (*TSF*, p. 147). Replaying a dilemma over waking and sleeping, consciousness and unconsciousness, and being and non-being at the close of Keats's 'Ode to a Nightingale', Quentin's symbol for uncertain modes of being draws on an earlier moment in Keats's springtime ode, where the speaker guesses, in 'embalmed darkness', at 'each sweet scent / Wherewith the seasonable month endows' (ll. 43–4). Inflected through both Quentin's passion for Keats and Tennyson and Faulkner's own fascination with Keats's odes, especially 'Ode on a Grecian Urn', the dramatisation of Quentin's consciousness is one that is orientated towards its own death.[32] Bereft of 'celestial light', in Wordsworthian terms, Quentin's sense of self has 'become shadowy paradoxical' and prone to being 'in darkness lost, the darkness of the grave' ('Ode: Intimations of Immortality', l. 116).

Beneath the echo of Keats in Quentin's associative and synaesthetic symbol of 'unrest', Faulkner's passage recalls the Wordsworthian 'shadowy recollections' that define Caddy's absence for Benjy as much as they do for Quentin. Quentin's further observation about the pungency of the river and the play of light on the water at twilight suggestively conjures with the touchstones and differences between Quentin's narrative (dangerously over-determined by clock time) and Benjy's (unregulated 'timeless') account: 'I could smell the curves of the river beyond the dusk and I saw the last light supine and tranquil upon tide-flats like pieces of broken mirror . . . How [Benjamin] used to sit before that mirror. Refuge unfailing in which conflict tempered silenced reconciled' (*TSF*, p. 147). Twilight affords Quentin tranquillity through its promise of transformation and the prospect of non-existence; a final ending to his troubled mind, splintered by time and his own sense of failure, like those 'pieces of a broken mirror'. The alternate and compelling reality (and memory) of the whole mirror, from Quentin's perspective, permitted Benjy a temporary refuge of 'tempered silence' similar to that respite offered to Quentin by the dusky light on the river. Unlike the imagined unity of 'tempered silenced reconciled', this twilit respite is fragmentary, fleeting and beautiful, like the fractals of light and, by extension, self that Quentin pictures 'a little like butterflies hovering a long way off'

(*TSF*, p. 147). They also recall, like those 'pieces of broken mirror', the 'fragments of glass' (*TSF*, p. 69) that result from Quentin's vehemently destructive resistance to clock time, measured by his father's watch, the clock tower and bells throughout the day.

Quentin's poetic, often grandiloquent expression seeks to evade the brute facts of his own and his family's situation in an attempt to mask his inability to act in any meaningful way (even his sexual awakening and incestuous relations with Caddy are fanciful), especially one that will register in his father's eyes. Unable to translate words into deeds (either to live up to parental expectations or to preserve Caddy's honour), Quentin is imprisoned by his own inadequacies, time and circumstance to the extent that he recognises that the 'Peacefullest words' are 'I was. I am not' (*TSF*, p. 150). This death wish is anticipated by Quentin's awareness of numerous shadows, including his own shadow which, reminiscent of the breaking of his father's watch, he treads self-destructively 'into the pavement' (*TSF*, p. 86).[33] Throughout his section Quentin repeatedly imagines fading 'into twilight and the sense of water peaceful and swift beyond' (*TSF*, p. 146). Such shadows and imagined shadowy existences gesture towards Quentin's past, present and future ghostly selves. Prompted by his observation of yet another panoply of shadows, among them an outline of a schooner moving 'like a ghost in broad day', this triptych of images crystallises in Quentin's recollection of the saying 'a drowned man's shadow was watching for him in the water all the time' (*TSF*, p. 77).[34] This shadow and the myriad others in Quentin's account recall the implied fatal twilight in which the misguided 'fools' find their 'dusty death' and tragic demise in Macbeth's soliloquy. Quentin's suicide is never narrated and Benjy's narrative is all but silent, but the signifying absence and darkness of their respective muted narratives are given visible shape, in Faulkner's *The Sound and the Fury*, by these imagistic flickers of light on water, shadow play and the half-light of twilight.

Byron and Faulkner: Shifting Shades, Nature and Subjectivity

Twin oppositions characterise the narrative modes of Benjy and Quentin, as much as twin opposites define the inverse qualities of two readily identifiable key Romantic characters, Byron Bunch and Percy Grimm, in Faulkner's later novel *Light in August*.[35] Bunch's state of social alienation, eventually healed by an act of love, resonates to some degree with the exilic Byron and Grimm's fervour for religion, and military action inverts Shelley's idealism to the point of violent justice. To varying degrees Faulkner's major characters in *Light in August* are shunned by society or remain outsiders. Unable to escape the past and the death of his wife, and rejected by his congregation, the high-minded Reverend Hightower is, according to Faulkner, antithetical to the orphaned and self-victimised Joe Christmas, who has no past.[36] Christmas's wanderings, after his murder of Joanna Burden, end violently at the hands of Grimm. By contrast, Lena Grove is also a victim, but she is permitted to continue quietly on her journey with her newborn child. Whereas Lena represents a heterodox celebration of fertility and life, Joanna signifies sterility and a life-denying Calvinist extremism. Accompanying Lena on her travels at the close of the novel, Bunch embodies a nobility of spirit that Lucas Burch (his surname a near synonym of Bunch's own) is incapable of as the feckless absentee father of Lena's child.[37]

Faulkner's direct borrowings of the names of Lord George Gordon Byron and Percy Bysshe Shelley have been documented by commentators alongside many of his other textual borrowings from Blake, Wordsworth and Keats.[38] Allusions to Blake in Faulkner's *Light in August* signal that these paired opposites of characters and their oppositional values are not straightforward antitheses, but that they should be construed as Blakean antinomies, comprised from subtle gradations of difference, which reveal the interpenetration of states of existence, nature and individual responses to them in order to 'shew the contrary states of the human soul'.[39] These differing attitudes to the shifting shades of self and nature provide Faulkner's *Light in August* with its formal unity and belie a peculiarly Byronic inflection of Romantic inheritance in the novel.

Imagery of shadow and light reinforces a Nietzschean transvaluation of these oppositional values,[40] including innocence and experience, good and evil, stasis and process, black and white, as well as, geographically, North and South, along which a reading of *Light in August* might be constructed. Joe Christmas's miscegenation embodies this transvaluation of values, and his consequent inability to fit (or be fitted) into conventionally defined societal and moral Southern categories renders him a troubled and troubling spectral presence in the novel, as if he were 'a phantom, a spirit, strayed out of its own world, and lost'.[41] Approaching his moment of illuminated vision, Reverend Hightower reflects on his past, presented as a cast of phantoms comprising 'his father, his mother, and an old negro woman' (*LA*, p. 356). Such reflections lead Hightower to realise the fluid insubstantiality of his own subjectivity, as he finds that those shifting faces of his congregation 'seem to be mirrors in which he watches himself' (*LA*, p. 367). These mirroring and intermingling oppositions trace out the ghostly world of past and present selves that haunt the characters in *Light in August* and find fullest expression in Faulkner's description of Byron Bunch and Brown as inversely reflected planetary objects on discrete, but not dissimilar, pathways that pass 'one another *as though* on opposite orbits and with an effect as of phantoms or apparitions' (*LA*, p. 332, emphasis added).[42] The phantasmagoria of Hightower's solipsism, in which he sees himself as 'a shadowy figure among shadows' (*LA*, p. 366) caught between the paradoxes of youthful ambition, recalls Quentin's own existential crisis, in *The Sound and the Fury*, that manifests itself as 'shadowy paradoxical'. It is in 'the shadow of the bridge' that Quentin's desired suicidal release from the temporal and the contradictions of existence fuses, in his mind, with the desiccation of a single leaf which, if left in the 'water . . . after awhile will be gone and the delicate fibres waving slow as the motion of sleep' (*TSF*, p. 100), whereas Hightower's revelatory transcendence of the corporeal is a metaphorical 'final flood' that leaves 'his body empty and lighter than a forgotten leaf and even more trivial than flotsam lying spent' (*LA*, p. 370). Here Faulkner's image of the 'forgotten leaf' is indicative of the quality of Southern light that he claimed gave *Light in August* its published title and is associated for him with 'the middle of the month when suddenly there's a foretaste of the fall, it's cool, there's a lambence, a luminous quality to the light . . .'.[43] That Faulkner associates Hightower's release from the bodily and the temporal with a 'forgotten leaf' finds a Byronic antecedent in Manfred's inability to forget the past and the death of Astarte when he recollects that in her face 'there is now no living hue / But a strange hectic – / like the unnatural red / Which Autumn plants upon the perished leaf' (*Manfred*, I, i, ll. 98–101). This Byronic image is echoed by Christmas who, registering a change in his ill-fated relationship with Joanna (her desire for a child), remarks, 'But the shadow of autumn was upon her' (*LA*, p. 197). Forgetting and remembering are closely entwined for the tragic-stricken consciousness of Byron's Manfred, as they are for both Hightower and Christmas, whereby the act of forgetting becomes for Manfred a form of poetic remembering or, in Faulknerian terms, 'Memory believes before knowing remembers' (*LA*, p. 91).

Despite the evident religious and Dantean overtures of Hell, Purgatory and Paradise that trace out the revolutions of his illuminating 'wheel of thinking' (*LA*, p. 367),[44] Hightower's last vision that reconciles him to his past private and public failures also bears the hallmark of one of Byron's most striking images, from *The Giaour*, of self-victimisation and remorse. Originating in the fabled ability of the scorpion to fatally wound itself with its own sting, Byron's image finds an analogy for those self-inflicted injuries that result from a consciousness wracked by guilt and its attendant feelings of remorse: 'The Mind that broods o'er guilty woes / Is like the Scorpion girt by fire / In circle narrowing as it glows / The flames around their captive close . . .' (*The Giaour*, ll. 422–5). The circling and encircling glow of self-torturing infernal fire resonates with Faulkner's more desperate image of how Hightower's 'sand-clutched wheel of thinking turns on with the slow implacability of a mediaeval torture instrument' (*LA*, p. 369) and foreshadows Hightower's subsequent softened, angelic vision of 'a faint glow like a halo' (*LA*, p. 369). Byron's relentless likening of a 'desperate brain' to a 'Scorpion girt by fire' and bereft of hope concludes, fatally, that 'So writhes the mind Remorse has riven / Unfit for earth, undoomed for heaven / Darkness above, despair beneath / Around it flame, within it death!' (*The Giaour*, ll. 435–8).

Faulkner's description accentuates a more hopeful terminal moment of release and reconciliation in which numerous faces, including Hightower's wife's, Christmas's, Bunch's, Lena's and even that of the avenging Percy Grimm, at first, a part of 'an inextricable . . . compositeness', 'free themselves one from another, then fade and blend again' (*LA*, p. 370):

> The wheel whirls on. It is going fast and smooth now, because it is freed now of burden, of vehicle, axle, all. In the lambent suspension of August into which night is about to fully come, it seems to engender and surround itself with a faint glow like a halo. The halo is full of faces. The faces are not shaped with suffering, not shaped with anything; not horror, pain, not even reproach. They are peaceful, as though they have escaped into an apotheosis; his own among them. (*LA*, p. 369)

Hightower's final instance of liberation and apotheosis into the realm of the atemporal is ushered in by a series of natural similes which, consisting of 'a long sighing of wind in trees . . . borne now upon a cloud of phantom dust' and a 'tumult' of 'soundless yelling' like 'a crest . . . jagged with the wild heads of horses' (*LA*, p. 370), elaborate upon Faulkner's metaphor of a flotsam-tossed leaf. Nature's ever-changing action and noises, as in Christmas's perception of the dark 'intervals filled with a myriad voices' (*LA*, p. 83) or Hightower's sensitivity to how 'Beyond the open window the sound of insects has not ceased, has not faltered' (*LA*, p. 294), are a perpetually ever-present reminder that permanent stasis lies beyond temporality in the infinity of Hightower's vision of the 'Now' and that all other forms of arrest are transitory moments in the becoming of the lived 'now' (*LA*, p. 370).

It is against the 'steady insects whirr' (*LA*, p. 291) that Bunch, and others in *Light in August*, attempts to assert the permanence of selfhood and singularity of voice, only to find that both are unstable entities eroded by nature's ceaseless actions and continual 'whirr'. This failure to assert an identity is found in its most extreme form in Christmas, who can never recover his origins, and reaches a climax, for Bunch, in a moment of uncertainty about his own identity: '*you say that you are Byron Bunch . . . you are just the one that calls yourself Byron Bunch today, now, this minute . . .*' (*LA*, p. 319).

Such an instance of profound self-doubt is shared by a crisis of poetic selfhood dramatised poetically by Bunch's nineteenth-century namesake, Byron. Byron's treatment of subjectivity marks out an extraordinary imaginative mobility that permits competing and contradictory perspectives on selfhood to coalesce. These contradictory Byronic perspectives (as well as positive and negative external and internal forces that form them) on a mobile series of personae are vital to the imaginatively productive dynamic of Byron's poetics, committed, as they are, to representing the self in all of its extremities, potentialities and limitations. In Byron's *Childe Harold's Pilgrimage*, the lines blur between actuality and the imagined, between the biographical and the fictional personae, as Byron takes up the celebration of 'The wandering outlaw of his own dark mind' (*CH*, III, 3, l. 20) early in Canto III. Byronic selfhood, as 'A ruin amidst ruins' (*CH*, IV, 186, l. 219), is no stranger to the wreck of formerly inhabited selves or modes of being.

Faulkner and Byron share a similar artistic concern for dramatising the workings of consciousness and subjectivity through the spatiality of the external world. Faulkner's preoccupation with this connection between architectural spaces, shapes and subjective states is hinted at by his drafts of *Light in August*, which suggest that its working title, after Alfred Tennyson's *In Memoriam*, had been *Dark House*.[45] Consequently, Faulkner's use of natural imagery reaches beyond parallels between Byron Bunch and the Romantic poet Byron, and shared factual details of their self-imposed exile and social alienation. Prefacing the moment of Bunch's anxieties over self-identity, a key passage points to the ironic and parodic textual touchstones between Byron Bunch and Byron.[46] Such an instance successfully illustrates the extent to which Faulkner engages with Byron's literary imagination in *Don Juan* and *Childe Harold's Pilgrimage*. Metaphorically, the passage from chapter 18 is again focalised through Bunch and concerned with one of Byron's favourite subjects, the sea:

> The hill rises, cresting. He has never seen the sea, and so he thinks. 'It is like the edge of nothing. Like once I passed it I would just ride off into nothing. Where the trees would look like and be called by something else except trees, and men would like and be called something else except folks. And Byron Bunch he wouldn't even have to be or not be Byron Bunch. Byron Bunch and his mule not anything with falling fast, until they would take fire like the Reverend Hightower says about them rocks running so fast in space that they take fire and burn up and there aint even a cinder to have hit the ground.'
>
> But then from beyond the hill crest there begins to rise that which he knows is there: the trees which are trees, the terrific and the tedious distance which, being moved by blood, he must compass forever and ever between two inescapable horizons of the implacable earth. Steadily, they rise, not portentous, not threatful. That's it. They are oblivious of him . . . 'Well,' he thinks, 'if that's all it is, I reckon I might as well have the pleasure of not being able to bear looking back too.' He halts the mule and turns into the saddle. (*LA*, pp. 318–19)

Comedic, quixotic elements of the mode of Byron's *Don Juan*, which itself partakes of the picaresque, abound, not least because Bunch's ironic and meditative reflections on his life's situation take place atop a mule. That Faulkner fuses the trees and hills with the sea in Bunch's mind is also telling of the Byronic origins of this passage, as it recasts a series of reflections, admittedly on an Italian panorama, of 'a pleasure in the pathless woods' and a 'rapture on the lonely shore' (*CH*, IV, 178, ll. 1594–5) a few stanzas before his ecstatic encounter with the ocean. Byron's speaker prefers the 'deep sea' and the 'music in its roar' to 'society', simultaneously desiring 'To mingle with the Universe, and feel / What I can e'er express, yet cannot all conceal' (*CH*, IV, 178, ll. 1596–7, 1601–2) and shunning the self-destructive tendencies of humanity which, by comparison with the ocean's wrecks, leave only, fleetingly, 'A shadow of man's ravage' (*CH*, IV, 178, l. 1607).

Byron's measure of 'A shadow of man's ravage' is equally a fitting epithet for the self-destruction at the heart of the victimised and self-victimising Christmas who is, finally, crucified. Christmas's self-lacerating sexual entanglement with the hard, flinty, masculine Calvinist Joanna Burden exacerbates his own existential crisis of self-identity to threaten what remains of his solidity of being.[47] Such a crisis precipitates Christmas's murder of Joanna and the burning of her house to conceal the crime, as well as his own subsequent violent death in Hightower's kitchen. Tragically, Christmas is initially denied appropriate social relations (as an orphan and foster-child of mixed race) which he eventually, wilfully and defiantly, feels compelled to deny for himself. Christmas's wilful defiance resists both Southern racial stereotypes and straightforward morality. Through Christmas's refusal to flee and evade the guilt of his crime by appearing '"in broad daylight, on a Saturday with the town full of folks"' in Mottstown, as an anonymous inhabitant reports, '"It was like he never knew he was a murderer, let alone a nigger too"' (*LA*, p. 263). Christmas's identity does not fit into any Southern self-serving, prejudicial, moral and social categories, as he 'never acted like either a nigger or a white man' (*LA*, p. 263). A smartly dressed Christmas in his act of self-surrender visibly challenges the perpetuated myth of the African American as social pariah and sexual defiler of the virginal South.[48]

Christmas's visible presence 'in broad daylight' illuminates the invisible contradictions that are fundamental to the prejudicial categories of the white townsfolk of Mottstown and Jefferson in particular and the South in general. They mistakenly assume that these ill-founded social and moral categories describe a metaphysically grounded natural, hierarchical state of affairs in the world when, really, they are merely the measure of their own self-interested investment in maintaining the social and economic status quo. An earlier description of Christmas makes visible this absurd conflation of societal and natural values and questions the validity of these strict categories and their racial discriminations, as he passes 'between the homes of white people, from street lamp to street lamp, the heavy shadows of oak and maple leaves sliding like scraps of black velvet across his white shirt' (*LA*, p. 87). Ironically, the artificial light of society (signified by the street lamp) accentuates nature's 'heavy shadows' which, dappling across 'his white shirt', reveal Christmas's true natural ethnicity that defies the imposition of societal distinctions between black and white. The scene anticipates Christmas's final realisation of a self, partaking of 'peace and unhaste and quiet', which is 'moulded', intuitively, by nature's 'compulsions' that put him in touch with 'its actual shape and feel' (*LA*, p. 254).

With different emphases, Bunch's association with natural imagery is similar in kind. He keeps society at arm's length and rejects conventional social or moral values in favour of his own principles forged, ultimately, out of his renewed connection with life, no matter how faltering his attempts to live life on his own terms. Symbolically, Bunch's reluctance to engage with the processes of life is expressed through his ignorance of the ocean ('He has never seen the sea') and his aversion to immersing himself in the 'metaphorical "sea"'[49] of the 'hill crest' and its undulating landscape, which both 'Steadily . . . rise' and remain 'oblivious of him'. In this context, the fact that Bunch's dread of the sea turns him to think of 'the edge of nothing' has been interpreted as an ironic inversion of Byron's poetic celebration of the eternal vitality of the sea ('I have loved thee, Ocean!' (IV, 184, l. 1603)) in *Childe Harold's Pilgrimage*. Towards the close of Canto IV, an energetic, even sexualised, 'wantoned' (*CH*, IV, 184, l. 1651) abandon to the breakers of the overtly feminised sea unites the speaker's past exuberance as a boy (*CH*, IV, 184, l. 1650) with his adult fears. Recent fears of being buffeted wherever 'the tempest's breath prevail' (*CH*, III, 2, l. 19), as flotsam and jetsam by the ocean's waves, coalesce into what Byron describes oxymoronically as a 'pleasing fear'. Without doubt the sea, where 'Time writes no wrinkles on thine azure brow' (*CH*, IV, 183, l. 1636), represents, for Byron, vitality and eternity, but the 'pleasing fear' (*CH*, IV, 184, l. 1653) that it evokes equally speaks to the sea as an ever-changing, erosive and capricious elemental force. Byron's ocean is an enduring and transitory presence, a preserving and destructive force, one to be contended with, as well as celebrated and feared.

The indeterminacy of these contradictory attitudes towards the ocean by Byron in Cantos III and IV of *Childe Harold's Pilgrimage* does not necessarily detract from Faulkner's ironic evocation of Byron. Instead these ambivalences suggestively resonate with Byron Bunch's own particular situation and have ramifications for the wider concentric patterns of *Light in August*. The serio-comic sequence of Faulkner's novel, narrated through the eyes of an itinerant second-hand furniture salesman, witnesses a Bunch who, though his attentions are rebuffed by Lena Grove, is increasingly committed to affirm a Byronic desire 'To mingle with the Universe, and feel'. This commitment is embodied by Bunch's decision to travel with Lena, whose name (associated with Diana as earth-mother),[50] pregnancy and childbirth embody the enduring, timeless vitality of natural process.

Bunch's personal commitment to Lena displays something of the previous ambivalences of his own nature, as his affections towards her are caught at times between magnanimity and self-centredness. Recalling the conflicting attitudes of Byron's speaker in *Childe Harold's Pilgrimage*, Bunch does not fully know how to achieve such a truly harmonised (natural and social) state and finds himself unable to 'e'er express, yet cannot all conceal' what he now desires. To his credit, Bunch does not conform to normative social judgements and, intuitively, knows that Christmas ought to be saved and that Lena's honour needs preserving, even if his efforts to do so fail or fall short of the mark. Similarly, even if misdirected, the expectant Lena's romance quest for Lucas Burch (encountered by Christmas under the name of Joe Brown), the father of her child, at the start of the novel, the subsequent birth of her child and her departure from Jefferson at the close all point to the importance of, and need for, a reconnection between natural and social processes. This is evident in Bunch's insistence that Hightower is in attendance at the birth of Lena's child, a moment recorded by Bunch as also a reawakening of himself: 'Then he heard the child cry. Then he *knew*. Dawn was making fast' (*LA*, p. 301, emphasis added). Recalling the nativity, another episodic manifestation of light in August reminds Hightower and Bunch of the importance of social obligations and natural processes, as the child's birth makes flesh and blood incarnate. The yet unnamed child symbolises a blank cipher which, defying restrictive social and moral categorisation, demands a realignment of the social and natural orders.[51] Ultimately, there is a need for a more instinctive, collective, social responsibility, and this natural sense of obligation strikes an accord deep within Bunch's own ambivalent and often divided nature.

Comically, Bunch's relationship with Lena is unconsummated by the close of the novel but, as implied by the narrative of the second-hand furniture salesman and Hightower's earlier prediction, Bunch's redemption resides with his eventual union with the vitality of natural processes, life and Lena as his wife. Such a hopeful resolution is hinted at by Lena when, having rejected Bunch's advances, she remarks to him, '"Aint nobody never said for you to quit"' (*LA*, p. 380).[52] Symbolically, Lena provides Bunch with the prospect of emotional and physical sustenance, as well as a life to be lived which requires, as Lena knows first-hand, that '"A body does get around"' (*LA*, p. 381). Bunch's intuitive set of principles are akin to Lena's subjective state of a harmonious, earthbound, vital permanence around and through which the waters of life flow.[53]

The title of Faulkner's novel speaks to the enduring vitality of natural processes encapsulated by Lena's expectancy, as the phrase 'Light in August' has been attributed to Southern rural communities as describing a full-term pregnancy in livestock or horses.[54]

It is evocative of the burning of the Burden house, the flames (or smoke) from which are seen far and wide and variously interpreted by all of Faulkner's central characters in the novel.[55] It resonates, too, with that portentous and transformative 'luminous quality to the light' that Faulkner associated with 'Mississippi in August' (*FU*, p. 199). It equally captures the way that the transitional, often shadowy, shifting shades of twilight in *The Sound and the Fury* and *Light in August*, paradoxically, lend spatial and temporal definition to those barely perceptible ghostly selves that are frequently its denizens.

Much of Faulkner's fiction is preoccupied with isolated, ostracised or otherwise estranged figures that subsist on the margins of communities. These itinerant individuals resonate with those similarly displaced figures that populate the landscape of Wordsworth's poetry. These dispossessed Wordsworthian figures frequently return as revenants to assert their rights and identity and to voice their stories which would otherwise be silenced, forgotten and erased from communal memory by the passage of time. Faulkner's fiction is populated by its fair share of itinerants and spectral forms but, more importantly, when turning to Wordsworth, Faulkner discovers in 'The Idiot Boy' and the 'Ode: Intimations of Immortality' a Romantic (and pre-Bergsonian) model for expressing the self as a continuum of being and an innovative mode of temporal perception. Wordsworth's opposition to rational (or mechanical) time to foreground the temporal as a complex palimpsest and the centrality of lived experience provided a glossary of light and shadow for Faulkner's own imaginative structuring, in *The Sound and the Fury*, of the self as an entity shaped in, and absorbed by, time. A Byronic haunting and haunted sense of subjectivity still pervades Faulkner's *Light in August* and its concern with transformative instances of realisation and illumination which, although inextricable from the burden of the past, are primarily concerned with the spatial and relational definitions of the self. Faulkner valorises those characters that resist conventionally fixed categories, definitions and expectations of self and nature. They advocate instead a fluid, instinctive subjectivity that dissolves those rigid social, moral or metaphysical distinctions between observing self and observed natural world. To resist intuitively the imposition of these strict categories and divisions, socially, morally or intellectually, for Faulkner, is to resist the tyranny of abstract principles and to be attuned to the 'heart' of lived experience advocated and preserved by the 'inexhaustible voice', albeit surprisingly Romantic in tone, of Faulkner's artist.

Notes

1. Cleanth Brooks, *William Faulkner: Toward Yoknapatawpha and Beyond* (Baton Rouge: Louisiana State University Press, 1990), p. 32. Hereafter *TYB*.

2. See Robert M. Slabey, 'The "Romanticism" of *The Sound and the Fury*', *The Mississippi Quarterly* 16.3 (1963): 153; 146–59; Martin Bidney, 'Faulkner's Variations on Romantic Themes: Blake, Wordsworth, Byron, and Shelley in *Light in August*', *The Mississippi Quarterly* 38.3 (1985): 277–86. Hereafter 'FVR'. See also Dieter Meindl, 'Romantic Idealism and *The Wild Palms*', in *William Faulkner and Idealism*, ed. Michael Gresset and S. J. Patrick Samway (Jackson: University Press of Mississippi, 1983), p. 88; pp. 86–94.

3. Faulkner was interested in the genre of the ghost story. Dean Faulkner Wells recounts a number of ghost stories that she recalls being told by her uncle, William Faulkner. See Faulkner Wells, *Ghosts of Rowan Oak: William Faulkner's Ghost Stories for Children* (Oxford, MS: Yoknapatawpha, 1980).

4. Paul de Man, *The Rhetoric of Romanticism* (New York: Columbia University Press, 1984), p. 259.

5. For an account of the spectres that haunt de Manian deconstruction see Tilottama Rajan, 'Displacing Post-Structuralism: Romanticism after Paul de Man', *Studies in Romanticism* 24.4 (1991): 451–74.

6. Cleanth Brooks offers a measured assessment of the influence of Henri Bergson on William Faulkner's fiction and identifies the equally likely 'influence of Nietzsche rather than Bergson' (*TYB*, p. 262). See *TYB*, pp. 253–65.

7. William Faulkner, 'Nobel Prize Address', in *The Portable William Faulkner*, ed. Malcolm Cowley (1948; London: Penguin-Viking, 1977), p. 724. Hereafter *PWF*.

8. The last stanza speaks of the 'ensanguine skies' that usher in the 'fall of the remorseful day'. See A. E. Housman, *A Shropshire Lad and Other Poems*, ed. Archie Burnett, intro. Nick Laird, afterword Jack Sparrow (Harmondsworth: Penguin, 2014), p. 277.

9. William Wordsworth, Preface (1798) to *Lyrical Ballads*, in Wordsworth and Samuel Taylor Coleridge, *Lyrical Ballads*, ed. R. L. Brett and A. R. Jones (London: Methuen, 1963), p. 259.

10. William Wordsworth, *The Prelude: A Parallel Text*, ed. James C. Maxwell (Harmondsworth: Penguin, 1982), XI, ll. 325–6.

11. William Wordsworth, *The Waggoner*, in *Poetical Works of William Wordsworth*, vol. 1 (London: Moxon, 1886), p. 308.

12. Andrew Bennett argues that 'by insisting on this return or repair, Wordsworth undermines the efficacy of that return by dissolving the crucial distinction between event and representation: he cannot *actually* have "repaired" or returned to these spectacles and sounds since

so many of them . . . are ephemeral and can be returned to only in memory, in representation'. See Bennett, *Wordsworth Writing* (Cambridge: Cambridge University Press, 2007), p. 160.

13. William Shakespeare, *Hamlet*, ed. Ann Thompson and Neil Taylor (London: Bloomsbury, 2018), I, iv, ll. 43–4. All quotations are from this edition.

14. See Jonathan Wordsworth's editorial note 43 to p. 486 of *The Prelude: The Four Texts (1795, 1799, 1805, 1850)*, ed. Jonathan Wordsworth (Harmondsworth: Penguin, 1995).

15. Geoffrey Hartman, *The Unremarkable Wordsworth*, foreword D. G. Marshall (Minneapolis: University of Minnesota Press, 1987), p. 133.

16. David Simpson, *Wordsworth, Commodification and Social Concern* (Cambridge: Cambridge University Press, 2009), pp. 143–73.

17. Mary Jacobus's sense of Wordsworth's death-orientated poetics speaks to similar concerns in two other recent studies. See Jacobus, *Romantic Things: A Tree, a Rock, a Cloud* (Chicago: University of Chicago Press, 2012), p. 3; Kurt Fosso, *Buried Communities: Wordsworth and the Bonds of Mourning* (Albany: State University of New York Press, 2004); Paul H. Fry, *Wordsworth and the Poetry of What We Are* (New Haven: Yale University Press, 2008).

18. See Susan Wolfson, *Romantic Shades and Shadows* (Baltimore: Johns Hopkins University Press, 2018).

19. William Shakespeare, *Macbeth*, ed. Kenneth Muir, Arden Shakespeare (London: Routledge, 1988), V, v, ll. 26–8. All quotations are from this edition.

20. Idiocy here is understood as something that defies precise scientific definition and, as Martin Halliwell argues, 'can more accurately be said to refer to a range of human experiences and traits that are difficult to classify, ultimately deriving from neurological impairment, but often reflected in forms of asocial behaviour that can be visually mimicked' (p. 1). See Halliwell, *Images of Idiocy: The Figure of the Idiot in Modern Fiction and Film* (London: Routledge, 2016), especially the first chapter on 'Romantic and Victorian Idiots'.

21. Michael Fredrickson helpfully identifies the date of Benjy's opening narration, 7 April, as synonymous with the date of Wordsworth's birth – of which this year, 2020, marks the 250th anniversary. See Fredrickson, 'A Note on "The Idiot Boy" as a Possible Source for *The Sound and the Fury*', *Minnesota Review* 6 (1966): 368; 368–70. Hereafter 'NPS'. See Juliet Barker, *Wordsworth: A Life* (London: Viking, 2000), pp. 1–2. Fredrickson lays important groundwork for establishing a connection between the depictions of idiocy in Wordsworth and Faulkner, especially the importance of timelessness to mental perceptions of both Wordsworth's Johnny and Faulkner's Benjy. My emphasis here is on the importance of clock time, the significance of twilight and the ghostly as depicted in Wordsworth's poem. I agree, too, with Martin Bidney

that Wordsworth left a distinctive mark as 'a poet Faulkner strongly admired' ('FVR', p. 279).

22. William Faulkner, *The Sound and the Fury* (1929; London: Picador, 1993), p. 277. Hereafter *TSF*. All quotations are from this edition.

23. Fredrickson recognises Benjy's vindication and triumph as the key narrator of the events of Faulkner's *The Sound and the Fury* as occasioned by Luster's break with 'precedent' by turning left ('NPS', p. 369), but without noting the probable resonance the episode has with Wordsworth's 'The Idiot Boy'.

24. Compare with Rebecca Rio-Jelliffe, *Obscurity's Myriad Components: The Theory and Practice of William Faulkner* (Lewisburg: Bucknell University Press, 2001), p. 99. Hereafter *OMC*.

25. On the subject of Faulkner's working title for *The Sound and the Fury*, see Michael Millgate, *The Achievement of William Faulkner* (London: Random, 1966), p. 86. Also see Ann Priddy, *Bloom's How to Write about William Faulkner*, intro. Harold Bloom (New York: Infobase, 2010), p. 74. For a discussion of the significance of twilight in Faulkner's prose and poetry, as well as the Romantic influence of Keats, see also Max Putzel, *Genius of Place: William Faulkner's Triumphant Beginnings* (Baton Rouge: Louisiana State University Press, 1985), p. 231.

26. Theresa M. Towner has recently and eloquently summed up the question behind Faulkner's allusion to Shakespeare's *Macbeth* as 'What if your language, any language, is just sound and fury that signifies nothing? If Macbeth was right, why write at all?' (p. 24). See Towner, *The Cambridge Introduction to William Faulkner* (Cambridge: Cambridge University Press, 2008). Hereafter *IWF*.

27. See Kenneth Muir's commentary on V, v, ll. 23ff., *Macbeth*, pp. 153–4.

28. Drawing on Tzvetan Todorov, Rebecca Rio-Jelliffe rightly observes of the unspoken voice in *The Sound and the Fury* that 'Literature . . . becomes language empowered in form that surpasses the word and infuses silence' (*OMC*, p. 88).

29. I note Theresa M. Towner's caution that we 'read the novel as a product of Faulkner's imagination in the late 1920s and the Appendix as a product of his imagination in the mid-1940s' (*IWF*, p. 23).

30. William Faulkner, '1699–1945. Appendix: The Compsons', *PWF*, pp. 718–19.

31. For a discussion of light imagery in Wordsworth's 'Ode' and its legacy in the poetry of Byron and Shelley, see Mark Sandy, '"Lines of Light": Poetic Variations in Wordsworth, Byron, and Shelley', *Romanticism* 22.3 (2016): 260–8, Special Issue on 'Light in Literature', ed. Sarah Wootton.

32. Quentin's thoughts are saturated with the poetry of Keats and Tennyson. Despite Faulkner's often-cited life-long preoccupation with the dilemma of Keats's 'Ode on a Grecian Urn', the imagery of 'Ode to a Nightingale' is most pertinent here. Warwick Wadlington observes of Faulkner's depiction of Quentin's consciousness 'that it was an analogous performance

of the inner consciousness that Keats praised in the ode' (p. 195). See Wadlington, *Reading Faulknerian Tragedy* (Ithaca: Cornell University Press, 1987).

33. See A. Nicholas Fargnoli, Michael Golay and W. Hamblin, *A Critical Companion to William Faulkner: A Literary Reference to his Life and Work* (New York: Infobase, 2008), p. 284. Hereafter *CCWF*.

34. Cleanth Brooks emphasises the importance of this matrix of imagery in the novel and argues that it signals that Quentin gives himself over to the 'river of death' rather than the body of his sister, Caddy. See Brooks, *William Faulkner: The Yoknapatawpha Country* (Baton Rouge: Louisiana State University Press, 1991), p. 332. Hereafter *TYC*.

35. See Hugh M. Ruppersburg, 'Byron Bunch and Percy Grimm: Strange Twins of *Light in August*', *The Mississippi Quarterly* 30.3 (1970): 441–3, Special Issue on William Faulkner.

36. Faulkner writes that he sought 'to underline the tragedy of Christmas by the tragedy of [Hightower's] antithesis'. See Frederick Landis Gwynn and Joseph Leo Blotner, eds, *Faulkner in the University* (Charlottesville: University of Virginia Press, 1959), p. 72. Hereafter *FU*.

37. These unifying and structural parallelisms are a commonplace in critical responses to Faulkner's *Light in August*. See, for example, Brooks, *TYC*, pp. 47–74; Fargnoli et al., *CCWF*, pp. 155–6; Towner, *IWF*, pp. 35–7.

38. See Bidney, 'FVR', pp. 277–86.

39. William Blake, *Songs of Innocence and of Experience*, in *William Blake: Poetry and Prose*, ed. Mary V. Erdman (New York: Norton, 1979). All quotations are from this edition. Martin Bidney convincingly explores the complex worm motif in Blake's 'The Sick Rose' and its unfolding allusions in the narrative of Joe Christmas. See Bidney, 'FVR', pp. 277–9.

40. See Friedrich Nietzsche, *Beyond Good and Evil*, trans. R. J. Hollingdale (Harmondsworth: Penguin, 1990), [203], pp. 71–2. Numbers in square brackets refer to section numbers.

41. William Faulkner, *Light in August* (1932; London: Picador, 1991), p. 87. Hereafter *LA*. All quotations are from this edition.

42. See Olga W. Vickery, 'The Shadow and the Mirror: *Light in August*', in *Twentieth-Century Interpretations of 'Light in August'*, ed. David L. Minter (Englewood Cliffs, NJ: Prentice Hall, 1969), p. 26; pp. 25–41. Hereafter *TWCI*.

43. See Gwynn and Blotner, *FU*, p. 199.

44. See Richard Chase, 'Faulkner's *Light in August*', in *TWCI*, pp. 23–4; pp. 17–24. See also Darrel Abel, 'Frozen Movement in *Light in August*', in *TWCI*, pp. 52–3; pp. 42–55.

45. See Michael Millgate, 'Faulkner's *Light in August*', in *TWCI*, p. 77; pp. 71–82. See also Rio-Jelliffe, *OMC*, p. 58.

46. See Bidney, 'FVR', pp. 282–3. For a psychologically inflected reading of mirror imagery in Faulkner's work more generally and *Light in August*

in particular see Doreen Fowler, *Faulkner: The Return of the Repressed* (Charlottesville: University of Virginia Press, 2001), pp. 71–2.

47. See William J. Sowder, *Existential-Phenomenological Readings of Faulkner* (Conway: UCA, 1991), p. 58.
48. Susan V. Donaldson observes, 'In a word, that anonymous white townsman is infuriated that Joe Christmas can be so easily misread in a world where the realm of the visible is subject to such rigid racial regulation and segmentation' (p. 111). See Donaldson, '*Light in August*, Faulkner's Angels of History, and the Culture of Jim Crow', in *Faulkner's Inheritance: Faulkner and Yoknapatawpha*, ed. Joseph R. Urgo and Ann J. Abadie (Jackson: University Press of Mississippi, 2005), pp. 101–25.
49. Bidney, 'FVR', p. 284.
50. See Millgate, 'Faulkner's *Light in August*', TWCI, p. 79.
51. See Arnold Weinstein, *Nobody's Home: Speech, Self, and Place in American Fiction: From Hawthorne to DeLillo* (Oxford: Oxford University Press, 1993), pp. 176–8.
52. See Brooks, *TYC*, pp. 73–4.
53. Compare with Brooks, *TYB*, pp. 262, 263.
54. See Millgate, 'Faulkner's *Light in August*', TWCI, p. 77.
55. See Fargnoli et al., CCWF, p. 155.

Part III

Romantic Transformations: Fictional Selves and Nature

Chapter 5

Fictions of the Self and Nature: Reading Romanticism in Saul Bellow

Attaining prominence in the post-war era, Saul Bellow is one of the most widely read and intellectually eclectic novelists of the Jewish American School.[1] Bellow's frequent references to Romanticism form a dominant design within his culturally diverse fiction.[2] The interwoven complex patterns of this literary and cultural fabric find expression in a moment of near epiphany, in *Herzog* (1964), characterised as 'webbed with golden lines'.[3] Bellow's image indicates the two levels on which his Romantic allusions operate. At one level, this 'webbed' pattern of 'golden lines'[4] suggests how Bellow interlaces his own prose with the poetry and philosophy of British Romanticism to govern readers' responses to his portrayal of epiphanies. At another, *Herzog*'s moment of interconnected vision signals Bellow's investment in a Coleridgean and Wordsworthian imagination that reveals the all-pervasive spirit of the 'One Life within us and abroad'.[5] This metaphysical dimension to Bellow's web of 'golden lines' finds a further affinity with P. B. Shelley's later notion of the 'web of being' (*Adonais*, ll. 481–2).

How central the English Romantic imagination is to Bellow's writing can be measured from two of his novels published sixteen years apart, *Henderson the Rain King* and *Humboldt's Gift*, which have both been read as extended meditations on Wordsworth's 'Ode: Intimations of Immortality'.[6] From the 1950s onwards, Bellow was concerned that contemporary existence was creating a restrictive and rational mode of thinking equivalent to Blake's 'mind forg'd manacles'.[7] These rational modes of knowledge deaden a Romantic belief in the transforming power of the imagination. Bellow solidified this view in a 1965 interview when he speculated, 'I wonder whether there will ever be enough tranquillity under modern circumstances to allow our contemporary Wordsworth to recollect anything.'[8]

Grasping at the Romantic Self: Bellow, Wordsworth and Keats

Bellow's investment in Romantic concepts of the imagination can be gauged from those unexpected yet crucial moments in his writing when he alludes to Romanticism. Bellow's least intellectually gifted protagonist, Tommy Wilhelm, the focus of Bellow's 1956 novella *Seize the Day*, finds himself quoting British Romantic poetry. Even Bellow's choice of title gestures towards a certain Romantic sensibility in its recommendation of *carpe diem*. On the brink of personal and financial ruin, Wilhelm recalls being read some lines from John Keats's *Endymion*:

> Is he [Dr Tamkin] trying to hypnotize or con me? Wilhelm wondered. To take my mind off selling? But even if I'm back at seven hundred bucks then where am I?
>
> As if in prayer, his lids coming down with raised veins, frayed out, on his significant eyes, Tamkin said, '"Here and now I see a button. Here and now I see the green thread."' Inch by inch he contemplated himself in order to show Wilhelm how calm it would make him. But Wilhelm was hearing Margaret's voice as she read, somewhat unwillingly,
>
> > Come, then, Sorrow!
> > I thought to leave thee,
> > And deceive thee,
> > But now of all the world I love thee best.[9]

Chavkin interprets these lines from Keats's 1817 poem as an embryonic version of his later attitude to suffering, expressed famously in the 'Vale of Soul-making' letter addressed to George and Georgiana Keats, where the suffering of existence no longer secures individuals an afterlife.[10] Instead, in less spiritual and more humanist terms, suffering is instrumental in shaping 'Intelligences' or souls into mature identities through 'a medium of a world like this' – a 'World of Pains' (*JKL*, 1, p. 192). Such a view is encapsulated by Keats's reversal of those words - which are spoken by Byron's Manfred - in a letter from spring 1818, when Keats declares that 'Sorrow is Wisdom' (*JKL*, 1, p. 279). Read in these Keatsian terms, Wilhelm's sense of suffering shapes, purposefully, the growth of an individual identity, so that his eventual emotional breakdown amidst a crowd of mourners at the end of the novella can be read as a powerful and emotional breakthrough:[11]

The flowers and lights fused ecstatically in Wilhelm's blind, wet eyes; the heavy sea-like music came up to his ears. It poured into him where he had hidden himself in the center of a crowd by the great and happy oblivion of tears. He heard it and sank deeper than sorrow, through torn sobs and cries toward the consummation of his heart's ultimate need. (*SD*, p. 118)

Wilhelm's capacity for an empathetic identification with the deceased stranger and the grieving loved ones is commensurate with a moment of Keatsian negative capability as his own ordinary egotistical self is obliterated – and cleansed, as the water imagery suggests both a baptism and birth of a new self – through this out-pouring of emotion. But these waters of baptism and creation are equally the waters of destructive flood (especially as Wilhelm is hydrophobic) and might signpost an emotional and psychological breakdown rather than a transcendent breakthrough of the 'heart's ultimate need'.

Elsewhere in *Seize the Day*, Romanticism's redemptive and sublime power of the imagination is presented with even greater qualification than affirmative readings of Bellow's Romantic tendencies permit. When Wilhelm recollects his more tranquil past, he creates a pastoral haven away from the claustrophobic pressures of contemporary city-life:

Wilhelm had kept a small apartment in Roxbury, two rooms in a large house with a small porch and garden, and on mornings of leisure in late spring weather like this, he used to sit expanded in a wicker chair with the sunlight pouring through the weave, and sunlight through the slug-eaten holes of the young hollyhocks and as deeply as the grass allowed into small . . . flowers. This peace (he forgot that that time had had its troubles, too), this peace was gone. (*SD*, p. 43)

Wilhelm's efforts to recollect and recast past biographical events through the truth, at least, of his own imagination verge on an affirmation of the interconnected nature of the universe, as he is interfused with the threads of 'sunlight pouring through the weave' that bind him to the leaves of the hollyhocks, the lush grass and those delicate, barely discernible flowers of nature. Yet this moment of Romantic transcendence is only partial, as the interfering voice of realism in parenthesis reminds us that this imagined loss of peace in a previous paradise is just that – imagined. This voice of limits and limitations, which speaks from outside of Wilhelm's imaginative act, ensures that the reinvigorating and redeeming potentiality of the Romantic imagination is kept in play alongside the harsh realities and contingencies of existence.

Bellow may be on the side of the Romantic imagination, but not without characteristic qualification and ambivalence.[12] He is a latter-day Romantic, but one with a seared consciousness. Bellow reaffirms as much, in his 1975 essay 'A World Too Much with Us', with the conviction that 'the imagination', as Bellow writes, 'I take to be indispensable to truth'.[13] In this same essay Bellow reinforces his concern about whether a Wordsworthian sensibility could survive in contemporary society and elaborates further his defence of the redeeming qualities of the imagination:

> Two centuries ago, the early romantic poets assumed that their minds were free, that they could know the good, that they could independently interpret and judge the entire creation, but those who still believe the imagination has such powers to penetrate and to know keep their belief to themselves. As we now understand knowledge, does imagination *know* anything? At the moment the educated world does not think so. But things have become dreary and humankind tired of itself because the collective fictions of alleged knowledge are used up. We now bore ourselves with what we think we now know. ('ATM', p. 6)

Bellow's caricaturing of modern-day thought recalls the mind-numbing 'Here-and-now' exercises advocated by the confidence man, Dr Tamkin, in *Seize the Day*. These require the participant to repeat the phrase 'here-and-now' (*SD*, p. 90) whilst focusing on a single object (in this case, a button and its thread on a corduroy shirt). Tamkin's pseudo-mystical, pseudo-philosophical, even pseudo-scientific mental exercise embodies precisely the over-rationalised and prescriptive modes of knowledge that Bellow regards as eroding our belief in the Romantic imagination. Tellingly, Tamkin admonishes that for his piece of quackery to be successful you must 'not let your imagination shoot ahead' (*SD*, p. 90). Throughout Bellow's novella, Tamkin espouses a quasi-psychological theory of a conflict within individuals between the 'real soul' and the socialised 'pretender soul' (*SD*, p. 70) which is reminiscent of Freud's theory of the struggle between Superego, Ego and Id. Parodying the widespread popularity in the States of psychoanalysis (after Freud had delivered the Clark University lectures in 1909),[14] Bellow moulds Tamkin into a modern-day mountebank of quasi-scientific and quasi-mystical pronouncements.

Dubbed as 'reality-instructors', Tamkin and his kind represent, for Bellow, the worst of modern humanity, who plug the spiritual void of the post-war period with fake mysticism and psychobabble. They are themselves the arch-exponents of a spiritual and emotional vacuity in twentieth-century America. These 'reality-instructors' trade, as Bellow notes in *Herzog*, in the stock 'commonplaces of the Wasteland outlook, the cheap mental stimulants of Alienation, the cant and rant of pipsqueaks about Inauthenticity and Forlornness' (*HZ*, p. 75). Tamkin is one of many Bellovian exponents of this bad faith of modern inauthentic and alienated humanity and seizes the day (or present moment) in precisely the wrong way.[15] Tamkin's claims to self-transcendence and the endurance of selfhood offer, at best, a mockery of Emersonian self-reliance.[16] By contrast Wilhelm's Romantic sensibilities and Keatsian empathy with suffering signpost a world of possibilities and knowledge accessible only through the power of the imagination, which can sanctify existence in all its mundane manifestations. Such a revelation is not open to the mock-mystical buffoonery of Dr Tamkin's 'Here-and-now' exercise which, rather self-centredly, focuses on his own button's 'green thread' and – mocking Wilhelm's attempted imaginative union with nature at Roxbury – falls comically short of a metaphysical thread or yarn that binds him to some greater transcendental chain of being which tentatively comprises, in Shelley's words, 'Nature's vast frame, the web of human things' (*Alastor*, l. 719).

Romantic Selfhood and Being: Bellow, Emerson, Wordsworth and Shelley

So far Bellow's allusions to British Romantic writers have been read as regulating responses to epiphanies in his fiction. Indeed, Bellow has often been regarded as an exponent of a Romantic sensibility with a peculiarly British inflection. Often those commentators who interpret Bellow within this British Romantic tradition identify his ability to make Romanticism's faith in the power of the imagination relevant to the contemporary concerns and anxieties of the early and late twentieth century.[17] Bellow's mature fiction is more than a conduit for British Romanticism, as he manages to fuse the central tenets of British Romantic sensibilities with those distinctive characteristics of American Romanticism or Transcendentalism. Revisiting

American Romanticism helps us to appreciate Bellow's unique brand of twentieth-century Romanticism.

By extending Tony Tanner's observations about American Transcendentalism, it is possible to register the distinctly American note of Bellow's Romanticism.[18] Outlining differences between American and European Romanticism, Tanner comments that 'Emerson may sound like Wordsworth when he talks of "that wonderful congruity which subsists between man and nature"', but 'above all it is the fluidity, the insubstantiality, the transparency of nature which is stressed' (*SNSM*, p. 32) by Ralph Waldo Emerson and not by William Wordsworth.[19] Published in 1836, Emerson's essay on *Nature*, with its famous declaration, stresses the selfless, intuitive disclosure of being as presence, which fuses together those Cartesian dualities of subject and object, mind and body, spirit and matter: 'I become a transparent eyeball. I am nothing; I see all; the currents of Universal Being circulate through me; I am part or [particle] of God' (*Nature*, *CWE*, p. 10).

Yet Wordsworth's use of place names in his description of the rural landscape often lends the scene a specificity of locale rarely found in Emerson's accounts of natural landscape.[20] Emerson appreciates the enormity of nature, but understands its material substance as malleable and open to being woven into the web of the true poet, for

> His [the poet's] imperial muse tosses the creation like a bauble from hand to hand . . . to embody any caprice shade of thought that is uppermost in his mind. The remotest spaces of nature are visited, and the farthest sundered things are brought together, by a subtle spiritual connection. We are made aware that magnitude of material things is merely relative, and all objects shrink and expand to serve the passion of the poet. (*Nature*, *CWE*, p. 32)

For Emerson, at least, the only point of anchorage in the endless ebb and flow of a continually expanding and contracting, fluidly dynamic universe is the fixity of the soul which finds its place in the vast, circulating current of 'Universal Being' through a fabrication of these delicate fictional designs – what Shelley understood some seventeen years earlier, in 'Mont Blanc', as those fleeting 'human mind's imaginings' that lend meaning and purpose to 'the everlasting universe of things' (l. 143, l. 1). Such poetic 'imaginings' are entirely necessary to ground the self, in Emerson's view; as he explains, 'we are not built like a ship to be tossed, but like a house to stand' (*Nature*, *CWE*, p. 30).

These last two Emersonian similes (of the cast-adrift ship buffeted by the open sea and the fixed, static structure of the house) have a direct bearing on Bellow's novel *Herzog*. If Emerson renegotiates the terms of Wordsworth's poetic vision, then Bellow fuses together elements from British and American Romanticism. Through his own fiction, Bellow transforms Emerson's and Shelley's notion of the 'web of being' as a fictional pattern read into the ever-changing and 'everlasting universe of things' ('Mont Blanc', l. 1). Waiting for a ferry, Bellow's Herzog finds himself caught up in a sublime moment of Romantic transcendence. Herzog's revelation, Bellow tells us, occurs when,

> In the mild end of the afternoon, later, at the waterside in Woods Hole, waiting for the ferry, he looked through the green darkness at the net of bright reflections on the bottom. He loved to think about the power of the sun, about light, about the ocean. The purity of the air moved him. There was no stain in the water, where schools of minnows swam. Herzog sighed and said to himself, 'Praise God – Praise God.' His breathing had become freer. His heart was greatly stirred by the open horizon; the deep colors; the faint iodine pungency of the Atlantic rising from weeds and molluscs; the white, fine, heavy sand; but principally by the green transparency as he looked down to the stony bottom webbed with golden lines. Never still. If this soul could cast a reflection so brilliant, and so intensely sweet, he might beg God to make such use of him. But that would be too simple. But that would be too childish. The actual sphere is not clear like this, but turbulent, angry. A vast human action is going on. Death watches. So if you have some happiness, conceal it. And when your heart is full, keep your mouth shut also. (*HZ*, pp. 91–2)

Here Bellow reimagines Wordsworth's sacred trinity of 'the light of setting suns / And the round ocean and the living air' that intimates 'a sense sublime / of something far more deeply interfused' (*Tintern Abbey*, ll. 97–8, 95–6). The play of light on water generates a number of tightly knit, intricate geometric patterns: firstly described as the 'net of bright reflections', secondly glimpsed in the 'stony bottom webbed with golden lines', and lastly present in Herzog's desire to 'cast a reflection so brilliant'.

Inverting the notion of casting a shadow, Herzog imagines his soul casting a reflection of such brilliance that its light breaks out of his corporeal form and penetrates the 'green darkness' and commingles with those webbed designs of light on the 'stony bottom'. 'Cast', then, suggests not just the imagined throwing of this luminous reflection, but the casting out of a fishing line or net with the intention that its own threads will be woven into the greater design of universal being projected on to the natural world through these webs of 'golden lines'. There is also the implied notion of weighing anchor, as Herzog's inner being casts around for a suitable place to tether itself to the ever-shifting but continually interconnected Shelleyan-Emersonian 'web of being'.

Herzog's almost realised transcendent moment (curtailed by his awareness of Death watching in the wings) is also both informed and framed by Blake's visionary poetry; Herzog always carries a New York pocket edition of Blake close to his heart (*HZ*, p. 80).[21] The Blake of *Songs of Innocence and of Experience*, as Bellow ruminates in the late autumn of 1959, was closer to his own heart than he had previously realised: 'Last night after reading Blake, the lost children and especially "A Little Girl Lost", I began to suspect he must have sunk deeply into my unconscious.'[22] Bellow's description that 'there was no stain in the water' echoes Blake's *Songs of Innocence*, where the Piper declares: 'And I made a rural pen, / And I stain'd the water clear, / And I wrote my happy songs / Every child may joy to hear' ('Introduction', ll. 1–4). Even Bellow's detail of the 'green darkness' recalls the 'darkening green' (l. 30) at the close of 'The Ecchoing Green' and ushers in Blake's realisation that beyond a child-like state of Innocence lies what Bellow construes as a Blakean 'second inno-cence . . . per experience, passing by way of lions' (*SBL*, p. 1182), the threat of age, experience and death.

Bellow's description of Herzog's failed Romantic epiphany is fur-ther illuminated when placed alongside the following two passages by Emerson, the first from his essay entitled 'Poetry and Imagination' and the second from his essay on *Nature*:

> [Nature] serves us best, when, on rare days, she speaks to the imagination, we feel that the huge heaven and earth are but a web drawn around us, that the light, skies, and mountains are but the painted vicissitudes of the soul.[23]
>
> I only wish to indicate the true position of nature in regard to man, wherein to establish man, all right education tends; as the ground which to attain is the object of human life, that is, of man's connection with nature. Culture inverts the vulgar views of nature, and brings the mind to call that apparent, which it uses to call real, and that real, which it uses to call visionary. Children, it is true, believe in the external world. (*Nature*, *CWE*, p. 36)

Bellow's Romanticism shares as much with Blake's visionary revelations of seeing 'a World in a Grain of Sand' ('Auguries of Innocence', l. 1) as it does with an Emersonian sense of the fluidity and unreality of the natural and external world, which only exists to be shaped and woven into an interconnected, web-like pattern. Bellow's portrayal of Herzog's aspiration to Romantic transcendence entertains the possibility of recapturing an innocent child-like state of consciousness, which will reawaken the adult Herzog to the mysterious although often hidden wonders of a divinely ordered universe, and, simultaneously, recognises with Emerson the childish simplicity of such a worldview. Bellow's Romanticism strains after the traditional Romantic belief in the sacredness of a given nature and fuses this with Emerson's understanding of the fragility of those fictional webs of interconnectedness woven out of the poet's perception that could give way to the 'apocalypse of the mind' (*Nature, CWE,* p. 53). In Bellow's ambivalently poised novel, Herzog (an academic and professional advocate of Romanticism) is either on the brink of a mental collapse, in the midst of a nervous breakdown or on the road to recovery from some sort of psychological crisis.

In an earlier passage, Bellow self-consciously interrogates the validity of Herzog's Romantic endeavour to locate himself within the vast 'web of being' through a series of his own 'human mind's imaginings'. Bellow's terminology echoes both Emerson's previously quoted account of the cosmos in his essay on *Nature* and Emerson's sense of how technological innovation is readily accommodated into the poet's vision of nature's vast 'web':

> Readers of poetry see the factory-village, and the railway, and fancy that the poetry of the landscape is broken up by these, – for these works of art are not yet consecrated in their reading; but the poet sees them fall within the great order not less than the bee-hive, or the spider's geometrical web. Nature adopts them very fast into her vital circles, and the gliding train of cars she loves like her own.[24]

Interfused with Shelley's 'Light whose smile kindles the Universe' (*Adonais,* l. 478), Bellow's passage – from *Herzog* – improvises around its Emersonian theme:

> Then the enamelled shells of the commuters' cars, and the heaped bodies of junk cars, the shapes of old New England mills with narrow, austere windows; villages, convents; tugboats moving in the swelling fabric-like water; and then plantations of pine, the needles on the ground of a life-giving russet color. So, thought Herzog, acknowledging that his imagination of the universe was elementary, the novae bursting and the worlds

coming into being, the invisible magnetic spokes by means of which bodies kept one another in orbit . . . Then after many billions of years, light years, this childlike but far from innocent creature, a straw hat on his head, and a heart in his breast, part pure, part wicked, who would try to form his own shaky picture of this magnificent web. (*HZ*, pp. 47–8)

Bellow's Herzog may be a scholar of European Romanticism, but he is inclined towards an Emersonian sensibility with a heightened sensitivity to 'his own shaky picture' of the 'magnificent web'. Into this fragile 'web of being', Herzog interweaves his own chaotic sense of the by-products of industrial development and the onset of a consumerist society, along with his giddying – and humbling – comprehension of the operations of astral bodies on a cosmic scale.

Against this endless ebb and flow of being, Emerson admonishes that we either tether our souls by casting a fictive web or, alternatively, we erect a 'house to stand'. Much of Bellow's novel is taken up with Herzog's writing of letters to famous scientists, philosophers, psychologists, social theorists, personal acquaintances and even God at one point. This frenetic, even incessant letter writing is punctuated by Herzog's recollection of purchasing a 'country house' with money inherited from his deceased father – unbeknown to Herzog at the time of purchase, the house in reality is a 'fix me up' in Ludeyville, Massachusetts. Similarly to his tireless letter writing, Herzog responds to the reality of the calamitous situation with fervent DIY tenacity in which 'He sat up nights studying the *Do-It-Yourself Encyclopedia*, and with hysterical passion he painted, patched, tarred gutters, plastered holes' and, eventually, 'a year of work saved the house from collapse' (*HZ*, p. 120).

At other junctures in the narrative, Bellow describes this New England property purchase as 'gloomy . . . with rotting Victorian ornaments' and 'bricks dropping from the foundations' (*HZ*, p. 120). But Bellow's concern is with more than just the material details of Herzog's 'country house', especially when Herzog's rural retreat is located in Massachusetts. Woods Hole, the coastal site of Herzog's first visionary episode, is also, by no coincidence, situated in the state of Massachusetts. There, with the founding of the Transcendental Club in Cambridge, on 8 September 1836, Massachusetts witnessed the genesis of Transcendentalism or American Romanticism. The house itself, with its 'rotting Victorian ornaments', clearly belongs to the nineteenth and not the twentieth century and, like Herzog's professional and emotional attachment to Romanticism in the modern world, it is outmoded. Indeed, the condition of Herzog's house as somewhat shaky but fundamentally sound – its whole structure is restored from a state of dilapidation within 'a year' – is suggestive. It extends the corollary between the physical state and well-being of the static form of the house and Herzog's own mental 'collapse' and possible psychic restoration (especially as the duration of Herzog's journey through mental collapse and possible recovery also lasts approximately one year). Readers must reconstruct the events of Herzog's life as he reconstructs the structure of his house in the Berkshires.[25] The Ludeyville house – unidentified on 'the Esso map' (*HZ*, p. 329) – is Herzog's last retreat at the novel's close. Herzog is both inside and outside societal and geographic margins – on the psychic map, but location unspecified.

Finally, in Massachusetts, Herzog, having ceased writing his unsent letters to numerous addressees, communes with the natural rhythms and goings-on of life, and lapses into the silence of '[n]ot a single word' (*HZ*, p. 341). Read solely through Emerson, Herzog's retreat to his repaired 'country house' offers a safe haven for his soul or mind from the endless flux of the external world and provides a static anchorage-point – like his previously attempted uncertain fictions of the 'magnificent web' – from which he can appreciate his own position in the universe. Yet Herzog's final retreat into the rural house in Ludeyville blends, as does Wilhelm's pastoral idyll of Roxbury in *Seize the Day*, a sense of Wordsworth's physical and mental 'eye made quiet by the power of harmony' with Emerson's restless awareness of those 'currents of Universal Being [that] circulate through me'. For instance, when Herzog reflects on Ludeyville and its environs,

> *Everywhere on earth, the model of natural creation seems to be the ocean. The mountains certainly look that way, glossy, plunging and that haughty blue color. And even these scrappy lawns. What keeps these red brick houses from collapse on these billows is their inner staleness. I smell it yawning through the screens. The odor of souls is a brace to the walls. Otherwise the wrinkling of the hills would make them crumble.*
> (*HZ*, p. 339, original italic)

There is awareness that any anchorage-point – whether fictional web or house – provides only a temporary respite from the ceaseless undulating motions of the universe. Even if these fictional houses or webs provide a momentary stay in an otherwise randomly chaotic existence, they cannot be clung to or inhabited forever as they run the risk of stifling the souls that they seek to sustain and shelter. It is conceivable that the ideological or aesthetic house of European and American Romanticism itself could one day become subject to this preserving yet corrosive 'inner staleness'. Herzog's faith in Romanticism, echoing Bellow's own, is born of a resistance to modern-day nihilism and yet, even in the peaceful respite of the Berkshires, he is conscious that 'this rest and well-being were only a momentary difference in the strange lining or variable silk between life and void' (*HZ*, p. 326). Whatever 'momentary difference' is arrested from between the 'life and void' is entirely internal – a question of Herzog's inner, transitory sense of his right relation to the universe (a Keatsian glimpse of 'ethereal existence' (*JKL*, 1, p. 301)) – as the over-run garden is a reminder that the external world remains as endlessly chaotic as ever and ever-waiting to be shaped by the observer's imagination.

Romantic Selves Recast: Bellow, Wordsworth, Emerson and Shelley

This Bellovian tension between self and nature, between outer and inner world, is coloured by Emerson's view that 'Nature is not fixed but fluid. Spirit alters, molds, makes it', but, as Emerson qualifies, it is only 'fluid', 'volatile' and 'obedient' to one of 'pure spirit' (*Nature*, *CWE*, p. 44). In terms that are more affirmative than Bellow's Romantic tendencies in *Herzog*, Emerson's essay continues that such a 'spirit builds itself a house; and beyond its house, a world; and beyond its world, a heaven' (*Nature*, *CWE*, p. 44). In the intervening years between *Herzog* and *Mr Sammler's Planet* (1970), Bellow moves towards a darker and less optimistic view of Romanticism.[26] Aligning himself with the aged speaker of Emerson's poem 'Terminus', who acknowledges that 'It is time to be old' and, like a bird 'in a gale', 'trim myself to the storm of time', Bellow describes himself as passively isolated from the 'large "cultural" trends' of the current historical moment. In the same letter, dated 24 September 1977, Bellow elaborates:

> I am passive, registering what's wrong in what this civilization of ours thinks when it speaks of Nature, God, the soul, and it cuts me off from all organized views. It doesn't cut me off at all from the deeper being of people – in fact that's where my reaction against these organized views begin. (*SBL*, p. 350)

Twenty or so years earlier Bellow expressed a similar commitment to the inwardness of individual character, 'the deeper being of people'.

Reflecting again on Emerson, on this occasion writing about 'the remoteness of the high minded transcendentalists from worldly activities', Bellow affirms the 'intelligence of imagining' over other more organised 'forms of intelligence' (*SBL*, pp. 121–2). Bellow's distinction between different kinds of intelligences and their vital role in shaping selfhood resonates with Keats's insistence that true selves are forged out of 'intelligences' through their tempering by an external world of suffering. What Bellow identifies as an 'intelligence of imagining' signals an investment in the aesthetic as a revelatory mode of knowing with the capacity to reveal the true nature of self and world. Bellow's formulation and sentiment equally chimes with Shelley's claim, in *A Defence of Poetry*, that poetry 'purges from our inward sight the film of familiarity that obscures from us the wonder of our being. It compels us to feel what we perceive, and to know that which we imagine' (*SPP*, p. 533).

By the 1970s, Bellow strongly believed that any kind of imaginative insight into the essence of our consciousness, true selfhood and depth of being had been sacrificed to the false idol of the superficial. Bellow's essay 'A World Too Much with Us', published in 1975, traces since the Romantics a decline of belief in the power of imagination and the ability of its creations to constitute a form of knowledge. Bellow's central claim turns on a crucial change, exacerbated by contemporary society, in post-Romantic configurations of the interrelations between imagination and knowledge, which finds compressed expression in Bellow's handwritten draft of the essay, where he pens: 'those who believe in [imagination's] power are today comparatively few. It does not stand before the creation to judge or praise it as it once did. As we now understand knowledge, does imagination know anything?'[27] The power, reach and significance of the imagination has been diminished, if not eradicated, by overly rationalised and scientific 'organised views'. Such forms of knowledge do not countenance the view that, as Bellow avers in his published essay, the 'imagination is an indispensable truth' ('ATM', p. 6) and a means by which the ordinary world can communicate to us the remarkable and sublime. Bellow strongly felt, as the opening of 'A World Too Much with Us' announces, 'that we were giving our hearts away, and that we saw less and less in the external world, in nature, that the heart could respond to' ('ATM', p. 1).

These darkening views of the fate of the imagination and the cultural project of Romanticism are integral to the weft of Bellow's *Mr Sammler's Planet*, set in 1969 and published in 1970. In *Mr Sammler's Planet*, Bellow's septuagenarian protagonist, a Holocaust survivor, who has witnessed the murder of his wife, recollects the days he spent in hiding in a Polish cemetery. Artur Sammler recounts an attempted imaginative communion with the natural world which, similar to Herzog's experience, questions the childish naivety of such a world-view. There is, as in *Herzog*, a straining after Wordsworth's sense of 'something far more deeply interfused' (*Tintern Abbey*, l. 100) and a desire to sanctify every living, breathing thing in existence even in the most extreme of circumstances, mingled with self-doubt, uncertainty and a sense of the foolishness of the entire Romantic venture:

> It was in Poland, in wartime, particularly during three or four months when Sammler was hidden in a mausoleum, that he first began to turn to the external world for curious ciphers and portents. The dead life of that summer and into autumn when he had been a portent watcher, and very childish, for many larger forms of meaning had been stamped out, and a straw, or a spider thread or a stain, a beetle or a sparrow had to be interpreted. Symbols everywhere, and metaphysical messages.[28]

It is not clear that Sammler's forced (as opposed to Herzog's self-imposed) retreat from the world and communion with nature brings about, no matter how fleetingly, any restorative effects; the 'spider thread' no more than 'a stain' (in contrast to the absence of 'stain' in Herzog's first near moment of transcendence) provides the imagination with the stuff from which to create an anchor-point for the soul. Nature, as Emerson understood it, may be malleable to the poetic mind, but in Bellow's darker Romanticism there is every chance that its 'metaphysical messages' will remain inscrutable or irrelevant. Bellow still advocates imaginative intuition as the means through which the human spirit or soul can partly create and partly discover that which is most vital, but he is reluctant to align this imaginative form with the modern-day pedant's over-rationalised definition of Romanticism. These reservations are evident at the start of the novel:

> Being right was largely a matter of explanations. Intellectual man had become an explaining creature. Fathers to children, wives to husbands, lecturers to listeners, experts to laymen, colleagues to colleagues, doctors to patients, man to his soul, explained. The roots of this, the causes of the other, the source of events, the history, the structure, the reasons why. For the most part, in one ear and out the other. The soul wanted what it wanted. It had its own natural knowledge. It sat unhappily on superstructures of explanation, poor bird not knowing where to fly. (*MSP*, pp. 1–2)

By the close of the novel, Sammler comprehends what constitutes this intuitive 'natural knowledge' of the soul, as he realises that the world of ordinary existence becomes sacrosanct in and for itself without recourse to abstract metaphysics, theology or philosophy – those superstructures of explanation. Bellow's late Romanticism advocates instead an instinctive 'natural knowledge' that recognises that the divine resides within the human breast and teaches us that we have an obligation to our fellow humanity and a duty to discover, in Shelley's words, the 'sustaining Love' woven through the 'web of being' (*Adonais*, ll. 481–2). Sammler articulates this belief in his prayer for his deceased uncle:

> He [Elya Gruner] was aware that he must meet, and he did meet – through all the confusion and degraded clowning of this life through which we are speeding – he did meet the terms of his contract. The terms which, in his inmost heart, each man knows. As I know mine. As all know. For that is the truth of it – that we all know God, that we know, that we know, we know, we know. (*MSP*, p. 313)

Even if the spiritual comforts of the natural world are less certain, Bellow's tempered Romanticism ultimately resists the potentially solipsistic retreat of Herzog and the nihilism of the last century to foreground our wider communal and social obligations to one another as human beings and Blakean and Emersonian sense of the divine within and to be once again connected with Shelley's interwoven 'web of being'.

This fascination with the Romantic image of an interconnected web of self and world persists, albeit somewhat tarnished, in Bellow's final novel, *Ravelstein* (2000), which ranks alongside *Herzog* and *Humboldt's Gift* (1975) as one of Bellow's novels of ideas.[29] The authorial figure and narrator, Chick, fondly recalls in *Ravelstein* his ideas about 'modern disenchantment' and how they were paraphrased by his deceased friend, Abe Ravelstein:

> Under the debris of modern ideas the world was still there to be rediscovered. And [Ravelstein's] way of putting it was that the gray net of abstraction covering the world in order to simplify and explain it in a way that served our cultural needs has *become* the world in our eyes. We needed to have alternate visions, a diversity of views – and he meant views not bossed by ideas. . . . We need to know – our deep human need, however, can't be satisfied by . . . terms. . . . The right words would be a great help. But even more, a gift for reading reality – the impulse to put your loving face to it and press your hands against it.[30]

Ravelstein's gloss squarely identifies the root of the problem as being with those ready-made, neatly packaged, 'modern ideas' and their related abstract terminology that increasingly distances the self from the world and hampers our ability to imaginatively read 'reality' and revive our intuitive senses to a tactile encounter with its 'loving face'. What emerges as the central sermon here is that we have closed out freedom of thought (those 'views not bossed by ideas') in favour of a 'gray net of abstraction', which offers simplifications and explanations of the 'world' instead of an actual, vital encounter with external experience. Ravelstein's gloss of Chick's anxieties about the modern condition and culture, that 'the gray net of abstraction . . . has *become* the world in our eyes', recalls Bellow's own indictments of modern sensibility in 'A World Too Much with Us'. Ravelstein's choice of words reduces the Emersonian image of the web of existence to a dull, unedifying net.

Nature is waiting for us somewhere beyond the reductionism of culture, forever *in potentia* as a series of indecipherable and endlessly deferred signs that remain meaningless to the 'modern condition' as we have neglected our 'gift for reading'. This deadening of Romantic impulses is a popular and recurring theme in Bellow's essays, lectures and fiction from the 1970s to the new millennium. Emersonian and Shelleyan ideas and motifs often fuse together in the crucible of Bellow's imagination to striking effect. In *Herzog*, sexual and capricious desire result in parodies of Emersonian transcendence in the declaration 'Hang your agony on a star (*HZ*, p. 22) and a Shelleyan loss of vision: 'I fall upon the thorns of life. I bleed. And what next? I get laid, I take a short holiday, but very soon after I fall upon those same thorns of life with gratification in pain or suffering in joy' (*HZ*, p. 214).[31] Shelleyan imaginative falling away and 'ideal eroticism' (gratified or disappointed) had formed a life-long association for Bellow who, reminiscing about sexual awakening as a Chicago teenager, with a degree of both amusement and self-parody, equates such hopeful and thwarted desire with the sensual frisson of Shelley's final stanza of 'The Indian Serenade': 'Oh lift me from the grass / I die! I faint! I fail! / Let thy love in kisses rain / On my lips and eyelids pale' (ll. 17–20).[32]

For all of Bellow's Wordsworthian inflections in *Humboldt's Gift*, the novel also witnesses Charlie Citrine, an aspiring artist and quasi-Bellovian figure, advocate the significance of imagination as a mode of knowing through terms that are explicitly drawn from the Romanticism(s) of Emerson and Shelley:[33]

> An artist sometimes tries to see how close he can become to being a river or a star, playing at becoming one or the other – entering into the forms

of the phenomena painted or described. Someone has even written of an astronomer keeping a drove of stars, the cattle of his mind, in the meadows of space. The imaginative soul works in that way, and why should poetry refuse to be knowledge? For Shelley, Adonais in death became part of the loveliness he had made more lovely. According to Goethe the blue of the sky *was* the theory. There was a thought in blue. The blue became blue when human vision received it.[34]

Bound together by an intricately woven web of associations, Citrine's defence of imaginative power originates in Emerson's praise for the sublimity and permanence of the stars in *Nature*, but the Emersonian thought of many stars gives sway to the thought of the single metaphorical star of Shelley's Adonais, whose soul 'like a star / Beacons from the abode where the Eternal are' (*Adonais*, ll. 494–5). In Citrine's associative web of thoughts, there is a natural progression from *Adonais* to Goethe's theory of colour perception, especially as Shelley's elegy finds in Rome's azure skies a 'fitting charnel-roof' for the deceased Keats, who lies beneath the 'vault of blue Italian day' (ll. 59–60).

Bellow's allusion to Shelley's elegy and its depiction of the absorption of Keats as Adonais into the natural world reinforces the empathetic, negatively capable power of the imagination avowed by Citrine in the passage. This is reinforced further by the reference to Goethe's colour theory and its advocacy of 'human vision' as the active ingredient in the realisation of the blueness of blue as blue. For artists, there remains an inexplicable yet productive tension between self and other, between ideal and real, between sympathetic engagement with an array of subjects ('playing at becoming one or another') and their artistic desire to render those subjects as objects ('the phenomena painted or described'). This selfless identification of artists with their chosen subject (a specification of Citrine's 'imaginative soul') speaks directly to Shelley's carefully poised poetic balancing act as elegist in *Adonais*. Shelley must at once empathetically rejuvenate every fibre of the once living now expired Keats and selfishly fashion Keats into Shelley's own image of a posthumous poet.

Ideal or imperfect love is, as Shelley advocates in *Adonais*, the generative and sustaining force of the universe even when 'blindly wove' through the fabric of the 'web of being' (ll. 478–82). Empathy and selfishness are indistinguishable aspects of love, which, for Shelley, is manifest as a self-interested sympathy that craves that 'another's nerves should vibrate to our own, that the beams of their eyes should kindle at once mix and melt in our own'

(*SPP*, p. 503). Love, then, is both an idealised quest for a 'corresponding antitype' and the tragic realisation, as Shelley writes in the Preface to *Alastor*, that the poet only 'images to himself the Being whom he loves' (*SPP*, p. 73).

In *Ravelstein*, Chick's account fashions the life of Abe Ravelstein into what Shelley terms a 'corresponding antitype'. As the larger-than-life character of monumental achievement, Ravelstein is an idealised and magnified projection of Chick's own modest aspirations. With the only exception of age, according to Chick's own account, Ravelstein exceeds Chick as a writer, a thinker and a pursuer of intellectual passions and physical appetites. Shelley's auto-erotic poetics of desire is central to the Platonic ideas of love and the soul or character at stake in Bellow's *Ravelstein*.

Chick is a biographer of the last days of his fictional acquaintance with Ravelstein, an elegist for Ravelstein and a thinly veiled avatar for Bellow himself. Bellow, in *Ravelstein*, records his friendship with the deceased cultural critic, philosopher and author of *The Closing of the American Mind* (1987), Allan Bloom. Bellow here is both memoir writer and novelist, life-long friend and eulogist. He recounts in his eulogy how Bloom, on visits to Vermont, 'never failed to quote the *Phaedrus* at me' about Socrates's reluctance to leave Athens. Bellow records, too, how Bloom both exhibited a depth of feeling aligned with 'Platonic Eros' and demanded an intellectual rigour that did not succumb to 'artificial euphorias imposed upon us by managers and manipulators'.[35] The contradictory impulses towards, on one hand, the nobility of a Socratic commitment to the intellectual and immaterial pursuits of the mind or soul and, on the other, a sensual delight in the sensuous, superficial, coarse material forms of the world are the defining architectural principles of Bellow's design in *Ravelstein*.

Chick's threefold narratorial role in *Ravelstein*, as a novelist, a memoir writer and an elegist, is replicated in the connotations of his name as fledgling, boy (in Yiddish) and attractive woman. The threefold significance of Chick's name and role as narrator adumbrates the three typologies of love which, represented by his triangulated relationships with Vela, Ravelstein and Rosamund (Ravelstein's graduate student and Chick's lover), blur distinctions between its heteronormative, homoerotic and Platonic forms.[36] Chick recalls the enthusiasm instilled in him by Ravelstein's passionate discourse on Platonic conceptions of love:

> Like all, or most, of the students of my generation I had read Plato's *Symposium*. Wonderful entertainment, I thought. But I was sent back

to it by Ravelstein. Not literally *sent*. But if you were continually in his company you had to go back to the *Symposium* repeatedly. To be human was to be severed, mutilated. Man is incomplete. Zeus is a tyrant. Mount Olympus is a tyranny. The work of humankind in its severed state is to seek the missing half. And after many generations your true counterpart is simply not to be found . . . And the quest for your lost half is hopeless. The sexual embrace gives temporary self-forgetting but the painful knowledge of mutilation is permanent. (*R*, p. 24, original emphasis)

By implication Ravelstein's inventive reading of Plato – which extrapolates the general principle that 'mankind suffered' because we 'seek the missing half, longing to be whole again' (*R*, p. 24) – is Platonic in spirit, but not Platonic in conception. Ravelstein as a reader of Plato proves himself to be sympathetic to the idealising impulse of Shelley's poet-figure who 'images to himself the Being whom he loves' in the full knowledge of the tragedy that such a quest 'in vain for a prototype of his conception' (*SPP*, p. 73) constitutes.

Throughout Bellow's *Ravelstein*, love in its varied forms may be Platonic in origin, but the extrapolation of its attendant perplexities and 'painful' self-knowledge is wholly Romantic in execution. Shelley, as an avid reader, translator and attentive respondent to Plato, especially the Plato of the *Symposium* and the *Ion*, simultaneously appreciates and resists a Platonic elevation of the 'Beauty which is in souls' as 'more excellent than that which is in forms'. Shelley is sensitive to Plato's ability to create oppositions between the intellectual or spiritual and the sensuous world of manifest forms only in order to dismantle them. Shelley's definition of love as a 'universal thirst' shares in this (Platonic) deconstructive impulse and is expressed in Shelley's sinewy syntax as, in Michael O'Neill's words, 'a fusion or redefinition that will not allow words to sit back comfortably in semantic armchairs'.[37]

Shelley's resistance to orthodox worldviews and reductive taxonomies resonates with Bellow's own concerns, in *Ravelstein*, about the superficiality of modern culture and his celebration of both multiple, chimerical forms of love and characters whose individual depth (or soul) defies the 'gray net' of reductionism. Ravelstein's 'vital force' cannot be contained by these mundanities even if his idealised notion of love must be tempered by the reality of sensual, sexual encounters (embodied in the figure of Nikki) and his intellect must be circumscribed by the physical (biological) world and the inevitability of death. Chick's deep spiritual and physical connection with Rosamund, after a loveless marriage to Vela, and his own near-death

experience (from which Rosamund nurses him back to health following near-fatal food poisoning) signify the necessity of tempering
the ideal with the real, the mind with the body. The idealised depiction of Rosamund encapsulates the two opposing, yet complemen-
tary, notions of 'Rousseauan romantic love and . . . Platonic Eros'
(*R*, p. 231) that Bellow wrestles with in *Ravelstein*.

If Chick's relationship with Rosamund is a physical manifestation
of the type of love idealised by Ravelstein, then Ravelstein's idealised
conception of love exceeds the boundaries of heteronormative and
monogamist relations.[38] Chick's elegiac narrative frame or fictional
memoir acts as a reflection of, and conduit for, these extreme contrary impulses that comprise that 'vital force' of Ravelstein's extraordinary personality:

> I am doing what I can with the facts. He [Ravelstein] lived by his ideas.
> His knowledge was real, and he could document it, chapter and verse.
> He was there to give aid, to clarify and *move*, and to make certain if
> he could that the greatness of humankind would not entirely evapo-
> rate in bourgeois well-being, et cetera. There was nothing of the aver-
> age in Ravelstein's life. He did not accept dullness and boredom. Nor
> was depression tolerated. He did not put up with low moods. Troubles
> when he had them were physical. His dental problems at one time were
> severe. (*R*, pp. 53–4, original emphasis)

Ravelstein, according to Chick's portrait, 'lived by his ideas' and was
intolerant of mediocrity and the lacklustre. Intellectually and spiritually, Ravelstein sought to preserve the 'greatness of humankind'
from the deadening effects of shallow modern culture and facile
'bourgeois well-being'. Ravelstein's dislike of these forms of social
decorum and niceties which, for him, mask deep-seated prejudices of
class and antisemitism can be gauged from his careless table manners
that demand 'An experienced hostess [to] spread newspapers under
his chair' (*R*, p. 38). These indecorous eating habits also symbolise
Ravelstein's apparent aloofness from the materiality of the physical
world, as well as the vital need for physical sustenance of the body to
sustain the life of the mind.

Ravelstein may live the life of the mind, but he still feels the allure
of, and delights in, the crass humour, talk 'about celebrities' (*R*, p. 137)
and material products of this superficial culture, including a variety of
'beautiful objects', such as 'Quimper antique plates', a 'Jensen tea-
pot' (*R*, p. 20), an expensive 'new Lavin jacket' (*R*, p. 35), purchased
impulsively in Paris only to be 'soiled' by a coffee stain moments later,

and an array of designer neckties 'dotted with cigarette burns' (*R*, p. 41).[39] Metaphorically, these accidental stains of Ravelstein's sartorial finery, his messy eating habits and his dental problems signal that the mind cannot evade the body, that the ideal exists in response to the real, that Platonic Eros is inseparable from sensuous forms, and that the vital presence of life is defined by the negation and absence of death.

Chick's awareness of death and his own infirmities, as well as those of Ravelstein, provides, as does their shared Jewish heritage, another important touchstone between them. Chick's later claim that he possessed 'a good grasp of reality and my defects' and was mindful of 'the approach of death' (*R*, p. 105) is disproportionately enlarged in his earlier reflection on Ravelstein's capacity for self-knowledge, who 'obsessively knew what it was to be sunk by his faults or errors. But before he went under he would describe Plato's Cave to you' (*R*, p. 20). Shelley's role as self-appointed mourner for Keats in the pastoral elegy *Adonais* is instructive here, as Shelley deliberately fashions his weakened portraiture of Keats into a Shelleyan poet for posterity for both his own and Keats's literary survival. Similarly, in *Ravelstein*, Chick as novelist, biographer or memoir writer and elegist both accentuates the weaknesses, 'faults and errors' of his chosen subject and makes them his own to ensure Ravelstein's posthumous survival (and Chick's own) in the face of the 'universal gradual progress toward oblivion' (*R*, p. 161).

Symbolically, Chick's near-death experience from severe food poisoning becomes a means of taking on and transforming Ravelstein's own suffering and death from AIDS – 'reckless sex habits' (*R*, p. 189) – and thereby expunging any social slur, prejudice or condemnation from the circumstances of Ravelstein's demise.[40] This symbolic substitution is the ultimate expression of the Platonic fraternity formed between Ravelstein and Chick. Chick's narrative creates a visionary company of love that shapes and reshapes the deceased Ravelstein into a perpetual moment of presence like 'music in which ideas are dissolved, reflecting these ideas in the form of feeling' (*R*, p. 232). After all love, for Shelley, functions as a mirror whose surface reflects only the forms of purity and brightness: 'a soul within a soul' (*SPP*, p. 504). Through a shifting series of narrative doublings and reduplications, Chick honours the terms of his promise to act as a faithful Boswell to Ravelstein's Johnson (*R*, p. 6) and by so doing fulfils his own dictum that 'You don't easily give up a creature like Ravelstein to death' (*R*, p. 235). Ravelstein's posthumous endurance is dependent, paradoxically, on his simultaneity with and difference from the human sphere through Chick's reinvention of Ravelstein as a transcendent 'creature'.

Chick fulfils his promise as a writer by ensconcing Ravelstein in a series of self-enclosing and enclosed idealising fictions.[41] Even in death Ravelstein is not 'forgotten', and transcending conventional expectation, in Chick's words, 'claimed and filled a more conspicuous space in Rosamund's life as well as mine' (*R*, p. 161). Like Keats as the mythologised figure of Adonais in Shelley's elegy, Ravelstein as Bellow's fictionalised version of Bloom remains a luminary in the firmament of time beckoning – or 'gesturing' (*R*, p. 233) – to us from afar.

British and American Romanticism may not be the sole governing ideologues of Bellow's fictional mosaic, but they profoundly shaped his imaginative vision.[42] Yet Emerson's and Wordsworth's poetic reflections on the interconnection between the visionary and natural worlds influenced Bellow's own post-Romantic negotiations with the self and world. Often delighting in these distinctive Romantic revelatory modes, Bellow tested the prophetic claims of American and British Romanticism for the twentieth century to advocate a collective humanism as an antidote to our modern, alienated condition. Finally, then, reconsidering Bellow's Romanticism reminds us that as a novelist he was and still remains an exponent of the awakening power of Romantic Eros or love which, as Shelley understood, 'is that powerful attraction towards all we conceive, or fear, or hope beyond ourselves' that forms 'the bond and the sanction which not only connects man with man, but with every thing which exists' (*SPP*, p. 503).[43] Rather than reinforcing an escape from selfhood through an idealised vision of interconnectedness, Shelley's 'On Love' confronts the inevitable reality of being imprisoned in a self which, by acutely feeling its own isolated and alienated condition, provides an alternative, darker, mode of reconnection with others and the surrounding environment.[44] Refracted through such Romantic sensibilities, Bellow emerges as the latter-day sceptical yet hopeful explorer, defender and preserver of our 'soul within our soul'.[45]

Notes

1. Max F. Schulz compares the Jewish American School to the Lake Poets. See Schulz, *Radical Sophistication: Studies in Contemporary Jewish-American Novelists* (Athens: Ohio University Press, 1969), p. 3. Hereafter *RS*.
2. Allan Chavkin has explored Bellow and Romanticism. See Chavkin, 'The Romantic Imagination of Saul Bellow', in *English Romanticism*

and Modern Fiction, ed. Allan Chavkin (New York: AMS, 1993), pp. 113–38. Hereafter 'RIB'. See also Chavkin, 'Bellow and English Romanticism', in *Saul Bellow in the 1980s: A Collection of Critical Essays*, ed. Gloria L. Cronin and L. H. Goldman (East Lansing: Michigan State University Press, 1989), pp. 67–79. Hereafter 'BER'.

3. Saul Bellow, *Herzog* (Harmondsworth: Penguin, 1965), p. 91. Hereafter *HZ*. All quotations are from this edition.

4. For a discussion of the 'web' motif see Edmond Schraepen, '*Herzog*: Disconnection and Connection', in *Saul Bellow and his Work*, ed. Edmond Schraepen (Brussels: Centrum voor Tall-en Literatuurweten-schap, 1978), pp. 73–88.

5. Samuel Taylor Coleridge, *Coleridge's Poems*, 1912, 2 vols, ed. E. H. Coleridge (Oxford: Oxford University Press, 2000), I, p. 101, l. 26.

6. See Jeff Campbell, 'Bellow's Intimations of Immortality: *Henderson the Rain King*', *Studies in the Novel* 1 (1969): 323–33; David Majdiak, 'The Romantic Self and *Henderson the Rain King*', *Bucknell Review* 19 (1971): 125–46. See also Allan Chavkin, '*Humboldt's Gift* and the Romantic Imagination', *Philological Quarterly* 62 (1983): 1–19.

7. William Blake, *Blake's Poetry and Designs: The Authoritative Texts*, ed. Mary Lynn Johnson and John E. Grant (New York: Norton, 1979), 'London', ll. 8, 53. All quotations are from this edition unless other-wise stated.

8. Gordon Lloyd Harper, 'The Art of Fiction: Saul Bellow', *Paris Review* 9 (1966): 49–73; rpt 'Saul Bellow: An Interview', in *Saul Bellow: A Collection of Critical Essays*, ed. Earl Rovit (Englewood Cliffs, NJ: Prentice Hall, 1975), p. 14.

9. Saul Bellow, *Seize the Day* (1956; Harmondsworth: Penguin, 1988), p. 90. Hereafter *SD*. All quotations are from this edition.

10. Chavkin, 'RIB', p. 118.

11. For example, see Schulz, *RS*, p. 145 and Singh Sukkbir, *The Survivor in Contemporary American Fiction: Saul Bellow, Bernard Malamud, John Updike, and Kurt Vonnegut* (Delhi: BR Publishing, 1991), pp. 3–4. See also Daniel Fuchs, *Saul Bellow: Vision and Revision* (Madison: University of Wisconsin Press, 1974), p. 83. Hereafter *SBVR*.

12. See Tony Tanner, *Saul Bellow* (London and Edinburgh: Boyd, 1965), p. 115. Hereafter *SB*. See also Chavkin, 'BER', p. 77; Fuchs, *SBVR*, p. 70.

13. Saul Bellow, 'A World Too Much with Us', *Critical Inquiry* 2 (1975): 5; 1–9. Hereafter 'ATM'.

14. See Saul Rosenzweig, *Freud, Jung, and Hall the King-maker: The Historic Expedition to America (1909), with G. Stanley Hall as host and William James as guest* (St. Louis, MS: Hogrefe & Huber, 1992).

15. On 'reality-instructors' see Jeanne Braham, *A Sort of Columbus: The American Voyages of Saul Bellow's Fiction* (Athens: Ohio University Press, 1984), p. 60. See especially chapter 3. See also Tanner, *SB*, pp. 94–5.

16. For an alternative reading of Tamkin as a more earnest exponent of Emerson's ideas see Helge N. Nilsen, 'Saul Bellow and Transcendentalism: From "The Victim" to "Herzog"', *College Language Association* 30.3 (1987): 311–12; 307–27.

17. Chavkin, 'BER', p. 77.

18. On Bellow and American Transcendentalism see M. Gilbert Porter, 'Hitch your Agony to a Star: Bellow's Transcendental Vision', in *Saul Bellow and his Work*, ed. Edmond Schraepen (Brussels: Centrum voor Tall-en Literatuurwetenschap, 1978), pp. 73–88. See also M. A. Quayum, *Saul Bellow and American Transcendentalism* (New York: Lang, 2004).

19. In Chapter 2 and the coda, my readings of Emerson and Thoreau in this study argue for the recognition of affinities between American and British Romanticism.

20. Tanner, *SNSM*, pp. 32–3.

21. Schulz, *RS*, p. 111.

22. Saul Bellow, 'To Richard Stern', 3 November 1959, in *Saul Bellow: Letters*, ed. Benjamin Taylor (Harmondsworth: Viking-Penguin, 2010), p. 182. Hereafter *SBL*. All quotations are from this edition.

23. Ralph Waldo Emerson, *The Complete Prose Works of Ralph Waldo Emerson* (London: Ward, Lock, and Co., 1803), p. 579.

24. Ralph Waldo Emerson, *The Complete Works of Ralph Waldo Emerson: Essays Second Series*, vol. 3, ed. Alfred R. Ferguson and Jean Ferguson Carr, historical intro. Joseph Slater and textual intro. Jean Ferguson Carr (Cambridge, MA: Belknap Press, 1983), p. 11.

25. On Herzog's reconstruction in New England, see Peter Hyland, *Saul Bellow*, Macmillan Modern Novelists Series (London: Macmillan, 1992), p. 66.

26. For readings of this kind see Jonathan Wilson, *On Bellow's Planet: Readings from the Dark Side* (London: Fairleigh Dickinson University Press, 1985).

27. Saul Bellow, draft of 'A World Too Much with Us', holograph draft (c. 1975), Series III: Writings 2, 'Essays and Articles', Box 93, Folder 5, Saul Bellow Papers, Special Collections Research Center, University of Chicago, p. 15.

28. Saul Bellow, *Mr Sammler's Planet* (1970; Harmondsworth: Penguin, 1972), pp. 89–90. Hereafter *MSP*. All quotations are from this edition.

29. For a recent reading of the Platonic themes in Bellow's *Humboldt's Gift* and *Ravelstein* see Willis Salomon, 'Saul Bellow on the Soul: Character and the Spirit of Culture in *Humboldt's Gift* and *Ravelstein*', *Partial Answers: Journals of Literature and the History of Ideas* 14.1 (2016): 127–40.

30. Saul Bellow, *Ravelstein* (Harmondsworth: Penguin, 2000), p. 203. Hereafter *R*. All quotations are from this edition.

31. See Paul Lévy, 'Women and Gender in Bellow's Fiction: *Herzog*', in *The Cambridge Companion to Saul Bellow*, ed. Victoria Aarons

(Cambridge: Cambridge University Press, 2017), p. 117; pp. 108–19. Hereafter *CSB*.

32. See Saul Bellow, 'Boston Lecture', 9 September 1993, Series III: Writings 1, 'Public Speaking and Engagements', Box 90, Folder 5, Saul Bellow Papers, Special Collections Research Center, University of Chicago, p. 1.

33. For other Romantic and intellectual influences see S. Lillian Kremer, '*Humboldt's Gift* and Bellow's Intellectual Protagonists', in *CSB*, pp. 76–7; pp. 68–80.

34. Saul Bellow, *Humboldt's Gift* (1975; Harmondsworth: Penguin, 2007), p. 363 (original emphasis).

35. See Saul Bellow, 'Eulogy for Allan Bloom', 9 October 1992, photo-copied typescript, Series III: Writings 1, 'Public Speaking and Engage-ments', Box 90, Folder 2, Saul Bellow Papers, Special Collections Research Center, University of Chicago, pp. 4, 1.

36. Chick's name, according to Leah Garrett, is 'in Yiddish/English a "boy-stick": a word combining the English "boy" with Yiddish diminutive "tshik" to mean young man' (p. 175). For an excellent account of the significance of Chick's role see Garrett, 'Late Bellow: *Ravelstein* and the Novel of Ideas', in *CSB*, pp. 171–81. For an account of Chick's nar-rative as an instance of a poetics of disappointment see Michael Mack, *Disappointment: From Spinoza to Contemporary Literature* (London: Bloomsbury, 2020), pp. 128–36. I am grateful to the author for permis-sion to read this work in proof.

37. Shelley quotations are from the Bodleian Shelley Manuscript, XV, 36–5 and XX, 402–5 respectively (qtd by Michael O'Neill). For Michael O'Neill's observation and sense of Shelley's productive resistance to Plato see O'Neill, *Shelleyan Reimaginings and Influence: New Rela-tions* (Oxford: Oxford University Press, 2019), p. 30; pp. 29–45.

38. See Garrett, 'Late Bellow: *Ravelstein* and the Novel of Ideas', *CSB*, pp. 173–4.

39. For a proliferation of the expensive and luxury items with which Ravelstein surrounds himself see Zachary Leader, *The Life of Saul Bellow: Love and Strife 1965–2005* (London: Cape, 2019), p. 586. Hereafter *LSB*.

40. Leah Garrett offers a persuasive account, drawing on Susan Sontag, of this symbolic transference between Chick and Ravelstein. Garrett outlines the controversy that ensued from Bellow's suggestion that Ravelstein dies from AIDS with the implication that the disease had caused Allan Bloom's death. See Garrett, 'Late Bellow: *Ravelstein* and the Novel of Ideas', *CSB*, pp. 176, 178–80. Both Garrett and Zachary Leader document Bellow's profound sense of hurt that the accusations of his portrayal of Ravelstein's death triggered, but also Bellow's insis-tence on disclosing the details of Bloom's death as part of *Ravelstein*. See Leader, *LSB*, pp. 579–86.

41. Compare with Shelley's treatment of the observing of antelope in *Epipsychidion* and *Alastor*; see Mark Sandy, 'Quest Poetry', in *The Oxford Handbook of Percy Bysshe Shelley*, ed. Michael O'Neill and Anthony Howe with the assistance of Madeleine Callaghan (Oxford: Oxford University Press, 2013), p. 283; pp. 272–88. See also Timothy Morton, *EWN*, p. 202.
42. Chavkin, 'BER', p. 75.
43. For a study of Romantic notions of love and Shelley's poetics of Eros see William A. Ulmer, *Shelleyan Eros: The Rhetoric of Romantic Love* (Princeton: Princeton University Press, 1990).
44. See Morton, *EWN*, pp. 200–1.
45. For a discussion of Bellow's prose style and an examination of inner soul in his fiction see Vidyan Ravinthiran, 'Race, Style, and the Soul of Saul Bellow's Prose', *Essays in Criticism* 16.4 (2016): 488–517.

Reimagined Pastoral Poetics: Narrative Structures and the Environment in Toni Morrison, Thoreau and Wordsworth

To avoid critical comparisons that might distract from the African American inflection of her writing, Toni Morrison claims she has resisted using literary allusion to canonical authors in her work. However, given her background and formal literary qualifications, her insistence does not guarantee the absence of such allusion.[1] Critics have recognised Morrison's awareness of an integrated sense of community and her episodic encounters with nature and the sublime as indebted to American Romanticism, as well as identifying echoes of William Blake, William Wordsworth, P. B. Shelley and John Keats.[2] Recognising verbal echoes and reimaginings of Romantic concerns and episodes from Wordsworth's *The Prelude* (1850), Martin Bidney reminds us that Morrison has been and continues to be an attentive respondent to Wordsworth.[3]

The approach offered here explores the profound influence that Wordsworth's fascination with *genera mixta*, as exemplified in his elegiac vision of the pastoral and poetic experimentation with lyrical ballads, exerted on Morrison's novels *Beloved* (1987), *A Mercy* (2008) and *Home* (2012). This account of Morrison's engagement with Wordsworth resists a tendency to regard her as a contemporary advocate of Romantic ideological beliefs, artistic conventions or practices. Reading the three works by Morrison as meditations on and transformations of Wordsworth's own ambivalent treatment of the pastoral finds affinity with anti-pastoral elements in the poetics of Robert Frost and Derek Walcott. Through such an interpretation, Morrison emerges as a subtle respondent to the pastoral and to Wordsworth, one who is attuned to the complex, nuanced and darker misgivings of Wordsworth's idealising and compensatory poetics.

Given the historical, geographical and topographical differences between Wordsworth and Morrison, definitions of the pastoral are no less critical and difficult than those of Romanticism itself. From its inception, the idealising pastoral mode celebrated the idyllic, harmonious, rural existence, but was frequently self-conscious about its use of generic conventions and resistance to the anti-pastoral of the urban and modern.[4] To complicate matters further, Wordsworth's Romantic pastoral poetry of personal reaction to and interaction with a sublimely uncultivated landscape is distinct from the writings of Ralph Waldo Emerson and Henry David Thoreau. Their version of the American pastoral has been characterised as celebrating rural industriousness and naturalising technological innovation in their responses to nature. Within the American tradition, the site of the pastoral is infrequently aligned with the idealising imagination and epiphany and more often with the realities of aggressive colonial ownership of the land and its people.[5]

The reception of Morrison's novels as Faulknerian pastoral – surprisingly termed in John Updike's review of *A Mercy* as a 'dreamy wilderness'[6] – attests to a creative and literary genealogy that reaches back through Faulkner to an earlier American Romanticism and its literary negotiations with Wordsworth. Works by Thoreau and Emerson provide a vital conduit between the pastoral mode of British Romantic poetry and American letters that are indebted to Wordsworth's concept of nature, which discovers beauty, spiritual delight and revelation in the commonplaces of natural existence and everyday language.[7]

Morrison and Wordsworth's Voices

In the first few pages of *A Mercy*, Morrison announces her Wordsworthian inheritance through attention to how tales can empower a 'telling [that] can't hurt you'[8] and to the limitations of words and language from which stories are created. Criticism of Morrison's novel as a series of 'half-told tales'[9] indicates the Wordsworthian traits of her writing. Ironically, this negative characterisation of Morrison's work describes both her continuing engagement with partial perspectives, memory and self-discovery and the centrality of these concerns to Wordsworth's Romantic project.[10] Many of Wordsworth's pastoral poetic tales form a record of personal, familial, social, physical and transcendental loss. Equally, Wordsworth's poetry registers the multi-layered perspectives and processes that govern communal and individual memory.

Wordsworth's poems not only lend authenticity and immediacy to the human experiences they convey, but they also point to their provisional nature in both oral and written form as their authority is derived from legend, superstition and gossip. By her own admission, Morrison draws on these elements of 'lore . . . gossip . . . magic . . . [and] sentiment'[11] to voice those experiences silenced by traditional and dominant historical accounts. For Wordsworth, the poetic genre of the pastoral renders individual tales told by marginal rustics as the repository of communal memory and wider historical record; the genre self-consciously delights in multiple perspectives and ironies.[12] Morrison's fictional version of pastoral – hovering between the imaginary and historical reality – finds in Wordsworth a model for establishing a series of competing voices and perspectives to explore the latent tensions in the genre between nature's sympathetic compensatory power and unsympathetic indifference to human loss and grief.

Comprising multiple marginal voices and haunting presences, Morrison's fiction reimagines Wordsworth's chance meetings with spectral figures on the social fringe (the Female Vagrant, the Leech-Gatherer, the Idiot Boy and the Discharged Soldier),[13] a distinctly Wordsworthian preoccupation that Morrison shares with Faulkner. If Faulkner's fiction tends to affirm the transcendent and revelatory power of nature afforded to Wordsworth's solitary figures, then Morrison's literary imagination questions nature and the part it plays in these Wordsworthian modes of transcendence and revelation. For Morrison, Wordsworth's recollections of these social misfits and outcasts reveal a duality of vision that opens up and closes down moments of personal transcendence and imaginative transformations of the ordinary. Morrison's sense of the world and self as both given and endlessly recreated reshapes Wordsworth's own anxiety about how 'all the mighty world / Of eye and ear [is] both what [we] half-create, / And what perceive' (*Tintern Abbey*, ll. 106–8). In *Beloved*, Morrison reimagines this Wordsworthian perspective through Denver, who is even more extreme in her conviction that 'she does not know where her body stops' and conceives of her self as something 'breakable, meltable and cold'.[14] And Scully's account of Florens, the primary narrator of *A Mercy*, 'marching down the road – whether ghost or soldier – he knew she had become untouchable' (*M*, p. 150) explicitly recalls Wordsworth's encounter with the dispossessed, wandering, 'ghastly' figure (*Prelude*, IV, l. 458) of the Discharged Soldier on the open road.

Even though some twenty years separate the publication of *Beloved* and *A Mercy* – and 200 years or more separate the historical settings of the novels – both works confirm Morrison's continued fascination with Wordsworth's pastoral poetry and the workings of multiple voices, perspectives and memories. Set in the America of the 1690s, according to Morrison 'two years before the Salem witch trails',[15] the penultimate section of *A Mercy* draws to a close with a rhapsodic meditation on the potentially restorative power of language, memory and nature:

> What will I do with my nights when the telling stops? Dreaming will not come again. Sudden I am remembering. You won't read my telling. You read the world but not the letters of talk. You don't know how to. . . . If you never read this, no one will. These careful words, closed up and wide open, will talk to themselves. Round and round, side to side, bottom to top, top to bottom all across the room. Or. Or perhaps no. Perhaps these words need the air that is out in the world. Need to fly up then fall, fall like ash over acres of primrose and mallow. Over a turquoise lake, beyond the eternal hemlocks, through clouds cut by rainbow and flavor the soil of the earth. (*M*, pp. 158–9)

There is a momentary belief in the potency of words, even without an interpreter, to overcome Florens's anxiety that what she can 'read or cipher is useless now' (*M*, p. 155). Words can generate meaning through, and in spite of, their topsy-turvy arrangement in the claustrophobic and stifling 'room' of 'the big, awing house' (*M*, p. 159). Morrison invests a physicality in these words that recalls the same tactility of language evident in Beloved's spelling of her name, 'slowly as though the letters were being formed as she spoke them' (*BL*, p. 52). There are Romantic overtures here of the artist as poetic visionary fuelled by a Shelleyan aspiration to 'scatter, as from an unextinguished hearth / Ashes and sparks, my words among mankind!' ('Ode to the West Wind', ll. 66–7). This is also underpinned by a Romantic conceptualisation of language and nature, which invests these 'careful words' with the potential to be meaningful through contact with the natural 'air that is out in the world' and scatter them like 'ash' to replenish the 'soil'.

Morrison's Romantic aspiration toward and possible communication with a future audience is mediated through Italo Calvino's conviction that 'in the shape that chance and wind give the clouds', any prospective reader is 'already intent on recognizing figures'.[16] Morrison marks the dissemination of these shapes, figures, words and their rejuvenation through and of the soil on a painfully visceral scale; the phrase 'cut by rainbow' extends beyond merely severing the clouds to the shaping and 'carving [of] letters' (*M*, p. 158) and the 'forming of words' (*M*, p. 156) out of Florens's hard-won endeavour and experience.

In this same remarkable passage from *A Mercy*, Morrison reaches beyond Calvino and Shelley to Wordsworth, engaging with a Romantic duality of vision that oscillates between nature's compensatory power and unsympathetic indifference to grief and loss, and is central to Wordsworth's poetry and his account (a recasting of material from *The Ruined Cottage*) of the visionary Pedlar's coming of age in Book 1 of *The Excursion*:

> . . . he was o'erpowered
> By Nature, and his spirit was on fire
> With restless thoughts. His eye became disturbed,
> And many a time he wished the winds might rage
> When they were silent. Far more fondly now
> Than in his earlier season did he love
> Tempestuous nights, the uproar and the sounds
> That live in darkness. From his intellect,
> And from the stillness of abstracted thought,
> He sought repose in vain. I have heard him say
> That at this time he scanned the laws of light
> Amid the roar of torrents, where they send
> From hollow clefts up to the clearer air
> A cloud of mist, which in the shining sun
> Varies its rainbow hues. But vainly thus,
> And vainly by all other means he strove
> To mitigate the fever of his heart.[17]

Nature offers both reciprocation and antagonism to the Pedlar and his efforts to becalm and 'mitigate the fever of his heart'. Wordsworth's visionary Pedlar's 'restless thoughts', fiery 'spirit' and sensitivity to those 'sounds / That live in darkness' characterise his hope in, and misgivings about, nature's ability to soothe his anxiety or reveal the pattern of meaning of those 'laws of light'.

Morrison's reference to Wordsworth's imaginative dilemma is no casual allusion. This Wordsworthian ambivalence toward nature – expressed through the poetry's shifting intangible 'rainbow hues' – is compressed into the steely beauty of Morrison's phrase 'cut by rainbow'. A similar forceful aesthetic sensibility is elaborated by Florens's reflection on the autumnal leaves of 'blood and brass' that there is a natural 'color so loud it hurts the eye and for relief I must stare at the heavens high above the tree line' (*M*, p. 156). From Lina's partial view, this observation confirms her perception of Florens as 'mindless as fern in wind' (*M*, p. 42). But this simile also captures the tactility of Florens's sensory vision and her capacity for imaginative visionary insight, which defines her as a self-conscious Romantic artist who uses 'pebbles to shape words on smooth flat rock' (*M*, p. 4). Unlike Lina, who holds to the view that 'We never shape the world' (*M*, p. 69), Florens glimpses the elating and terrible prospect that the present circumstances and power relations of self and world, self and other, might be configured differently.

In *A Mercy*, these power relations and hierarchies transcend identifiers of race and sexuality, so that those subjugated subjects include, as Morrison makes explicit, a 'Native American, or a white homosexual couple', or even the 'white mistress in *A Mercy* [who], though not enslaved, was purchased in an arranged marriage' (*TOO*, p. 52).[18] The identities of both Florens and her mistress are determined by those socio-economic relations embodied in Jacob Vaark as husband and master who, in Florens's mind, is represented as 'Another animal that shapes choice' and closely fused with an earlier chance sighting of a stag. Verbal echoes of Wordsworth's *The White Doe of Rylstone* shape Florens's imaginative reconfiguration of the self and world, without fixed relations and identities. Morrison recasts Wordsworth's poem in her recount of Florens's 'memory' of an extraordinary encounter with the animal world:

> To my left is a hill. High, very high. Climbing over it all, up up, are scarlet flowers I never see before. Everywhere choking with their own leaves. The scent is sweet. I put my hand in to gather a few blossoms. I hear something behind me and turn to see a stag moving up the rock side. His is great. And grand. Standing there between the beckoning wall of perfume and the stag I wonder what else the world may show me. It is as though I am loose to do what I choose, the stag, the wall of flowers. I am a little scare of this looseness. Is that how free feels? I don't like it. I don't want to be free of you because I am live only with you. (*M*, pp. 67–8)

Wordsworth's white doe, presumably because of the preoccupations of Florens's thoughts with her slave master, Jacob, is translated into a stag and Emily, central to the Northumberland legend that is the kernel of *The White Doe of Rylstone*, is supplanted by the presence of Florens. Her gathering of a 'few blossoms' recalls the environs bestrewn with 'wild-rose blossoms fair' through which Wordsworth's doe glides as effortlessly as thought and as 'Soft and silent as a dream'.[19] The subtleties of the outward action of Wordsworth's doe find a corollary with the barely perceptible workings of thought and dream, so that her gait is likened to 'steps of thought' (*White Doe*, l. 428). Morrison's stag, for all its masculine grandeur, encapsulates, through its capacity to materialise and dematerialise in and out of existence ('the world may show me') at a whim, something of the same graceful and passive agency ascribed to Wordsworth's white doe.[20] The stag's transgression of physical and spatial boundaries foreshadows the apparitional, yet indistinct, 'ghostly blaze' of Jacob as a revenant who 'floated for a while . . . disappeared, then moved ever so slowly from window to window' (*M*, p. 142). Momentarily, at least, Florens's feelings of liberation ('looseness') align with the freedom of the stag, which transcends the earthly limitations of the property boundaries of the 'new house' and the topographical obstacles of the 'very high' (*M*, p. 67) hill. That the 'stag bounds away' (*M*, p. 68) at the end of the encounter makes concrete the boundless, transcendent quality which so terrifies Florens with its 'looseness' and the prospect of being freed from the otherness of the 'you' that defines her. Like Wordsworth's white doe, the stag signifies a 'softened remembrance of [the] pain and sorrow' (*White Doe*, l. 242) of the power relations that define Florens's past and present identity and situation.

The unfettered freedom of the stag recalls Florens's appealing and frightening vision of the lake's boundless, deepest blue that 'is more than sky, more than any blue' (*M*, p. 135). This episodic dream is couched in anxiety and hesitancy for Florens, because she fears that she might 'not get the beautiful blue of what I want' and, worse still, that the absence of her reflection in the water reduces her to 'not even a shadow there' (*M*, p. 136). Florens's dream dramatises Morrison's claim that 'The resources available to us for . . . access to each other, for vaulting the blue air that separates us, are few but powerful: language, image, and experience' (*TOO*, p. 35).

With a defiant, phoenix-like declaration (reminiscent of the triumphantly emergent reborn selfhood of Sylvia Plath's 'Lady Lazarus'[21]), 'Feathers lifting, I unfold', Florens resists the annihilation of her non-existent shadowy self as being of 'no consequence in your world' (*M*, p. 140). Such a shadowy, absent self defies traditional notions of categorisation, ownership and governance, which seek to define the otherness in relation to ourselves and force the Other, as Morrison writes, 'back into our mirrors' (*TOO*, p. 39). Florens is determined to nurture her story so that its significance blossoms (as her name suggests) into being and so that her tale, no matter how painful, realises an authentic entrance into the world. In *Beloved*, Sethe is a reluctant storyteller who understands 'the profound satisfaction Beloved got from [her] storytelling' and, eventually, the restorative power of language to recover memory even if 'everything in it was painful or lost' (*BL*, p. 58). Florens as artist *manqué* is alert to the transformative healing power of language, where 'when the letters are memory we make whole words' (*M*, p. 4), but she also recognises with Lina the limitations of words that in the wrong hands can negatively define existence so that 'we never shape the world' (*M*, p. 69). *A Mercy* resists this reductive view of language by making its readers aware that Florens's artistic perspective is one of many perspectives and must compete with stories seen and told by Jacob Vaark, his wife Rebekka, Lina, Sorrow and Florens's own mother. *A Mercy* mirrors the structural principle of *Beloved*, adopting a model of multiple voices, perspectives and half-told tales. Bound by their revelation of a series of events and sense of location, these partially told stories circle around and encircle a specific spot of time, space and place in memory, as does Wordsworth's poetry.[22]

Morrison, Wordsworth and Writing the Ruined House

For Wordsworth, the site of memory is a site of loss. One such 'cheerless spot' (l. 60) is occupied by *The Ruined Cottage*, a poem Wordsworth revised and incorporated into Book 1 of *The Excursion*, to which Morrison alludes. *The Ruined Cottage* focuses on a maternal figure, Margaret, and her tragedy of familial and domestic decline, irrecoverable human loss and grief. Coincidentally, Margaret Garner, the historical person whose life provides the kernel of Morrison's story in *Beloved*, finds a namesake in Wordsworth's grief-stricken cottage-dweller. In Wordsworth's poem, Margaret's personal suffering is exacerbated by the departure of her husband, who enlists in the militia to fight in a colonial war in the Americas.

Taking her cue from the significance Wordsworth afforded to a tale of maternal loss and a ruined cottage, Morrison places the ruined and ruinous household structures at the narrative centres of *A Mercy* and *Beloved*. These works remould the subject of Wordsworth's *The Ruined Cottage* by focusing on tragic females who, owing to a very different set of economic and social factors, have suffered the destruction or disintegration of their families and become the inheritors of dysfunctional domestic spheres. Romantic and post-Romantic responses to ruined domestic structures and their spectral inhabitants can be construed as interrogations of Emily Dickinson's conundrum that 'Nature is a Haunted House – but Art – a House that tries to be Haunted'.[23]

Evidently, Morrison is not alone in taking her literary bearings from William Wordsworth's treatment of disintegrating domesticity. Morrison's meditation on the ruins of house and home is part of Wordsworth's Romantic legacy, albeit refracted through the twentieth-century poetic responses of Frost and Walcott to Wordsworth's *The Ruined Cottage*. Although different in their colonial perspective, style and tone, Frost's 'The Black Cottage', published in *North of Boston* (1914), and Walcott's 'Ruins of a Great House', first collected in *In a Green Night* (1962), reflect on their respective ruined structures, issues of property and the legalities of ownership.[24]

The poems by Frost and Walcott both question physical or spiritual senses of belonging. Elsewhere, Frost formulates this preoccupation as 'all there is is belonging and belongings'.[25] 'Belonging' and its attendant word 'belongings' suggest the connection between individuals, their situations and their possessions. More widely, these terms relate to how finding a place at home, in society or in the wider universe of nature involves a delineation of boundaries between familial, social, civilised and economic groupings of people. The impulse to belong is driven by a desire to find a connection with the people and the world around us. Ironically, laying claim to our territory, social group or possessions is divisive and heightens our sense of disconnection and alienation both socially and existentially.

Thematically and structurally, 'The Black Cottage' is indebted to Wordsworth's *The Ruined Cottage*, but Frost's poem interrogates the dark, underlying, existential misgivings Wordsworth has about his own poetry's unified vision of nature. Although vehemently opposed to Frost's colonial sympathies, Morrison shares similar reservations about Wordsworth's concept of nature, and senses the darker implications of a 'chearful faith' in the doctrine that 'Nature never did betray / The heart *that loved her*' (*Tintern Abbey*, ll. 134, 122–3, emphasis added). Morrison and Frost emphasise the fact that nature, as Wordsworth's lines imply, offers no consolation in the face of suffering, grief and tragedy to the wavering and uncertain heart. Nature is an indifferent, obdurate force which, as Robert Faggen suggests, does not discriminate between human and non-human existence; it is endlessly at war with power structures and hierarchies. Ultimately, nature lays waste to life's inequalities.[26]

Frost's black cottage in its abandoned state symbolises how human aspirations toward social order and spiritual connection are eroded by the debilitating effects of war and racially and economically divisive human relations. Set against this bleak vision of conflict and disconnection, those questions raised by Frost about ownership and possession of the dilapidated cottage are all the more acute. Gradually, 'The Black Cottage' presents two sons who retain economic possession of their deceased mother's property and are bereft of any Wordsworthian sentimental attachment to their childhood home. This lack of sentimentality is reinforced by the surprisingly cynical speech of the minister, who declares, 'why abandon a belief / Merely because it ceases to be true',[27] and chillingly observes:

> Everything's as she left it when she died.
> Her sons won't sell the house or the things in it.
> They say they mean to come and summer here
> Where they were boys. They haven't come this year.
> They live so far away – one is out West –
> It will be hard for them to keep their word. (ll. 15–20)

By the close of Frost's poem, the minister and poet-narrator are driven away by a hostile nature represented by the 'fierce heads' of threatening bees ('The Black Cottage', l. 112). The tragedy of 'The Black Cottage' is that its decaying structure is left utterly abandoned – the two sons and everyone else 'so far away' – without anyone or anything left to recognise or memorialise the suffering and waste that has occurred, except for the reflection of a preternatural and indifferent 'sunset . . . on the windows' (l. 127).

Like Morrison, Walcott resists the colonial sentiment of Frost's poetry. Walcott's allusion to Andrew Marvell's seventeenth-century poem 'Bermudas'[28] in the choice of title for his first collection of poems – *In a Green Night* – captures the continuing presence in the twentieth century of the pastoral mode and its associated Romantic sensibilities. Walcott's title also hints at the complexity of the poetics and politics of belonging and place set in play by the poetry of Wordsworth and Frost. In 'Ruins of a Great House', this concern is especially evident when Walcott writes with an unexpected regret for the loss of aesthetic grandeur. Instigated by the collapse of colonial wealth and power, Walcott observes that 'Marble like Greece, like Faulkner's South in stone / Deciduous beauty prospered and is gone'.[29] Like the ephemeral inhabitants, whose delicate 'moth-like' existences have mingled with the 'candle-dust' ('Ruins of a Great House', l. 2), the power and the pastoral beauty of the former 'Great House' have faded to a haunting echo of bygone days of glory. All that now remains is the quickened stench of death and decay of the corpse and 'leprosy of empire' ('Ruins of a Great House', l. 10) which Walcott's elegiac tone laments.

Recalling aspects of Walcott's *disjecta membra* of this Great House' ('Ruins of a Great House', l. 1), Morrison's 'grand house' in *A Mercy* symbolises a troubled and troubling pastoral paradise founded on rum trade profits and the exploited 'remote labor force in Barbados' (*M*, p. 33). The disorderly dejection and ruination of the once orderly peace of Walcott's colonial 'Great House' is silently expressed through the 'mouths of those gate cherubs streaked with stain' ('Ruins of a Great House', l. 4). With its ominous wrought-iron serpentine-design gates, 'the grand house of many rooms rising above the hill of fog' (*M*, p. 33) that Jacob dreamed of constructing in *A Mercy* is left at his death as an incomplete and ruinous structure. The 'third and presumably final house' is an aggressive assault on the natural world; Lina notes that its construction 'distorted sunlight' and 'required the death of fifty trees . . . without asking their permission' (*M*, pp. 41–2).

This unfinished structure substitutes the killed trees with its own 'profane monument to [Jacob] himself' (*M*, p. 42) and the European mindset that thrives on one successive project or scheme after another. In opposition to this mechanistic worldview, Lina has moments of visionary attachment to the natural world, which can send 'sudden a sheet of sparrows [to] fall from the skies and settle in the trees' so that 'the trees seem to sprout birds, not leaves at all'. These moments of spiritual connection are fleeting, for nature can just as easily withdraw from humanity, symbolised by the 'sudden and silent' departure of the sparrows (*M*, p. 69).

By the close of *A Mercy*, the ruined and ruinous form of Jacob's house is reclaimed by the natural world, as 'all manner of small life enters the windows along with cutting wind', and 'spiders reign in comfort and robins make their nests' (*M*, p. 156). These descriptions of nature's destructive reclaiming of the space occupied by the colonial house point up those sympathies Morrison shares with Frost and Walcott and the legacy of Wordsworth that lies behind their poetry. For Morrison and Wordsworth, the ruined and the ruinous articulate grief and frustrate the hope for consolation following moments of destroyed human connections and relations.

Such moments occur when, according to Wordsworth, 'a bond / Of brotherhood is broken' (*The Ruined Cottage*, ll. 84–5), as well as through the tragedy and potential comfort that, as he writes in 'Simon Lee', 'Such stores as silent thought can bring' (l. 74). Wordsworth's ballad of 'Simon Lee', by the poem's own admission, is a tale much like Margaret's in *The Ruined Cottage* – it 'is no tale' unless the listener or reader chooses to 'make it' one ('Simon Lee', ll. 79–80). In *A Mercy*, Florens's 'disorderly' formed words (p. 156) similarly challenge the reader with her claim that 'If you never read this, no one will' (p. 159). We are also reminded here of the closing refrain of 'It was not a story to pass on' in the final few pages of Morrison's *Beloved* (*BL*, pp. 274–5). 'No one', as Morrison has commented, 'tells the story about himself or herself unless forced.'[30]

Paradoxically, for both Morrison and Wordsworth, the fragmented and fragmentary are broken signs that voice through their incomplete condition the unspoken 'tale of silent suffering' (*The Ruined Cottage*, l. 233):

> When I stooped to drink,
> A spider's web hung to the water's edge,
> And on the wet and slimy foot-stone lay
> The useless fragment of a wooden bowl;
> It moved my very heart. (*The Ruined Cottage*, ll. 88–92)

Such a profound sense of disconnection between the assured woven design of a spider's web and the human futility implied by the 'useless fragment of a wooden bowl' delineates the disparity and hoped-for connection between the spheres of natural and human activity that shape Wordsworth's poetic pattern. Such an uncertain connection between nature and humanity is crystallised in the Pedlar's claim that he 'eyed its waters till we *seemed* to feel / One sadness, they and I' (*The Ruined Cottage*, ll. 83–4, emphasis added).[31] The inclusion of the seemingly insignificant spider's web at the water's edge typifies Wordsworth's attention to minute detail and sense of place as a means to dramatise the inward personal suffering and ruination at the core of *The Ruined Cottage*, which accords with Morrison's reimagining of these Wordsworthian and Faulknerian concerns central to her fiction.[32]

Place, Memory and Loss in Morrison and Wordsworth

A preoccupation with memory, history and individual and communal identity manifests itself through Morrison's and Wordsworth's treatment of the specificity of location. Physical presence and place as the site of memory – or 'rememory' – are as inextricable from one another in Morrison's fiction as they are in Wordsworth's poetry. In *Beloved*, Sethe explains that 'if a house burns down, it's gone, but the place – the picture of it – stays, and not just in my rememory, but out there, in the world' (*BL*, p. 36). Thinking of the horrors of Sweet Home Farm, Sethe elaborates to Denver this notion of the intrinsic connection between location and memory:

> Where I was before I came here, that place is real. It's never going away. Even if the whole farm – every tree and grass blade of it dies. The picture is still there and what is more, if you go there – you who never was there – if you go there and stand in the place where it was, it will happen again; it will be there for you, waiting for you. So, Denver, you can't never go there. Never. Because even though it's all over – over and done with – it's going to always be there waiting for you. (*BL*, p. 36)

Morrison is concerned with more than the persistence of memory, as she is alert to the tangible presence of the past in the present and the hauntingly disruptive influence of characters' own memories and those of others that are never or only partially articulated or recovered. Morrison captures something of this ever-present haunting otherness in her reflection on writing more generally, and her novel *Beloved* in particular:

> Narrative fiction provides a controlled wilderness, an opportunity to be and to become the Other. The stranger. With sympathy, with clarity, and the risk of self-examination. In this iteration from me the author, Beloved the girl, the haunter, is the ultimate Other. Clamoring, forever clamoring for a kiss. (*TOO*, p. 91)

Distinct from Updike's 'dreamy wilderness', Morrison's fiction as a 'controlled wilderness' presents repressed or partial memories of the self that gesture toward the possibility of recovering a collective, redemptive body of experience as much as they suggest that all recollections of the past are perspectival, fractured and fragmented. The partial and fragmentary workings of memory, as well as its deliberately obfuscating effects, are foregrounded in Morrison's recent novel, *Home*, set primarily in the early 1950s, by establishing a tension between Frank Money's claimed recollection and how his memory will be written down: '*Since you're set on telling my story, whatever you think and whatever you write down, know this.*

I really forgot about the burial. I only remembered the horses.'[33] Frank's anxiety may be genuine, but the credibility of his claim is open to question given that the events of *Home* are bookended by two burial scenes, one witnessed by Frank and his sister, Cee, as children and the other conducted by them as adults at the close of the novel. His unsuccessful repression of the buried man is hinted at by the apparitional appearance of the 'little man in the pale blue zoot suit' (*H*, p. 33), in later life, besides Frank on a train and at his bedside as a 'new dream ghost company' (*H*, p. 34). That Cee also glimpses the same 'small man in a funny suit swinging a watch chain' (*H*, p. 144), when she and Frank rebury the 'small bones' (*H*, p. 143) of the male corpse at the end of the novel, suggests that the presence of this figure is more than a figment of Frank's own mind and represents a collective pathology,[34] an embodiment of a shared, repressed, traumatic childhood event and selfhood for brother and sister alike.

Estrangement from both the past and place pervades *Home*, a theme that announces itself in Morrison's selection, from her own earlier writing, of the novel's poetic epigraph, which reads: 'This house is strange / Its shadows lie / Say, tell me, why does its lock fit my key?' Frank has been a stranger in many places at different points in his life but, ultimately, his source of separation is spiritual or psychological and resides within. 'There are no strangers,' as Morrison attests:

> There are only versions of ourselves, many of which we have not embraced, most of which we wish to protect ourselves from. For the stranger is not foreign, [it] is random; not alien but remembered . . . (*TOO*, p. 38)

This process of wariness about the stranger within and beyond ourselves is not easily disentangled from issues of race but, as Morrison reflects on the composition of *Home* and *God Save the Child*, 'writing non-colorist literature about black people is a task I have found both liberating and hard' (*TOO*, p. 51). In *Home*, Morrison's intention, slightly thwarted at the behest of her editor, was 'to create a work in which color was erased but could be easily assumed if the reader paid close attention to the codes' (*TOO*, p. 51). Frank's reluctance to return home, *'the worst place in the world, worse than any battlefield'* (*H*, p. 83, original italic), is a consequence of his personal history, which is inextricably bound up with his racial identity. He is motivated, though, by a desire to recapture his role as elder brother and protect Cee from a present-day unknown fatal threat.

Frank's quest to rescue Cee, the *'first person he took responsibility for'* when he was a child, is as much a bid to recover his own self-worth, because '*Deep down inside her lived my secret picture self – a strong good me tied to the memory of those horses and a burial of a stranger*' (*H*, p. 104, original italic). Frank's often uncertain grasp on actuality and lack of a unified sense of self stem from his traumatic childhood, compounded by the horrors of battle he experienced in the Korean War. Cee's own trauma as a child is exacerbated by being subjected to Dr Beau's grotesque medical experimentations. Bound together by their shared trauma of childhood, Frank ascribes Cee with a ghostliness that speaks to his own insubstantiality: '*When you write this down, know this: she was a shadow for most of my life, a presence marking its own absence, or maybe mine*' (*H*, p. 103, original italic). Frank's uncertainty about what constitutes the self and world is counterbalanced by his desire to establish what can be objectively known of his subjectively immersive experience. Such an impulsive attitude towards the objective causes Frank (and us as readers) to question the reliability of his narration. What at first had appeared to be uncertainty over the actual belies a deliberate concealment of a deeper trauma pertaining to Frank's wartime experiences and his (sexually charged) estrangement from himself and his killing of a Korean girl: '*I have to tell the whole truth. I lied to you and I lied to me. I hid it from you because I hid it from me*' (*H*, p. 133, original italic).

Morrison's meditation on what physically, spiritually and emotionally constitutes a place of belonging, a home, is haunted by retrospective and proleptic acts of infanticide in the form of a spectral murdered Korean infant and the ghost of Cee's child never to be born (her sterility a consequence of Dr Beau's medical malpractice). Competing perspectives over a probable act of infanticide form the kernel of Wordsworth's lyrical ballad *The Thorn*. In *Home*, Morrison's oscillation between the objectively known and the subjectively experienced recalls the divided, paradoxical perspective of the narrator of *The Thorn*, who is, as Wordsworth's 'Note' to the poem attests, 'prone to superstition' (*WMW*, p. 593), although tirelessly committed to seeking out the truth of the tragedy of Martha Ray and her child. Recalling the narrative technique of *The Ruined Cottage*, Wordsworth's embedding of multiple points of view within the eccentric outer narrative frame of the retired sea captain in *The Thorn*, simultaneously, creates an aesthetic distance from the full horror of the ballad's tragedy and startles the reader with painful glimpses into its tragic events.

Central to Wordsworth's *The Thorn* is the uncontestable fact of an infant's death, but the precise cause, nature and circumstance of the child's demise are never fully established. Signs of the child's untimely demise are marked everywhere on the surrounding landscape seen through the susceptible mind's eye of Wordsworth's narrator, who reckons that 'Not higher than a two years' child / It stands erect, this aged Thorn' (ll. 5–6) and that the nearby moss in 'all its beauteous dyes / Is like an infant's grave in size' (ll. 55–6). Likened to a tombstone, the thorn becomes a site of memorial to the deceased child and the place to which Martha, reportedly, routinely returns to grieve for her loss. Uncertainty and hearsay blend, in the mind of Wordsworth's narrator, with attention to specific details to convey a semblance of the factual that predisposes any potential observer's mind to the haunting legend of the spot: 'Some say, if to the pond you go / And fix on it a steady view / The shadow of a babe you trace / A baby and a baby's face / And that it looks at you' (ll. 225–9). Wordsworth's haunting, shadowy, presently absent, deceased child, whose presence is infused into the natural environs, is reconfigured in Morrison's *Home*. Having been told of her life-long sterility by Miss Ethel Fordham, Cee traces the 'toothless smile' of the baby she will never carry 'in a green pepper' and 'a cloud curved in such a way' (*H*, p. 132). This spectral absent-presence of the *'baby girl'* never to be born to Cee and the *'little girl'* shot by Frank become synonymous with one another in Frank's mind, so that the unborn child, whose absence is felt *'through the house, in the air, the clouds'*, is not the *'little girl . . . waiting around to be born'* but the one *'already dead'* (*H*, p. 133, original italic).

The final scene of Morrison's *Home* concerns the exhumation and reburial of the corpse, whose hasty burial Frank and Cee had accidentally witnessed as children. Recalling Wordsworth's 'aged Thorn' that 'stands erect . . . like a stone' (*The Thorn*, l. 10), they reinter the body at the foot of a tombstone provided by nature in the form of a 'sweet bay tree' (*H*, p. 144). Similarly to Wordsworth's opening description in *The Thorn*, Morrison instils the tree, which is *'hurt'* or 'split down the middle, beheaded, undead' (*H*, p. 147, original italic, p. 144), with symbolic qualities that speak to both Cee's present, sterile, yet enduring condition and the haunting presence of the child she will never bear. This connection between the wounded state of the tree and Cee's barrenness is underscored by one of Morrison's final images of the tree's 'olive-green leaves . . . wild in the glow of a fat cherry-red sun' (*H*, p. 145). Martha Ray as the wronged 'Woman in a scarlet cloak' (*The Thorn*, l. 68) and the death of her infant are associated throughout Wordsworth's *The Thorn* with the moss that is thought to be 'spotted red / With the drops of that poor infant's blood' (*The Thorn*, ll. 129–30). Morrison's striking contrast between 'olive-green' and 'cherry-red' is a reconfiguration of the exclamation of Wordsworth's narrator about the redness of the moss: 'Ah me!

what lovely tints are there / Of olive green and scarlet bright / In spikes, in branches, and in stars' (*The Thorn*, ll. 49–51).

In *Home*, the plight of Cee, who has been taken advantage of and abandoned by Prince and biologically wronged by Dr Beau, reimagines the ruination of the jilted Martha Ray. Morrison's 'cherry-red' is a reminder of both the physiological harm – 'blood and pain' (*H*, p. 122) – inflicted on Cee and the life-blood she will never be able to give to a child. The 'cherry-red sun' equally symbolises how the 'sun's violent rays' (*H*, p. 124) were a curative to Cee's 'remaining womb sickness' within the vicinity of Miss Ethel's backyard, populated with 'royal scarlet berries shining in the morning rain' (*H*, p. 130). Nature, as Miss Ethel knows, has the potential to be both a source of spiritual and physical salve and a destructive, indifferent aggressor: 'For her the whole predatory world threatened her garden, competing with its nourishment, its beauty, its benefits, and its demands' (*H*, p. 130).

Nature's protective role is hinted at in the opening and closing scenes of *Home*, when Frank and Cee are afforded a safe vantage point by 'peeping through the grass' (*H*, p. 4) at the illicit burial of the man and on their return, many years later, they are reminded of past dangers by 'mere shadow warnings poking through tall grass' (*H*, p. 143). Paradoxically, a single blade of grass becomes an emblem of their shared childhood memory of this trauma, one of many horrors in Lotus, Georgia, and that specific physical and temporal spot, where the *'moon was a cantaloupe by the time we felt safe enough to disturb even one blade of grass'* (*H*, pp. 4–5, original italic). Here, as in Wordsworth's *The Thorn* and at other moments in Morrison's *Home*, collective and individual memory blur.

Elsewhere Morrison's description in *Beloved* of the minutiae of the dying 'grass blade' resonates with a passage toward the close of *The Ruined Cottage* in which Wordsworth meditates on the tensions between individual and collective memory:

> I well remember that those very plumes,
> Those weeds, and the high spear-grass on that wall,
> By mist and silent rain-drops silvered o'er,
> As once I passed did to my heart convey
> So still an image of tranquility . . . (ll. 513–17)

Finding a parallel between this episode and another in *The Prelude* (VIII, ll. 544–59), Bidney reads the 'image of tranquility' offered by Wordsworth's 'high spear' as a tentative variation of a Wordsworthian 'pattern whereby a center is linked to a radiant higher sphere or circumference' to 'offer epiphanies of consola-tion'.[35] Such a reading elides how Wordsworth's narrator's sym-pathy with Margaret's past places him at odds with nature's 'still season of repose and peace' (*The Ruined Cottage*, l. 185). This conflict is evident in his earlier question – 'why should a tear be in an old man's eye?' (*The Ruined Cottage*, l. 188) – which gives way to grief and the unquiet activity of a troubled mind. At best, Wordsworth's 'image of tranquility' is wrested from 'sympathies . . . that', as we are told earlier, 'steal upon the meditative mind / And grow with thought' (*The Ruined Cottage*, ll. 79, 81–2).

Margaret's presence is remembered and evoked by Armytage (referred to as the Pedlar in later revised versions) at the expense of fashioning her into a kindred spirit who, in his recollection, increas-ingly resembles those 'poets [that] in their elegies and songs / Lament . . . the departed' (*The Ruined Cottage*, ll. 74–5). Wordsworth's pas-toral elegies are, then, about the unreliability of memory to recapture a specific time, place and individual. Aware of these darker uncer-tainties, Wordsworth's poetry calls into question the 'chearful faith' (l. 134) invested in the harmony of memory advocated at the end of *Tintern Abbey*, where we read, 'If solitude, or fear, or pain, or grief, / Should be thy portion, with what healing thoughts / Of tender joy wilt thou remember me' (ll. 143–5).

This pattern of sceptical questioning is repeated in *The Ruined Cottage* when Armytage's faithful assertions about nature's ability to transcend 'ruin', 'change' and 'grief' (l. 521) invite the traveller-poet and reader to both share in his interconnected sympathetic vision and circumscribe our capacity for human sympathy. The traveller-poet and reader must delimit those feelings that, Arymtage instructs his audience, are so vital to the circulation of Margaret's tale and its survival in the communal memory of future generations:

> 'My Friend, enough to sorrow have you given,
> The purposes of wisdom ask no more;
> Be wise and chearful, and no longer read
> The forms of things with an unworthy eye.
> She sleeps in the calm earth, and peace is here.' (ll. 508–12)

Crucial to this passage is the idea of perspective and reading nature and the 'forms of things' correctly with a worthy as opposed to an 'unworthy eye'. By implication, to consider Margaret's 'resting-place' as anything other than a spiritual union with nature is to see with an 'unworthy eye' that lacks the imaginative vision to learn from Margaret's tragic sufferings. Armytage's account of the 'unworthy eye' suggests that the worthy eye recommends a particular way of seeing the 'forms of things' and promotes a reciprocal relationship between the natural and the human world.[36] Wordsworth's use of a double frame narrative makes possible the aesthetic distance necessary to extract such an instructive lesson and equally makes impossible the critical distance required to evaluate the truth of that purported lesson, as the end of one frame is indistinguishable from the beginning of the other.[37] Simultaneously, Wordsworth's presentation of Armytage's point of view admits the possibility of an alternative and less visionary mode of seeing, capable only of recognising disjuncture rather than similitude between humanity, nature and art.

Morrison, Wordsworth and Spectral Dwellers

Morrison's earlier insistence, in *Beloved*, that the 'picture is still there' indicates, as does Wordsworth's wresting of the 'image of tranquility' and 'peace', a self-conscious artistry about those figural substitutions that evoke a collective and individual sense of irretrievable loss. Alternatively, such figurations equally point up the impossibility of that collective and individual recollection and recuperation. Storytelling is, as Morrison claims, 'the collective sharing of . . . information [which] heals the individual – and the collective'.[38] Morrison's passage from *Beloved* taps into how, in Wordsworth's *The Ruined Cottage*, the raindrop-bejewelled 'high spear-grass' (l. 515) serves as much as 'an image of tranquility' as those unpopulated 'silent walls' of the ruined cottage act as a physical, albeit transient, monument to the reality of the desolate 'resting-place', the 'last human tenant of these ruined walls' (*The Ruined Cottage*, l. 492). Such a site of human desolation, Frost darkly reminds us in 'Directive', is 'broken off / Like graveyard marble sculpture in the weather, / There is a house that is no more a house' (ll. 3–5).

Wordsworth's 'ruined walls' testify to Margaret's suffering and are a sign that her presence still haunts both the poem's 'cheerless spot' (*The Ruined Cottage*, l. 60) and its poetic structure. Wordsworth's fascination with the figure of the revenant is shared by Morrison, who depicts Beloved's return to the house at 124 Bluestone Road as a visceral yet spectral presence and Jacob Vaark, in *A Mercy*, as 'climbing out of his grave to visit his beautiful house', to spend 'haunting time there' where there had been 'no previous tenants' (*M*, p. 141).

Wordsworth's description of Margaret as 'the last human tenant' and Morrison's observation that before Jacob there had been 'no previous tenants' suggest that their mutual interest, shared by the poetry of Frost and Walcott, in the workings and figuration of memory is connected with architectural structures, each in varying degrees of repair or construction, and questions of ownership and belonging. Morrison and Wordsworth are alert to how the subject is enmeshed in the complexities of the potential recovery and limitations of personal and historical memory, but they also recognise how the subject is entangled in the economics of property and possession. In what Samira Kawash has understood as an entwining of 'person' and 'property', Morrison's writing points to a 'foundational distinction between subject possessing and object possessed – converg[ing] in the structure and the substance of the house'.[39] Such an economic system in which the possessor (the subject) and the possessed (the object) are intractable and interchangeable permits the subject to become the possessed object, the terms of slavery itself.

To reinstate the subject's authority and autonomy, Wordsworth and Morrison reconfigure writing as an act of reading fractured or partial signs glimpsed only through multiple interpretations of those fragmentary remainders of a larger whole or utterance. Although responding to historically different economic pressures, the internalised tragedy of Wordsworth's fragmentary, elegiac poetry about the dispossessed, the peripatetic and the socially marginal resonates with Morrison's artistic temperament and sense of social injustice. Morrison translates the darker features of Wordsworth's rural poetics, inflected through Emerson's and Thoreau's urbanised pastoral modes, into her own version of the American pastoral – a 'controlled wilderness' – to map those uncharted spaces of suffering. This reimagining of Wordsworth's pastoral tales and tellers enables Morrison to speak of what could not be spoken, to pass on those stories that could not be 'passed on'.

Notes

1. For a discussion of this issue see Michael Nowlin, 'Toni Morrison's *Jazz* and Racial Dreams of the American Writer', *American Literature* 71.1 (1999): 151–74. For an insightful collection of recent readings of Toni Morrison's fiction see *MELUS* 36.2 (2011), Special Issue on Toni Morrison: New Directions, ed. Kathryn Nicol and Jennifer Terry.

2. See Martin Bidney, 'Creating a Feminist-Communitarian Romanticism in *Beloved*: Toni Morrison's New Uses for Blake, Keats, and Wordsworth', *Papers on Language and Literature* 36.3 (2000): 271–301. Bidney reads *Beloved* for the reworking of the plots of episodic moments in *The Prelude*; he does not acknowledge the centrality of Wordsworth's *The Ruined Cottage* (c. 1797), later revised and incorporated into Book 1 of *The Excursion*, to Morrison's writing. Jan Stryz reads Toni Morrison as an inheritor of American Transcendentalism or Romanticism. See Stryz, 'The Other Ghost in *Beloved*: The Specter of *The Scarlett Letter*', in *The New Romanticism: A Collection of Critical Essays*, ed. Eberhard Alsen (New York: Garland, 2000), pp. 137–58.

3. For example, Toni Morrison's essay 'Romancing the Shadow' has been included in *The New Romanticism: A Collection of Critical Essays*, ed. Eberhard Alsen (New York: Garland, 2000), pp. 51–69.

4. Richard Kerridge notes how ecocriticism has taken up a 'transformative approach to the pastoral [which] shows the extent to which it must resist and reform even those traditions and genres that support it' (p. 540). See Kerridge, 'Environmentalism and Ecocriticism', in *Literary Theory and Criticism: An Oxford Guide*, ed. Patricia Waugh (Oxford: Oxford University Press, 2006), pp. 530–43. For a discussion of the numerous forms of the pastoral, the genre's questioning of its own conventions, and the extent to which the 'pastoral' has become a contested concept see Terry Gifford, *Pastoral* (London: Routledge, 1999), pp. 1–12.

5. For an ecocritical account of Morrison's fiction in relation to American environmentalism see Kathleen R. Wallace and Karla Armbruster, 'The Novels of Toni Morrison: "Wild Wilderness Where There Was None"', in *Beyond Nature Writing: Expanding the Boundaries of Ecocriticism*, ed. Kathleen R. Wallace and Karla Armbruster (Charlottesville: University of Virginia Press, 2001), pp. 211–30. See also Greg Garrard, *Ecocriticism* (London: Routledge, 2004); Lawrence Buell, *The Environmental Imagination: Thoreau, Nature Writing, and the Formation of American Culture* (Cambridge, MA: Belknap-Harvard University Press, 1995); Annette Kolodny, *The Lay of the Land: Metaphor as History and Experience in American Life and Letters* (Chapel Hill: University of North Carolina Press, 1975).

6. John Updike, 'Dreamy Wilderness: Unmastered Women in Colonial Virginia', review of Toni Morrison, *A Mercy*, *The New Yorker*, 3 November 2008.

7. James C. McKusick argues for the centrality of English Romantic poetry to the American pastoral, ecocritical and environmental tradition. See McKusick, *Green Writing: Romanticism and Ecology* (New York: St. Martin's, 2000), pp. 1–11. See also Tony Tanner, *SNSM*, p. 32.

8. Toni Morrison, *A Mercy* (London: Chatto, 2008), p. 1. Hereafter *M*.

9. Hilary Mantel, 'How Sorrow Became Complete', review of Toni Morrison, *A Mercy*, *The Guardian*, 8 November 2008.

10. Recent critical studies on these aspects of Morrison's fiction include those by Rebecca Hope Ferguson, Lucille P. Fultz and Denise Heinze. See Ferguson, *Rewriting Black Identities: Transition and Exchange in the Novels of Toni Morrison* (Brussels: Lang, 2007); Fultz, *Toni Morrison: Playing with Difference* (Urbana: University of Illinois Press, 2003); Heinze, *The Dilemma of 'Double-Consciousness': Toni Morrison's Novels* (Athens: University of Georgia Press, 1993).

11. Toni Morrison, 'Memory, Creation, and Writing', *Thought* 59.235 (1984): 385–90.

12. Stuart Curran detects this 'multiperspectivism' in Wordsworth's use of the pastoral and further notes that 'Wordsworthian pastoral is self-conscious about its own making in a way that suggests a profound understanding of the nature and history of the form from Virgil on' (pp. 102, 107–16). See Curran, *Poetic Form and British Romanticism* (New York: Oxford University Press, 1986).

13. See Geoffrey H. Hartman, who identifies Lucy Gray and the Leech-Gatherer as instances of the recurring figure of the revenant in Wordsworth's poetry. See Hartman, *The Unremarkable Wordsworth*, foreword D. G. Marshall (Minneapolis: University of Minnesota Press, 1987), pp. 61–2. Morrison's interest in these Wordsworthian solitary figures is explicitly hinted at in the naming of Colonel Wordsworth Gray in her novel *Jazz*.

14. Toni Morrison, *Beloved* (London: Picador-Pan, 1988), p. 123. Hereafter *BL*. All quotations are from this edition.

15. Toni Morrison, *The Origin of Others*, The Charles Eliot Norton Lecture, 2016, foreword Ta-Neshisi Coates (Cambridge, MA: Harvard University Press, 2017), p. 52. Hereafter *TOO*. All quotations are from this edition.

16. Italo Calvino, *Invisible Cities*, trans. William Weaver (London: Vintage, 2001), p. 12.

17. William Wordsworth, *The Excursion*, ed. Sally Bushell, James A. Butler and Michael C. Jaye (Ithaca: Cornell University Press, 2007), ll. 187–203.

18. For a detailed discussion of slavery's legacies in the writings of Morrison and others see chapter 1 in Jennifer Terry, *Shuttles in the Rocking Loom: Mapping the Black Diaspora in African American and Caribbean Fiction* (Liverpool: Liverpool University Press, 2013).

19. William Wordsworth, *The White Doe of Rylstone*, in *The Poems of William Wordsworth: Collected Readings from the Cornell Edition*, ed. Jared Curtis (Grasmere: Humanities-Ebooks, 2011), p. 575, l. 123. All quotations are from this edition.

20. For a reading of gender action and passivity in Wordsworth's *The White Doe of Rylstone*, see Paul H. Fry, *Wordsworth and the Poetry of What We Are* (New Haven: Yale University Press, 2008), pp. 110–14.

21. Sylvia Plath's poem closes with the lines 'Out of the ash / I rise with my red hair / And I eat men like air'. See Plath, *Collected Poems* (London: Faber, 1981), pp. 244–7.

22. For an account of circular imagery in *Beloved* see Philip Page, 'Circularity in Toni Morrison's *Beloved*', Women Writers Issue of *African American Review* 26.1 (1992): 31–9.

23. Emily Dickinson, *The Letters of Emily Dickinson*, ed. Thomas H. Johnson and Theodora W. Ward (Cambridge, MA: Belknap, 1958), p. 263. Hereafter *EDL*.

24. I am grateful to my colleague, Jennifer Terry, for our discussion and helpful suggestions in relation to Morrison's fiction and Derek Walcott's poetry.

25. Robert Frost, 'Speaking of Loyalty', in *The Collected Prose of Robert Frost*, ed. Mark Richardson (Cambridge, MA: Belknap-Harvard University Press, 2007), p. 155, ll. 151–6.

26. See Robert Faggen, *Robert Frost and the Challenge of Darwin* (Ann Arbor: University of Michigan Press, 2001), pp. 282–8. For an account of Frost and Romanticism, see Mario L. D'Avanzo, *A Cloud of Other Poets: Robert Frost and the Romantics* (Lanham: University Press of America, 1991).

27. Robert Frost, 'The Black Cottage', in *The Collected Poems of Robert Frost*, ed. Edward Connery Lathem (London: Vintage, 2001), pp. 55–9, ll. 105–6. All quotations are from this edition.

28. 'He hangs in shades the orange bright / Like golden lamps in a green night.' See Andrew Marvell, 'Bermudas', in *The Complete Poems: Andrew Marvell*, ed. Elizabeth Story Donno (Harmondsworth: Penguin, 1987), p. 116, ll. 17–18. Marvell's poem depicts a paradise that will be corrupted by commercial self-interest.

29. Derek Walcott, 'Ruins of a Great House', in *Derek Walcott: Collected Poems, 1948–1984* (New York: Farrar, 1986), pp. 19–21, ll. 13–14.

30. Marsha Darling, 'In the Realm of Responsibility: A Conversation with Toni Morrison', *Women's Review of Books* 5 (1978): 5; 5–6.

31. See Mark Sandy, *Romanticism, Memory, and Mourning* (Farnham: Ashgate, 2013), pp. 33–46.

32. Kurt Fosso, for instance, maps the detail of the spider's web onto Margaret's weaving activity later in the poem to suggest that in the uncertain absence of her husband, her creations are akin to literary works of the elegist. Fosso reads weaving as a trope for writing and reading, which are themselves works of mourning. See Fosso, *Buried Communities: Wordsworth and the Bonds of Mourning* (Albany: State University of New York Press, 2004), pp. 103–11.

33. Toni Morrison, *Home* (London: Vintage, 2012), p. 5 (original italic). Hereafter *H*. All quotations are from this edition.

34. See Leah Hager Cohen, 'Point to Return', review of Toni Morrison, *Home*, *The New York Times*, 17 May 2012. Cohen suggests that Morrison's figure indicates there is 'no individual pathology'.

35. See Martin Bidney, *Patterns of Epiphany: From Wordsworth to Tolstoy, Pater, and Barrett Browning* (Carbondale: Southern Illinois University Press, 1997), p. 37.

36. James H. Averill reads *The Ruined Cottage* as promoting Wordsworth's idea of a sympathetic and reciprocal relationship between the human and the natural world without equivocation. See Averill, *Wordsworth and the Poetry of Human Suffering* (Ithaca: Cornell University Press, 1980), pp. 137–41.

37. Timothy Morton rightly observes of Wordsworth's *The Ruined Cottage*, 'The apparently simple act of double framing induces a sense of hesitation. Can we trust where the frame stops and where the next one starts, what is inside the frame, how truthful it is?' (*EWN*, p. 146).

38. Darling, 'In the Realm of Responsibility', p. 5.

39. Samira Kawash, 'Haunted Houses, Sinking Ships: Race, Architecture, and Identity in *Beloved* and *Middle Passage*', *The New Centennial Review* 1.3 (2001): 74; 67–87.

Nature without Self: Beauty, Death and Subjectivity in the Poetics of Walt Whitman, Emily Dickinson and Wallace Stevens

The enigmatical
Beauty of each beautiful enigma
Becomes amassed in a total double-thing.

Wallace Stevens, 'An Ordinary Evening in New Haven',
10, ll. 165–7

All over bouquets of roses,
O death! I cover you over with roses and early lilies;
But mostly and now the lilac that blooms first,
Copious, I break, I break the sprigs from the bushes;
With loaded arms I come, pouring for you,
For you and the coffins all of you, O death.

Walt Whitman, 'When Lilacs Last in the Dooryard
Bloom'd', ll. 149–54

Whitman, Nature's Beauty and Romanticism

These two epigraphs speak to a poetic concern with the 'double-thing' and enigma that beauty is. Walt Whitman's lines anticipate Wallace Stevens's later evocation of a powerfully ordinary and extra-ordinary beauty. Whitman's elegy, published in 1865, occasioned by the assassination of Abraham Lincoln, offers its readers the 'enigmatical / Beauty' of not just a single bouquet of roses, but a veritable bevy of them. Whitman's spiritual and psychic defence against death is infused with William Blake's visionary (and auto-erotic) poetics of a 'bed / Of crimson joy' in 'The Sick Rose' (ll. 5–6). Blake's own lyric mode is itself a provocative coalescence of allure and dread; a beauty consummated and ravished; innocent and experienced; corrupted and self-corrupted. Regrettably, poetic roses (as is evident in Blake's own enigmatic lyric) so often symbolise the transience or corruption of beauty. Whitman's poetical 'bouquets of roses' are no exception. Like the 'sprigs' of lilac vital to the elegy's unfolding poetic patterns, these 'bouquets of roses' commingle the delicate, the individual, the transcendent and a promise of new (spiritual) life with the numerous, abundant, fragile and transient. Whitman's poetic 'roses' are bestowed from the 'I' of the poet as mourner to each and every 'you' of the reader. The giving of these 'roses' is a symbol of the spiritual life to come and a reminder of the natural inevitability of the physical event of death itself. This passage occurs at a pivotal moment of Whitman's 'When Lilacs Last in the Dooryard Bloom'd' in which the grieving poet-speaker comes to realise the spiritual possibilities that death of the body might afford. This change in consciousness is traced in Whitman's offering of the roses by a shift from the particular to the universal. Earlier in Whitman's poem the lilac 'sprigs' were praised, like an individual rose, for their singular and particular beauty, but now they are valued for their 'Copious' abundance.

Confronted with, and confronting, death in its starkest terms in a godless universe, Stevens transforms such Romantic floral excess in his elegiac 'The Emperor of Ice-Cream' into those coldly alluring 'kitchen cups concupiscent curds'. By 1923 the desolating particulars of an individual death are, for Stevens, stripped of sentimentality and reduced to 'let the boys / Bring flowers in last month's newspapers. / Let be be finale of seem. / The only emperor is the emperor of ice-cream' (ll. 5–8). Here Stevens's refusal to go beyond the macabre facts of the matter quietly transforms the ordinary. With less quiet intent, what lends 'When Lilacs Last in the Dooryard Bloom'd' its imaginative power, and drives its cosmic drama, is Whitman's capacity to recover the extraordinary in the ordinary, to unearth the transcendent in the everyday, the spiritual in the material, the beautiful in a particular set of ugly circumstances. The dramatic impetus of Whitman's elegy perfectly illustrates Shelley's earlier sense, in *A Defence of Poetry*, that 'The story of particular facts is as a mirror which obscures and distorts that which should be beautiful: Poetry is a mirror which makes beautiful that which is distorted' (*SPP*, p. 515). That which the 'particular facts' both 'obscure' and 'distort' is recovered through the 'mirror' of poetry as beautiful; a beauty which, for Whitman and Shelley, partly exists in, and is invented through, the creative eye of the poet – a Romantic dilemma which, for all of his anti-Romantic brio, Stevens understood when he writes that it is only through the 'sight' of 'the necessary angel of earth' that 'you see the earth again' ('Angel Surrounded by Paysans', ll. 11–12). Stevens's imaginative recourse, in a chaotic cosmos, is to the anthropocentric; he sees the task of the poet to 'speak humanly from the height or from the depth / of human things'. But Stevens's 'acutest [form] of speech' ('Chocorua to its Neighbour', ll. 93–4) also points to affinities between his post-Romantic renewed visionary beauty and Romanticism itself.

The Beautiful and the Ordinary

It is this notion of the renewal of beauty and the beautiful which is rediscovered in Shelley's 'particular facts'. It is comparable to that which Stevens in a post-Romantic vein called 'the plain sense of things' and which Markus Poetzsch, a fairly recent critic of Romanticism, has termed a Wordsworthian 'visionary dreariness' of the ordinary.[1] A further aspect to mundane 'visionary dreariness' is explored by the work of the Harvard philosopher and aesthetician Stanley Cavell. He writes in *In the Quest of the Ordinary*:

> The everyday is ordinary because, after all, it is our habit, or habitat, but since that very habitation is from time to time perceptible to us – we who have constructed it – as extraordinary, we conceive that some place elsewhere . . . must be what romantics – of course including both E.T. and Nicholas Nickleby's alter ego Smike – called 'home'.[2]

Part of Cavell's larger claim is that Ralph Waldo Emerson and Henry David Thoreau sought to resist an impulse towards the sublime and to reconnect us with the beauty and wonders of ordinary, everyday existence. According to Cavell, American Romanticism resists a tendency towards abstraction – what he understands as the 'language of life' – and instead favours the 'life of language'.[3]

The fate of beauty and that of the ordinary in the Romantic imagination are entwined with one another. Whitman suggests that beauty, like a wild or cultivated rose, can be equally bestowed upon or discovered within a very ordinary and particular object or person. Writing in the 1881 edition (first edition published 1855) of *Leaves of Grass*, Whitman insists on the integral relationship between the poet, poetic language and the beautiful:

> All this time, and at all times, wait the words of true poems;
> The words of true poems do not merely please,
> The true poets are not followers of beauty, but the august masters
>   of beauty.
> ('Song of the Answerer', 2, ll. 65–7)

'Beauty' and the 'words of true poems' belong, recalling P. B. Shelley's sense that 'to be a poet is to apprehend the true and the beautiful' (*SPP*, p. 512), to pre-existent (almost Platonic) forms that survive through 'All this time' and 'at all times'. Poets are not, then, blind devotees, but 'august masters' who, paradoxically, partly create beauty and partly discover through their acts of imaginative creation an eternal order of both beauty and the 'words of true poems'. Faint echoes of Shelley's claim about the 'beauty' of poetic 'compositions' of those 'isolated fragments and portions' pertaining to the everlasting 'great poem' (*SPP*, p. 512) also inform Whitman's later assertion in 'Song of the Answerer' that the 'words of true poems' exceed the sum of their parts to 'give you more than poems' (2, l. 74).

Whether beauty is a pre-existent given in the natural universe of things or a quality that is bestowed upon our experience of the world, Whitman is keen elsewhere to stress the beautiful as an all-inclusive category that includes the transformative power of natural light, natural objects (both remarkable and unremarkable) and human activities and their manufactured products (manmade objects). In 'Poem of the Many in One', Whitman proclaims that, for the attuned sensibilities of the poet,

> The day-light is lit with more volatile light – the deep between the setting and rising sun goes deeper many fold,
>   Each precise object, condition, combination, process, exhibits a beauty – the multiplication-table its, old age its, the carpenter's trade its, the grand-opera its,
>   The huge-hulled clean-shaped Manhattan clipper at sea, under steam or full sail, gleams with unmatched beauty . . .[4]

Published in the second edition of *Leaves of Grass* and substantially revised as 'By Blue Ontario's Shore', the passage from 'Poem of Many in One' is representative of much of Whitman's poetic style with its reliance on panoramic, all-encompassing, sweeping lines of free verse (*vers libre*), which are made up of a dazzling array of objects, states of being and occupations. This habit of cataloguing in journalistic listings attributes to, and discovers within, each discrete 'object, condition, combination, process' an individual beauty of its own. More specifically, Whitman's lines recognise that the 'unmatched beauty' of the 'Manhattan clipper' is the collective product of the cumulative effect of each instance of discrete beauty of the ordinary object, event and process listed. In other words, the 'clean-shaped Manhattan clipper' is an instance, as the title of Whitman's poem suggests, of a consummation of 'Many in One'. Stevens would, in his own poetic lexicon, agree with Whitman about the multiplicity of the particulars of beauty, but he does so with arch-Romantic gusto when he observes that 'Beauty is momentary in the mind' ('Peter Quince at the Clavier', l. 51). Whitman's lines resonate, too, with William Wordsworth's conviction that there is 'a sense sublime / Of something far more deeply interfused / Whose dwelling is the light of setting suns' (*Tintern Abbey*, ll. 96–8). Emerson as an inheritor of British Romanticism intercedes between Whitman and Wordsworth to attest, in an essay on 'The Poet', that the artist's 'cheerfulness should be the gift of sunlight' and 'common influences' their 'delight' ('The Poet', *TPE*, p. 257).

That Whitman's poetry praises – in terms that recall and disavow Wordsworth's 'visionary gleam' ('Ode: Intimations of Immortality', l. 57) – the 'clean-shaped Manhattan clipper', gleaming 'with unmatched beauty', confirms these lines as a poetic embodiment of a different set of (non-Wordsworthian) sentiments found in Emerson's reflections on 'The Poet'.[5] Whitman's description chimes with Emerson's speculations about the relationship between the art of nature and the art (or products) of industrial progress. Nature, for Emerson, recognises and adopts the intricate and, by implication, those beautiful objects that are a product of industrial and human endeavour into her 'vital circles'. Similarly the task of the poet penetrates beyond the mere facts of ordinary things, because 'the poet' in Emerson's view

> alone knows the astronomy, chemistry, vegetation and animation, for he does not stop at these facts, but employs them as signs. He knows why the plain or meadow of space was strown with these flowers we call suns and moons and stars; why the great deep is adorned with animals, with men, and gods; for in every word he speaks he rides on them as the horses of thought. ('The Poet', *TPE*, p. 252)

Undoubtedly, Whitman's poetry was persistently alert to the beauty of the ordinary, the contingent and the mundane. As the 'Poem of Many in One' rejoices in the beauty of the 'carpenter's trade' and the delights of the 'grand opera', Whitman's later *Song of Myself* celebrates human life in all its manifestations in urban modern life, for as the poet declares in a moment of selfless egotism: 'Whatever interests the rest interests me . . . markets, newspapers, schools, / The mayor and councils, banks . . . real estate and personal estate' (*Song of Myself*, 42, ll. 1076–7).

That the everyday, the ordinary and the quotidian had the potential to grant imaginative access to some sense of beauty is not, as illustrated by Emerson and Whitman, American Romanticism's misapplication of British Romanticism's own idealised conception of the natural world to urban scenes and industrial manufacturing. In fact, it is an extension of Romanticism's dual conceptualisation of beauty as that which is both ever-present (awaiting imaginative discovery) in the surrounding world and created from our own experience of the world. Similarly poems, for Stevens, are an enactment of a momentary perception of a particular object which is transfigured through, and known in, the 'life of poetry' ('An Ordinary Evening in New Haven', 28, l. 498) and present us with 'An absence in reality, / Things as they are. Or so we say' ('Man with the Blue Guitar', 22, ll. 245–6).

In British Romanticism, this paradox is perhaps best expressed by Shelley's claim that the poetic imagination can both 'create for us a being within our being' and purge 'from our inward sight the film of familiarity which obscures from us the wonder of our being'. Shelley suggests that poetic revelation is rooted in a revitalised perception of our own selves and the world to rediscover beauty in the ordinary beyond the 'film of familiarity' (*SPP*, p. 533). In American Romanticism, as Cavell notes, this similar sense of the world is succinctly expressed by Thoreau's question, in *Walden*, about our perception of the world: 'Why do precisely these objects which we behold make a world?' (*TPT*, p. 471). This paradoxical tension is best exemplified by Emerson's own claim, in *Nature*, that it is only through the revelatory power of an active imagination and 'creative reading' that we will 'come to look at the world with new eyes' (*CWE*, p. 44). The 'sources', 'revelation', 'order' and arguably beauties of nature are found both through a sense of obligation or 'duty' to some higher pre-given spiritual calling and within the individual's 'own mind'. As Emerson writes, in *Nature*, 'all objects shrink and expand to serve the passion of the poet' (*CWE*, p. 32).

Whitman is alert to this imaginative malleability of our experience of the world. Whitman's poetry is as much concerned with revealing to its audience the beauty of a 'world' seen 'with new eyes' as it is with, in Emerson's terms, 'creatively seeing', singing and shaping into being a newly perceived world of continual change and process with which we must reconnect. One illuminating instance of this occurs in section 6 of Whitman's *Song of Myself*:

> A child said *What is the grass?* fetching it to me with full hands;
> How could I answer the child? I did not know what it is any more than he.
>
> I guess it must be the flag of my disposition, out of the hopeful green
>   stuff woven.
>
> Or I guess it is the handkerchief of the Lord,
> A scented gift and remembrancer designedly dropt,
> Bearing the owner's name someway in the corners, that we may see and
>   remark, and say *Whose?*
>
> Or I guess the grass is itself a child, the produced babe of the vegetation.
>
> Or I guess it is a uniform hieroglyphic,
> And it means, Sprouting alike in broad zones and narrow zones,
> Growing among black folks as among white . . .
> (*Song of Myself*, 6, ll. 98–107)

Again reminiscent of Blake's visionary *Songs of Innocence and of Experience*, the intuitive child in innocence and wonder perceives the natural, ordinary world anew and (prompted by the beautiful enigma) of a particular blade of grass asks the question which the experienced, overly habitual perception of the adult mind finds almost impossible, at first, to answer. For these different reasons both child and adult are confounded by the question with which they are presented. Perhaps the adult's mind is too attached to the 'language of life' as opposed to the 'life of language'. Whitman's lines permit competing, contradictory and co-existent perspectives on the possible meanings attributed to the unremarkable yet 'beautiful enigma' of the grass's 'green stuff woven'.[6]

Seamus Heaney's observation that Blake's 'The Sick Rose' extends to the reader 'an open invitation into its meaning rather than an assertion of it'[7] is also helpful for illuminating the workings of the blade of grass episode from Whitman's *Song of Myself*. In asking the question '*What is the grass?*', the child seems to be more closely attuned to the natural world around him and to the spiritual presence that flows through the whole material universe and prompts the adult to invent a series of imaginative guesses that renews his own sense of wonder and beauty at the offering of an ordinary blade of grass. The form of the beautiful design of the grass blade may be a 'handkerchief of the Lord' bearing his moniker, or the less religiously orthodox 'uniform hieroglyphic' of something roughly approximating Emerson's idea of the 'Over-Soul'. Recalling the emblem of copious 'roses' and sprigs of lilac present at the opening of this chapter, the grass, which grows everywhere, 'Sprouting alike in broad zones and narrow zones, / Growing among black folks as among white', also symbolises Whitman's poetic and social vision as an all-inclusive (democratic) one which, like those free-flowing expansive lists of his free verse, encompasses all geographic regions, religions, ages and social groups. As in Blake's prophetic claim 'To See a World in a Grain of Sand' ('Auguries of Innocence', l. 1), Whitman's poetics locate in the minutiae of the particulars of reality the generalities of the widest imaginable scheme of knowledge. For the visionary modes of Blake and Whitman, the macroscopic is no longer out there beyond the microscopic, because the general has become entirely subsumed into the local.[8]

Stevens, Post-Romantic Subjectivity, Nature and Beauty

In 'Last Looks at the Lilacs', Stevens objects to a Romantic fiat of a harmonised and beautiful interconnected organic universe by grafting Whitman's natural symbolism of the lilac into a twentieth-century setting (deliberately dropping the first consonant from 'valleys' and substituting the grasshopper with mechanical pincers) to ask to what end the rejuvenation of spring recurs: 'To what good, in the alleys of the lilacs, / O caliper, do you scratch your buttocks' (ll. 1–2).[9] 'Beauty', as Stevens remind us, 'is momentary in the mind' and the modern mind finds itself oppressed by the urban and industrial which, in Stevens's eyes, refuses to fit so easily into Emerson's organic and Romantic chain of being. Stevens's wryly amused questions return us, pointedly, to the reality of the mind and the mind in reality where there is only one prime mover. As Stevens remarks elsewhere, 'The magnificent cause of being, / The imagination, the one reality / In this imagined world' ('Another Weeping Woman', ll. 7–9).

It may be after all, as Stevens's poetry playfully indicates, that the beautiful intricacies of this single sprig of lilac or blade of grass are an instance of the Emersonian realisation that the 'sources of nature' ultimately abide in the visionary child's (and the poet's) 'own mind' (*Nature*, *CWE*, p. 55). The beautiful, for Whitman (and Shelley before him), is not simply a transcendent ideal form but instead inheres (or manifests itself) in those interstices of the complex transactions between

the often chaotic world of ordinary experience and the creative consciousness. Such a creative consciousness, simultaneously, perceives
in and bestows upon the world a sense of order, pattern, design and
above all beauty. Such a beauty is not abstracted from life, but an integral part of life. For Whitman, writing in the 1855 Preface to *Leaves of
Grass*, beauty is partially a product of universal (quasi-scientific) law,
which is as 'inevitable as life . . . it is exact and plumb as gravitation',[10]
and partially a result of an eternal human curiosity. Beauty can also in
these moments of imaginative recognition possess the ability to bring
about a change in the ingeniously inventive and perceiving consciousness of the poet; such a moment, for Shelley, occurs when 'we imagine
that which we know' and 'create for us a being within our being' (*SPP*,
p. 533). Through imaginative moments of this kind, beauty can be
rediscovered and recreated, according to Shelley and those American
inheritors of British Romanticism, in the 'particular facts' of the everyday world. Such a beauty that, with Wordsworth, is 'both what they
half-create, / And what perceive' (*Tintern Abbey*, ll. 107–8) has wider
implications for the relationship between self and world, at worst
courting a dangerous solipsism or, at best, making semi-permeable the
boundaries between perceiving subject and perceived object.

These philosophical dilemmas go to the heart of Whitman's own
semi-autobiographical 'growth of the poet's mind'.[11] In 'Out of the
Cradle Endlessly Rocking', the boy would-be poet is continually created (made into being) by the continuation of that same song through
which the poetic 'I' is 'chanter of pains and joys, uniter of here and
hereafter' (l. 20).[12] Inward intuitive desire and doubt are traced, initially, through the boy's outward empathetic engagement with the
natural world represented by the entwined song of two love-birds,
and then through the boy's equally sympathetic response to the tragic
drama of the presumed death of the she-mate that leaves the remaining he-bird to sing his own bereft, elegiac and remorseful song.

As Whitman's 'Out of the Cradle Endlessly Rocking' blurs temporal
modes, so it also blurs the boundaries between the boy's outward and
inward states, between the objective (visual and auditory) observations
and the subjective act of 'translating' both the joyful and the tragic birdsong presented in the poem. Both the original desire of 'Two feather'd
guests from Alabama' (l. 32) and the later tragic doubts of 'The solitary guest from Alabama' (l. 51) trace the would-be poet's own instinctive feelings of the possibility of love (growing) within the boy's own
heart which are, increasingly, tempered by a nagging awareness of the
intimate connection between love, transience and loss. Traces of John
Keats's negatively capable imagination are perceptible in Whitman's

treatment of the poem's unfolding central tragedy.[13] The would-be poet
both translates this bitter-sweet lesson from, and reads this lesson into,
the tragic love affair of the two birds. His creative consciousness affects,
and is affected by, his empathetic engagement with the natural world
through his endeavours to translate and come to apprehend the 'beautiful enigma' of the particular drama of the two birds, as representative
of the wider meaning of the ordinary condition of contingent reality
and those wider cycles of life and death. He translates the language of
nature and translates himself into being as the 'out-setting bard'.

> A word then, (for I will conquer it,)
> The word final, superior to all,
> Subtle, sent up – what is it? – I listen;
> Are you whispering it, and have been all the time, you sea-waves?
> Is that it from your liquid rims and wet sands?
>
> Whereto answering, the sea,
> Delaying not, hurrying not,
> Whisper'd me through the night, and very plainly before Daybreak,
> Lisp'd to me the low and delicious word death,
> And again death, death, death, death (ll. 160–9)

By implication, then, the poet's subjectivity is that which is whispered into a continual state of becoming (and, by extension, singing)
as 'the chanter of pains and joys, uniter of here and hereafter'. But in
these lines the contracted phrase 'Whisper'd me' (eliding the crucial
preposition 'to') finds an echo in the final line of the poem, where
'The sea whisper'd me'. This further verbally contracted phrase
both registers the crucial birth, albeit mournful, of the becoming
poet into a tragic poetic consciousness and fulfils the 'destiny of me'.

  If the revelation of the 'beautiful enigma' of the sea's dark 'clew' of
the 'delicious word death' is the spur to one dramatisation of poetic
self-creation, then the resistance of the ocean to disclose 'the secret of
the / murmuring I envy' is played out by the Whitmanesque imagination in another of Whitman's twilit American shoreline poems, 'As I
Ebb'd with the Ocean of Life'. Whitman, through a typically magis-
terial performance of poetic selfhood, as Michael O'Neill observes,
achieves 'operatic'[14] effect:

> As I inhale the impalpable breezes that set in upon me,
> As the ocean so mysterious rolls toward me closer and closer,
> I too but signify at the utmost a little wash'd-up drift,
> A few sands and dead leaves to gather,
> Gather, and merge myself as part of the sands and drift.

O baffled, balk'd, bent to the very earth,
Oppress'd with myself that I have dared to open my mouth,
Aware now that amid all that blab whose echoes recoil upon me I
    have not once had the least idea who or what I am,
But that before all my arrogant poems the real Me stands yet
    untouch'd, untold, altogether unreach'd,
Withdrawn far, mocking me with mock-congratulatory signs and
    bows,
With peals of distant ironical laughter at every word I have written,
Pointing in silence to these songs, and then to the sand beneath.
(ll. 20–31)

Through a description of a specific singularity of purpose and action ('I inhale'), Whitman's lines dramatise an illusory sense of an autonomous self-enclosed state of withdrawn isolation and, simultaneously, suggest such introspection is susceptible to (if not akin with) an outer landscape of fractured and fragmenting 'wash'd-up drift', 'dead leaves' and breaking billows of the 'mysterious' ocean. Concurrently, Whitman endeavours to preserve the boundaries between self ('the real Me') and world and dramatises a self decentred by the centripetal force of the ocean's gathering power – a power, ironically, that he also possesses as a beachcomber (a gatherer of driftwood). The merging of Whitman's 'myself' with 'part of the sands and drift' is both a wilful enactment of agency and an enforced (by the outer power of the ocean) merger and fracturing of the self.

Here the act of listening ('echoes', 'ironical laughter' and 'in silence'), favoured over that of watching, suggests an invisible affinity between inward and outward states which questions the solidity of the 'untouch'd' and 'Withdrawn' originally proposed. In spite of separation and withdrawal, the next section of 'As I Ebb'd with the Ocean of Life' establishes a further corollary between the tumultuous noise of the 'mocking' sea and the speaker's dejected state: both the poet and the sea are united through their mutual resentment for one another, so that 'We murmur alike reproachfully rolling sands and drift, knowing not why, / These little shreds indeed standing for you and me and all' (ll. 36–7). How seriously we should take these claims is hard to gauge but the poem does, in its concluding passage, provide a further moment of self-conscious theatricality that recognises the poet and his kind as 'Tufts of straw, sands, fragments / Buoy'd hither from many moods, one contradicting another' (ll. 61–2).

So the forlorn, increasingly fragmentary, although controlled and perfectly staged fragmenting self of Whitman's withdrawn speaker remains attuned to both the outward 'mocking' presence and 'fathomless workings' ('As I Ebb'd with the Ocean of Life', l. 65) of the sea and the inward, equally troubled, spurned condition of the poet. Eventually, the poet concedes that the 'mysterious' beauties of the world have eluded him, claiming that 'I perceive I have not really understood any thing, not a single object, and that no man ever can' (l. 32). This moment of self-proclaimed negative revelatory insight ('I perceive I have not . . .') is a tragic affirmation of the contingencies of ordinary existence, which permits the 'fathomless workings' of the ocean to retain their rather macabre, terrible beauty and mystery made all the dearer and more sought after by Whitman's sense that the poetic imagination refuses, in this instance, to access abstracted or transcendent beauty through any of the particular 'single object[s]' that comprise the chaotic flotsam and jetsam of life strewn along the shore. Such an imaginative refusal intensifies a reawakened sense of life from a world of dead concepts to a life of process and death.

This insistence upon, and persistence of, the beauty of the ordinary helps make sense of Whitman's claim, in his Preface to the 1855 edition of *Leaves of Grass*, that 'The sea is not surer of the shore or the shore of the sea than he [the Poet] is of the fruition of his and of all perfection and beauty' (Preface, p. 11). In 'As I Ebb'd with the Ocean of Life', Whitman's operatically staged withdrawal of the poetic 'real Me' and seeming failure of the poetic imagination effects an inverted consummation of self and other, noted by Gareth Reeves,[15] through a destructive display of an anatomisation of poetic self amidst the 'trail of drift and debris' (l. 43) of ordinary existence and death. A sense of the beauty of the ordinary, for Whitman, encapsulates all elements of life no matter how painful and once realised is a condition in which 'Nothing can jar him [the Poet] . . . suffering and darkness cannot – death and fear cannot' (Preface, p. 11).

The Centre and Circumference: Dickinson, Self and Nature

Emily Dickinson is no stranger to being a subtly unflinching navigator of human consciousness, its suffering and existential dread. Asked about her poetic influences, Dickinson famously declared that 'For Poets–I have Keats' (*EDL*, p. 404) but, as a poet, she was equally receptive of, and responsive to, the abstractions of Shelley's poetic imagery and thought.[16] When Dickinson pronounces that 'My Business is Circumference' (*EDL*, p. 268) she echoes Shelley's own proclamation, in

A Defence of Poetry, that 'Poetry is . . . at once the centre and circumference of knowledge' (*SPP*, p. 531). In one tightly knit poetic moment of 'There's a Certain Slant of Light', Dickinson captures with economic precision the speaker's metaphysical yearning for and sceptical doubt about the existence of an 'unseen Power' (l. 1) or 'Spirit of Beauty' (l. 13) in Shelley's 'Hymn to Intellectual Beauty'.[17] Through her exquisitely compressed quatrains of 'There's a Certain Slant of Light', Dickinson captures the wonder and awe of the power of nature, of seeing and not seeing a transcendental force at work in the material universe, of an intimately felt psychological experience and the wider perspective beyond a vanishing horizon. An interpenetration of self and world and intermingled light and landscape occurs:

> There's a certain Slant of light,
> Winter Afternoons –
> That oppresses, like the Heft
> Of Cathedral Tunes –
>
> Heavenly Hurt, it gives us –
> We can find no scar,
> But internal difference,
> Where the Meanings, are –
>
> None may teach it – Any –
> 'Tis the Seal Despair –
> An imperial affliction
> Sent us of the Air –
>
> When it comes, the Landscape listens –
> Shadows – hold their breath –
> When it goes, 'tis like the Distance
> On the look of Death –

Dickinson's succinct expression commingles the sacred and the secular, the human and natural world, as well as the external and internal. By the close of the poem the 'Landscape' is both out there in the world intently listening to the revelatory effect of 'a certain Slant of light' and an internalised psychic landscape constituted from 'internal difference'. For Dickinson, nature's revelatory power about the contingency of existence and mortality is freely given and far exceeds those doctrines ('None may teach it') of religious belief which are shackled to the oppressive 'Heft / Of Cathedral Tunes'. Even to the right-minded observer, nature's sublime and revelatory moments are themselves as fleeting as our own lives, occurring only when 'There's a certain Slant of light, / Winter Afternoons', in a specific season, in a certain place, at an appointed time, and when a particular observer's eye captures the effect of a particular ray of 'light'. The pared-down and particular visual and emotional focus of Dickinson's 'There's a Certain Slant of Light' at first seems reinforced by her use of tightly woven quatrains but, preferring nature's lesson to the restrictions of religious doctrine, her lines readily open out into a wider and ever-diminishing perspective – a near-impossible perspective from the edge of existence itself in which observing consciousness (the poem's centre) and observed landscape (the poem's outer circumference) become indivisible from one another.

By the final stanza of 'There's a Certain Slant of Light', shadow and light, sky and earth, sight and sound, internal and external collapse into one another to create the effect of the vanishing horizon. This vanishing point between sky and landscape on certain 'Winter Afternoons' reminds Dickinson of the vastness of 'Distance' (eternity) and, paradoxically, the ever-near proximity (transience) of 'Death' that can manifest itself at any given moment, just as 'a certain Slant of light' can in an instance transform a winter landscape into an inward and outward emblem of metaphysical and material 'Heavenly Hurt'. Such a visual transformation registers the possibility and impossibility of a spiritual afterlife, as well as reckoning with the fragile, fleeting moments of existence that compromise our uncertain mortal existences. For Dickinson, in 'There's a Certain Slant of Light', an encroaching darkness and a potential failure of light confront a conflicted poetic self with the inevitable event of its own demise and hold that tragic final moment in abeyance.

With a less overtly existential note, Dickinson's 'Wild Nights – Wild Nights!' beguiles the reader with a sexually and erotically charged fantasy, which entwines Keatsian sensuousness with Shelleyan abstraction. Through an intense sensuous and sensual luxuriance, Dickinson's lyric commingles sexual desire with abstract metaphysic, raw lust with the refinement of religious sentiment:

> Wild nights – Wild nights!
> Were I with thee,
> Wild nights should be
> Our luxury!
>
> Futile – the Winds –
> To a Heart in port –
> Done with the Compass –
> Done with the Chart!

Rowing in Eden –
Ah, the Sea!
Might I but moor – Tonight –
In Thee!

Dickinson's lyrical appeal, unity and sensual appeal with the entic-
ingly rich repetition of those highly evocative 'Wild nights – Wild
nights!' subtly combines the heady intoxication of the night with the
enchantment of the sea. Yet central to Dickinson's poem is a heart
conflicted, torn between competing sets of desires (sexual and spiritual) as they war within the speaker. A longing for erotic fulfilment
is evident in the speaker's desire (characterised by the conditional
'Were I with thee'), in the first stanza, to be united with those 'Wild
nights – Wild nights!' and the consummated 'luxury' they might
afford. This is a passionately sought-after consummation of physical
and emotional desires, but one that, in the event, is never arrived at.
As the middle section of Dickinson's poem announces, the efforts of
the wind to call the speaker back to the open sea of luxury and desire
are in vain and, ultimately, 'Futile'.

By the final stanza of 'Wild Nights – Wild Nights!', the ocean comes
to represent both that ever-sought yet unconsummated desire and the
reality of the poet-speaker's solitary and isolated state. This isolated
state at port rather than a-sail on the vast ocean is further symbolised by the declaration that as a seafarer the speaker is 'Done with
the Compass – / Done with the Chart!'. For all their intense appeal,
the speaker has never, in actuality, travailed those enchantingly sensuous waters of desire. The religious imagery of 'Rowing in Eden',
like the universalising image of the ocean, elevates physical sexual
desire in Dickinson's poem to a more abstract and rarefied register
and plane. 'Eden' as voyage's end is already irrecoverably lost somewhere in the unattainable past. By the close of 'Wild Nights – Wild
Nights!', the speaker's desire is still keenly felt ('Ah, the Sea!'), but
so, too, is the impossibility of ever realising or fulfilling that desire,
no matter how much the poet-speaker may wish to be moored in the
ocean. Dickinson's speaker is, and always has been, firmly tethered in
the harbourside. Ironically, then, what might at first appear to be a
consummation of the heart's desire in reality turns out to be a confir-
mation of the heart's desolation, isolation and unfulfilled emotional
and spiritual condition.[18]

As in 'Wild Nights – Wild Nights!', Dickinson's poetry frequently
enacts an imaginative and emotional encounter with the world and
its particulars that actively engages with wider existential universal

concerns. One exquisite instance occurs in 'From Cocoon forth a Butterfly', where Dickinson quietly observes of the creature 'Her pretty Parasol be seen / Contracting in a Field' in an image which deliberately commingles what might be seen – captured by the human gaze – and what construes the object of that gaze. The crucial verb is 'Contracting', as its meaning is suggestively twofold: first, the receding, ascending, iris-like patterned 'Parasol' of the butterfly's wing, and, second, the reflex of the human eye. Dickinson's play of verbal meanings relates to questions of what is visible and invisible in 'From Cocoon forth a Butterfly', which culminate in the poem's final image of the effect of the light of 'Sundown' that 'crept – a steady Tide –' to obliterate the 'Afternoon – and Butterfly –' as they (like those 'Men that made the Hay –') are 'Extinguished – in the Sea –'. Dickinson weaves together visual sight with those waves of darkening light and the waving ears of the cornfield through a homonym of 'see' and 'Sea', which imaginatively merges the observed natural scene and the observing subject to cast into doubt our ability to see truly the natural world, whether through visionary sight or our mundane eyes. Dickinson's poetic imaginings dwell in possibilities and impossibilities which, simultaneously and paradoxically, occupy and dissolve the self and world as the Shelleyan 'centre and circumference of knowledge'.

Stevens and the Enigma of Self, Beauty and the World

In a leisurely nautical poem, 'Sailing after Lunch', included in Wallace Stevens's 1936 collection *Ideas of Order*, the modern 'poet's prayer' captures perfectly this Romantic and post- (High) Romantic insistence on the proclaimed necessity and redundancy of Romantic imaginings and their engagement with the beauty of ordinary things: 'The romantic should be here. / The romantic should be there. / It ought to be everywhere. / But the romantic must never remain' (ll. 12–15). Characteristically, Stevens evokes and disavows those pervasive and persistent Romantic presences which, for him, still possess the power to afford momentary snapshots of beauty in the ordinary by lending 'That slight transcendence to the dirty sail' (l. 28). These creative renewals of Romantic inheritances and their imaginative reinventions in the twentieth century provide a riposte to what has been diagnosed as an ailing Romantic 'poetics of disappointment'.[19] Even Stevens, who insists here that the 'romantic must never remain', is willing to concede, in 'The Plain Sense of Things', that the 'absence of imagination had / Itself to be imagined' (ll. 13–14).[20] Poetry and the imagination have, after all, in Stevens's mind, to be 'one of the enlargements of life'.[21] If Whitman found beauties in our ordinary and transient condition, then Stevens recognised in a world without spiritual certainty (even in the funereal macabre of 'The Emperor of Ice-Cream') that 'Death is the mother of all Beauty' ('Sunday Morning', VI, l. 89). To conceive of poetry as the site of ordinary beauty and love, as Stevens writes in his reflections on poetics, *The Necessary Angel*, requires a strenuous imaginative (Romantic or High Romantic) acrobatic 'feat':

> But to be able to see the portal of literature, that is to say: the portal of the imagination, as a scene of normal love and normal beauty is, of itself, a feat of great imagination. (*NA*, p. 155)

On the one hand, what Stevens acknowledges here is the transformative power of the imagination to intensify our understanding of the world and our experience of the world by disclosing the contingent and fictive nature of those constructions – necessary, but competing fictions – that we invent to order reality and our place within that reality. On the other hand, this act of imaginative transformation is a disclosure, a deeper awareness of the way that things are; the way things are as they exist in the ordinary, in the real. But the real, for Stevens, is not an absolute because, as he ventures as his most 'intimidating thesis' in *The Necessary Angel*, 'that absolute fact includes everything that imagination includes' (*NA*, p. 60). Stevens illustrates his claim that 'absolute fact' is subjugated by the imagination with the following:

> For example, if we close our eyes and think of a place where it would be pleasant to spend a holiday, and if there slide across the black eyes, like a setting on stage, a rock that sparkles, a blue sea that lashes, and hemlocks in which the sun can merely fumble, this inevitably demonstrates, since the rock and sea, the wood and sun are those that have been familiar to us in Maine, that much of the world of fact is the equivalent of the world of the imagination, because it looks like it. (*NA*, p. 61)

It follows, then, that 'Poetry is the imagination of life' (*NA*, p. 65), as Stevens claims, because poetic imaginings are one of those 'enlargements of life' that provides a neutral lens – a colourless 'special illumination' – through which, and by the presence of its medium, we can see more intensely the beauty of things merely as they are. Things seen, that is, through the poetic imagination which 'Like light . . . adds nothing, except itself'. Still in High Romantic mode, Stevens comes close to an Emersonian or Shelleyan formulation about the imagination which recognises, as did those Romantics before him, the virtues and perils of a poetic imagining that has the 'power to possess the moment it perceives' (*NA*, p. 61).

One such instance of the Stevensian 'power' of the imagination to 'possess the moment it perceives' occurs in the final two stanzas of 'The Idea of Order at Key West' which, as the poem's title suggests, appeared in 1936 as part of the *Ideas of Order* volume:

> Ramon Fernandez, tell me, if you know,
> Why, when the singing ended and we turned
> Toward the town, tell why the glassy lights,
> The lights in the fishing boats at anchor there,
> As the night descended, tilting in the air,
> Mastered the night and portioned out the sea,
> Fixing emblazoned zones and fiery poles,
> Arranging, deepening, enchanting night.
>
> Oh! Blessed rage for order, pale Ramon,
> The maker's rage to order words of the sea,
> Words of the fragrant portals, dimly-starred,
> And of ourselves and of our origins,
> In ghostlier demarcations, keener sounds. (ll. 44–56)

These lines serve as a coda to the previous stanzas in which the poet-speaker and fellow companion, 'pale' Ramon, have had a chance visual encounter with a figure of a woman, randomly working along the shoreline and singing to herself. The figure of the woman is perceived, simultaneously, in and through a number of possible perspectives of Romantic and post-Romantic imaginings: she is both at one and not at one with the 'dark voice of the sea' (l. 22). From the opening of 'The Idea of Order at Key West' Stevens resists the temptation of pathetic fallacy and insists on a post-Romantic awareness that 'The sea was not a mask. No more was she' (l. 8). The poem actively encourages the separation of the woman's voice from the sound of 'grinding water' (l. 13) – for she 'sang beyond the genius of the sea' (l. 1) – and points to the empty futility of any kind of Romantic metaphor that might embody ('like a body wholly body, fluttering / Its empty sleeves' (ll. 3–4)) a figure or figuration of the spirit of the sea or coastal location. Even then, there is in the 'body wholly body' a self-conscious knowing about the operations of the Romantic imagination and its desire to venerate as something holy ('blessed') and something 'wholly' (complete) the embodied figure of the sea. Such a figure of the sea, unwoven in the moment of its weaving together, both denies and admits Romantic imaginative possibilities into Stevens's 'The Idea of Order at Key West'.

When the woman's 'song' ceases (l. 10), it is immediately substituted by another attempt by human consciousness to make order of the random and chaotic reality. In the absence of the 'song', this alternative mode of perception reconfigures the randomness of the 'glassy lights' of the 'fishing boats' in the harbour, so that they are arranged – deepened, enchanted – and invested with a renewed sense of 'blessed' order and beauty. Like the scattered pinpoints of stars in the night sky, the 'glassy lights' are formed in this moment of perception into constellations that 'mastered the night and portioned out the sea'. Such orderings of our experience of random particulars in reality are born of both a desire to discover some pre-existent 'rage for order' and our desire to order things in the world, to render meaningful (perhaps, in Whitmanesque vein) those 'words of the sea'. By appearing as a coda, the final two stanzas of the poem self-consciously comment on the process of figuration (which both resists and admits Romanticism's imaginative impulses) at work in the earlier sections of the poem. Stevens recognises in practice the fictive nature of all imaginative constructs and interpretations, including (as the poem's title implies) the fictional nature of his own sense of 'The Idea of Order at Key West'. These final few lines of the poem glance wistfully towards those 'Words of the fragrant portals', reminding us of the limitations of all fictional perspectives (Romantic or otherwise) on the world and a reminder, too, that there is something of ourselves and the ordinary which will remain a 'beautiful enigma' beyond, and barely perceptible in, those 'ghostlier demarcations, keener sounds'. These closing lines, as they bid adieu to Keats's own Romantic image of those 'Charmed magic casements, opening on the foam / Of perilous seas, in faery lands forlorn' ('Ode to a Nightingale', ll. 69–70), reinforce Stevens's desire to move beyond a heap of Romantic tropes that, in his words, are persistently 'everywhere' and 'should not remain'.

Those poetic difficulties and insights, dramatised in 'The Idea of Order at Key West', are succinctly stated at the end of Stevens's poem 'The Snow Man', which 'beholds / Nothing that is not there and the nothing that is' (ll. 11–12). We are asked to imagine as both there and not there the 'nothing' or 'no thing' which suggestively, but elusively, implies the presence of some thing or something. Yet whatever that elusive something might be can only be beholden by 'One [that] must have a mind of winter' (l. 1); a mind which is at once a blank (nothing) and an observing, creating consciousness that is something.

Such an observing consciousness which is, simultaneously, an identity and a non-identity approximates the malleable subjectivity of Keats's negatively capable poet. This Keatsian moment in Stevens seemingly permits a perfect union between the dissolving subject and the object of the natural world. For Helen Vendler, Stevens adopts Keats's perspective of the 'third eye' whereby 'In a perfect oneness with nature, the snowman-poet can put himself within the sphere of the universe and can take a celestial vantage point . . . at the heart of creation'.[22] Reminiscent of Dickinson, too, Stevens's self-identification with nature, like all negatively capable imaginings of a fusion of subject and object, points as much to similarities as it does to those differences between self and world. After all, to imagine the dissolution of the self as a non-identity is a position grounded in (or from within) a vantage point of self as identity. If, as in the poetic vision of Blake and Whitman, the general is never beyond the particular, then self (negatively capable or otherwise) does not have to imagine itself into a 'perfect oneness with nature' as each and every self cannot exist, and has never existed, beyond the processes of nature. Notions of critical distance from natural process are illusory because the observer, like Stevens's snowman, is not separate from but a constituent part of the environment that envelops indistinguishably the self (as mind) and the processes of the natural world (as winter).

'Identity', Timothy Morton writes (and Stevens might have added 'world'), 'is always a matter of resemblance.'[23] What haunts 'The Idea of Order at Key West' is Stevens's earlier claim about that other imagined and imaginary coastal location of Maine (at once Maine and any other similar coastal region in the world), where 'much of the world of fact is the equivalent of the world of the imagination, because it looks like it' (*NA*, p. 61). If the 'world of fact' and the 'world of the imagination' resemble one another, it is because of the impossibility of perceiving those objects and things in the world without, at some level, representing them. Even 'The Glass of Water' (in the poem of that name), for Stevens, teaches us that such an ordinary 'object is merely a state' (l. 3) of contradictions which both invites and frustrates imaginative speculations and metaphysics. We are made all the more keenly aware of the beautiful 'refractions' (l. 12) of 'The Glass of Water' – of the thing as it is – as we are made aware of how our creative perception of the object changes it irrecoverably. This complication is all too familiar to Stevens's figure of the musician, 'The Man with the Blue Guitar', who responds to the critical insistence of his audience that 'You do not play things as they are' by claiming, in a bluesy rhythmic set-piece, that 'Things as they are / Are changed upon the blue guitar' (1, ll. 4–6). Stevens elaborates on this problem in a letter, where he observes that the 'trouble is that poetry is largely a matter of transformation' and, as a result, it cannot seize the most ordinary of objects (a comb, slipper or toothbrush) 'without changing it and without concerning oneself with some extreme aspect of it'.[24]

Acts of representation, whether intentionally or not, transfigure 'Things as they are' no matter how ordinary. This difficulty of perception is, Stevens acknowledges in his poetry, a difficulty with the nature of poetic imagination itself which cannot resist finding in the less beautiful that 'slight transcendence to the dirty sail' ('Sailing after Lunch', l. 21), or bringing 'sudden rightnesses' to the twanging of a 'wiry string' ('Of Modern Poetry', ll. 20–1). 'The poem of the act of the mind,' Stevens concludes, in 'Of Modern Poetry', can find satisfaction, even beauty, in the figure 'of a man skating, a woman dancing, / a woman combing' (ll. 26–7). In these lines Stevens asks, with one of the last great Romantics, by alluding to W. B. Yeats's 'Among School Children', whether it is ever possible to disentangle the act of perception from the act of representation, for 'How can we know the dancer from the dance?'[25] This question alone both stimulates and productively vexes Romantic and post-Romantic negotiations with the beautiful which, ironically, turn out to be every bit as elusive, and as difficult, as those negotiations with the ordinary. Friedrich Nietzsche, the philosopher-poet who historically, at least, is an intermediary between the poetics of Whitman and Stevens, clarifies the difficulty of these negotiations:

> Man believes the world itself is filled with beauty – he *forgets* that it is he who has created it. He alone has bestowed beauty upon the world – alas! only a very human, all too human beauty . . .[26]

Nietzsche's sense of beauty is, for the listener of Stevens's 'The Man with the Blue Guitar', echoed in the musician's playing of 'A tune beyond us, yet ourselves' (1, l. 8). Encounters between the post-Romantic culture and Romanticism are often marked by a feeling of dispossession, a self-aware absence of authenticity and an unfulfilled longing. This type of angst characterises the poetics of Dickinson, Whitman and Stevens. Stevens's poetry offers one instance, in 'The Death of a Soldier', of how an aphoristic style achieves a Romantic lyrical unity of its own even as it subverts and makes strange a Romantic credo that once extolled lyric beauty in art and nature. Stevens casts a sceptical eye over the kaleidoscopic effect of temporal modes, in Keats's own 'To Autumn', which dissolves harvesting activities into the eternity of nature and the annual cycle of the seasons into the passage of a single day. For Stevens, the contraction of life and expectation of death is a symbiotic process that occurs in, and is encapsulated by, the simile 'As in the season of autumn'. Reserving the more Shelleyan verb 'falls' for the deceased soldier (and not the tumbling leaves of the season),[27] Stevens repeats the simile in the third stanza, where the death of a soldier is 'absolute and without memorial'.

Neither natural processes nor the fragility of beauty offer a memorial or transcendental consolation in the face of death, because both nature and beauty are perpetually open to the possibility of the inexorable reality of death of the self.[28] Romantic ideals can only be affirmed if they are redacted into succinct instances of the quotidian. Such post-Romantic acts of redaction constitute in themselves an extension of Romanticism's investment in the fragmentary and the everyday.

Romantic inheritors themselves, Whitman and Dickinson would have appreciated Stevens's chiasmic assertion that 'The enigmatical / Beauty of each beautiful enigma // Becomes amassed in a total double-thing' ('Ordinary Evening in New Haven', 10, ll. 165–7). As such the vital double gesture of the totality of the 'double-thing' represents a unity and disparity, a congruence between the observer and the observed which, echoing Wordsworth, both half-creates and half-perceives reality.[29] For post-Romantic poetics, this enigmatic 'double-thing', comprising the sacred and the profane, perceived and created, the real and non-real, the something and nothing, constitutes our elusory and inescapable sense of self, beauty, death and nature. This ineffable, though very real, sense of self and nature is succinctly expressed in the innumerable apertures and mirrored facets of Stevens's 'double-thing' and testifies to how such involutions of the transatlantic imagination can transform, yet never wholly exorcise, those Romantic negotiations between synchronously self-assertive and self-dissolving fictions of subjectivity and nature.

Notes

1. Wallace Stevens's phrase is taken from the poem of that title; see *Wallace Stevens: Collected Poems* (London: Faber, 1984), p. 502. See Markus Poetzsch, *Visionary Dreariness: Readings in Romanticism's Quotidian Sublime* (New York: Routledge, 2006).

2. Stanley Cavell, *In Quest of the Ordinary: Lines of Skepticism and Romanticism* (1998; Chicago: University of Chicago Press, 2004), p. 9.

3. Stanley Cavell, *Conditions Handsome and Unhandsome: The Constitution of Emersonian Perfectionism* (Chicago: University of Chicago Press, 1990), p. 21.

4. 'Poem of Many in One' (ll. 130–2) first appeared in *Leaves of Grass* (1856) and later appeared in the 1867 edition under the title 'As I Sat Alone by Blue Ontario's Shore'. See *Walt Whitman: The Complete Poems*, ed. Francis Murphy (Harmondsworth: Penguin, 1996), p. 826.

5. For an alternative view see D. J. Moores's reading of Wordsworth and Whitman as sharing a similar scientific and mystic vision, in *Mystical Discourse: A Transatlantic Bridge* (Leuven: Peeters, 2006), pp. 79–81.

6. Compare with Vivian R. Pollak's view that the blade of grass becomes the child. See Pollak, *The Erotic Whitman* (Berkeley: University of California Press, 2000), p. 110.

7. Quoted in Michael O'Neill, *The All-Sustaining Air: Romantic Legacies and Renewals in British, American, and Irish Poetry since 1900* (Oxford: Oxford University Press, 2007), p. 132. Hereafter *ASA*.

8. Timothy Morton offers an account of Blake's prophetic mode as a form of ecomimesis which seeks to convey a sense of 'knowledge that is somehow imprinted in the real' (p. 149). See Morton, *EWN*, pp. 148–9.

9. Compare with David Michael Hertz's reading. See Hertz, *Angels of Reality: Emersonian Unfoldings in Wright, Stevens, and Ives* (Carbondale: Southern Illinois University Press, 1993), pp. 44–5. For an account of the pastoral mode in Stevens, especially in relation to 'Credences of Summer', see also Malcolm Woodland, *Wallace Stevens and the Apocalyptic Mode* (Iowa City: University of Iowa Press, 2009), pp. 103–33.

10. Walt Whitman, Preface, *Leaves of Grass* (1855), ed. and intro. Malcolm Cowley (1976; Harmondsworth: Penguin, 1985), p. 11.

11. Phrase borrowed from Wordsworth's subtitle for *The Prelude*.

12. For an influential account of Whitman as a becoming poet see Paul Zweig, *Walt Whitman: The Making of the Poet* (New York: Basic, 1984).

13. See my account of Keats's imaginative influence on 'Out of the Cradle Endlessly Rocking' in Chapter 2, pp. 32–4.

14. See O'Neill, *ASA*, p. 187.

15. Gareth Reeves, 'Songs of the Self: Berryman's Whitman', *Romanticism* 14.1 (2008): 47–56.

16. See my discussion of Dickinson and Keats in Chapter 2, pp. 34–5.

17. Joanne Feit Diehl rightly observes that Dickinson was drawn to Shelley's images that forged a connection between physical world and abstract thought as a source for her own poetic structures and images to dramatise the 'life of the self' (p. 158). Additionally, Diehl notes that Dickinson

would have known Shelley through the edition printed as *Shelley: The Poetic Works* (Philadelphia: Grissy and Markley, 1853). See Diehl, *Dickinson and the Romantic Imagination* (Princeton: Princeton University Press, 1981), p. 137. Hereafter *DRI*.

18. This sense of separation, as Joanne Feit Diehl notes, is heightened by Dickinson's allusion to Shelley's poem 'Good-Night'. See Diehl, *DRI*, p. 159.

19. Laura Quinney, *The Poetics of Disappointment: Wordsworth to Ashbery* (Charlottesville: University of Virginia Press, 1999), p. 103. For a further account of Romantic presences in twentieth-century literature see my 'Introduction: The Persistence of Romantic Presences', in *Romantic Presences in the Twentieth Century*, ed. Mark Sandy (Farnham: Ashgate, 2012), pp. 1–12.

20. My following account of the ordinary and the beautiful in Stevens's poetry is indebted to the lucid, succinct and subtle account offered by Simon Critchley of how Stevens's 'poetry brings to us the [calming] realisation that things merely are' (p. iii). See Critchley, *Things Merely Are: Philosophy in the Poetry of Wallace Stevens* (London: Routledge, 2005).

21. Wallace Stevens, *The Necessary Angel: Essays on Reality and Imagination* (New York: Knopf, 1951), p. viii. Hereafter *NA*. All subsequent quotations are from this edition.

22. See Helen Vendler, *On Extended Wings: Wallace Stevens' Longer Poems* (Cambridge, MA: Harvard University Press, 1969), p. 283. Hereafter *OEW*.

23. See Timothy Morton's discussion of subjectivity, self and identity and theoretical models that press home too strongly the critical distance between the observing self and the natural world, *EWN*, p. 166; pp. 160–9.

24. Wallace Stevens, *Letters of Wallace Stevens*, ed. Holly Stevens, foreword Richard Howard (1966; Berkeley: University of California Press, 1989), p. 643.

25. W. B. Yeats, 'Among School Children', in *W. B. Yeats: The Major Works*, ed. Edward Larrissy (1997; Oxford: Oxford University Press, 2001), p. 115, l. 64. For a recent and persuasive account of Yeats as a Romantic legatee see Madeleine Callaghan, '"Strong Ghosts": Romantic Presences in Yeats's Poetry', in Sandy, *RPT*, pp. 27–42.

26. Friedrich Nietzsche, *Twilight of the Idols/The Anti-Christ*, trans. R. J. Hollingdale, intro. Michael Tanner (1968; Harmondsworth: Penguin, 1990), [19], p. 89. Numbers in square brackets refer to section numbers. For a detailed account of Nietzsche's influence on Stevens's formative poetry see Bobby Joe Leggett, *Early Stevens: The Nietzschean Intertext* (Durham, NC: Duke University Press, 1993).

27. Shelley's 'Ode to the West Wind' captures the hectic commotion of the leaves driven by the wind in an Italian autumn and finally describes the curbed imaginative aspiration of the poet-speaker as 'I fall upon the thorns of life' (l. 54).

28. For a detailed sense of how 'Beauty is the possibility of death' (p. 162) see Timothy Morton, 'Beauty Is Death', in *The Persistence of Beauty: Victorians to the Moderns*, ed. Michael O'Neill, Mark Sandy and Sarah Wootton (London: Chatto, 2015), pp. 151–62.
29. See Helen Vendler, who connects Stevens's image of the 'double-thing' with Wordsworth's observation in *Tintern Abbey* (ll. 107–8), *OEW*, pp. 278–9.

Bibliography

Aarons, Victoria. Ed. *The Cambridge Companion to Saul Bellow*. Cambridge: Cambridge University Press, 2017.

Alsen, Eberhard. Ed. *The New Romanticism: A Collection of Critical Essays*. New York: Garland, 2000.

Arsić, Branka. *Bird Relics: Grief and Vitalism in Thoreau*. Cambridge, MA: Harvard University Press, 2016.

Averill, James H. *Wordsworth and the Poetry of Human Suffering*. Ithaca: Cornell University Press, 1980.

Baker, Carlos. *The Echoing Green: Romanticism, Modernism, and the Phenomena of Transference Poetry*. Princeton: Princeton University Press, 1984.

Barker, Juliet. *Wordsworth: A Life*. London: Viking, 2000.

Barthes, Roland. *Roland Barthes by Roland Barthes*. Berkeley: University of California Press, 1994.

Bellow, Saul. 'Boston Lecture'. 9 September 1993. Series III: Writings 1. 'Public Speaking and Engagements'. Box 90. Folder 5. Saul Bellow Papers. Special Collections Research Center, University of Chicago.

Bellow, Saul. Draft of 'A World Too Much with Us'. Holograph draft (c. 1975). Series III: Writings 2. 'Essays and Articles'. Box 93. Folder 5. Saul Bellow Papers. Special Collections Research Center, University of Chicago.

Bellow, Saul. 'Eulogy for Allan Bloom'. 9 October 1992. Photocopied typescript. Series III: Writings 1. 'Public Speaking and Engagements'. Box 90. Folder 2. Saul Bellow Papers. Special Collections Research Center, University of Chicago.

Bellow, Saul. *Herzog*. Harmondsworth: Penguin, 1965.

Bellow, Saul. *Humboldt's Gift*. 1975; Harmondsworth: Penguin, 2007.

Bellow, Saul. *Mr Sammler's Planet*. 1970; Harmondsworth: Penguin, 1972.

Bellow, Saul. *Ravelstein*. Harmondsworth: Penguin, 2000.

Bellow, Saul. *Saul Bellow: Letters*. Ed. Benjamin Taylor. Harmondsworth: Viking-Penguin, 2010.

Bellow, Saul. *Seize the Day*. 1956; Harmondsworth: Penguin, 1988.

Bellow, Saul. 'A World Too Much with Us'. *Critical Inquiry* 2 (1975): 1–9.

Bennett, Andrew. *Wordsworth Writing*. Cambridge: Cambridge University Press, 2007.

Berman, Ronald. *The Great Gatsby and Fitzgerald's World of Ideas*. Tuscaloosa: University of Alabama Press, 1997.

Berman, Ronald. *The Great Gatsby and Modern Times*. Urbana and Chicago: Illinois University Press, 1996.

Berman, Ronald. '*The Great Gatsby* and the Twenties'. In *The Cambridge Companion to F. Scott Fitzgerald*. Ed. Ruth Prigozy. Cambridge: Cambridge University Press, 2002, pp. 79–94.

Berman, Ronald. *Modernity and Progress: Fitzgerald, Hemingway, Orwell*. Tuscaloosa: University of Alabama Press, 2005.

Bidney, Martin. 'Creating a Feminist-Communitarian Romanticism in *Beloved*: Toni Morrison's New Uses for Blake, Keats, and Wordsworth'. *Papers on Language and Literature* 36.3 (2000): 271–301.

Bidney, Martin. 'Faulkner's Variations on Romantic Themes: Blake, Wordsworth, Byron, and Shelley in *Light in August*'. *The Mississippi Quarterly* 38.3 (1985): 277–86.

Bidney, Martin. *Patterns of Epiphany: From Wordsworth to Tolstoy, Pater, and Barrett Browning*. Carbondale: Southern Illinois University Press, 1997.

Blake, William. *Blake's Poetry and Designs: The Authoritative Texts*. Ed. Mary Lynn Johnson and John E. Grant. New York: Norton, 1979.

Blake, William. *William Blake's Writings*. 2 vols. Ed. G. E. Bentley. Oxford: Clarendon, 1978.

Bloom, Harold. *The Anxiety of Influence: A Theory of Poetry*. 1973; Oxford: Oxford University Press, 1975.

Bloom, Harold. Ed. *Modern Critical Views of F. Scott Fitzgerald*. Bloom's Modern Critical Views Series. New York: Chelsea, 2013.

Bornstein, George. *Romantic and the Modern: Revaluations of Literary Tradition*. Pittsburgh: University of Pittsburgh Press, 1977.

Braham, Jeanne. *A Sort of Columbus: The American Voyages of Saul Bellow's Fiction*. Athens: Ohio University Press, 1984.

Bridgwater, Patrick. *Nietzsche in Anglosaxony*. Leicester: Leicester University Press, 1972.

Brooks, Cleanth. *William Faulkner: Toward Yoknapatawpha and Beyond*. Baton Rouge: Louisiana State University Press, 1990.

Brooks, Cleanth. *William Faulkner: The Yoknapatawpha Country*. Baton Rouge: Louisiana State University Press, 1991.

Bruccoli, Matthew J. *The Composition of 'Tender is the Night': A Study of the Manuscripts*. Pittsburgh: Pittsburgh University Press, 1963.

Bryer, Jackson R., Ruth Prigozy and Milton R. Stern. Eds. *F. Scott Fitzgerald in the Twenty-First Century*. Tuscaloosa: University of Alabama Press, 2003.

Buell, Lawrence. *The Environmental Imagination: Thoreau, Nature Writing, and the Formation of American Culture*. Cambridge, MA: Belknap-Harvard University Press, 1995.

Burke, Edmund. *A Philosophical Enquiry into the Origin of our Ideas of the Sublime and Beautiful*. Ed. Adam Phillips. Oxford: Oxford University Press, 1992.

Burroughs, Catherine B. 'Keats's Lamian Legacy: Romance and the Performance of Gender in *The Beautiful and Damned*'. In *F. Scott Fitzgerald: New Perspectives*. Ed. Jackson R. Bryer, Alan Margolies and Ruth Prigozy. Athens: University of Georgia Press, 2000, pp. 51–62.

Byron, George Gordon. *Lord Byron: The Major Works*. Ed. Jerome J. McGann. Oxford: Oxford University Press, 2008.

Byron, George Gordon. *The Works of Lord Byron, in verse and prose, including letters, journals, etc. With a sketch of his life*. New York: George Dearborn, 1836.

Calvino, Italo. *Invisible Cities*. Trans. William Weaver. London: Vintage, 2001.

Campbell, Jeff. 'Bellow's Intimations of Immortality: *Henderson the Rain King*'. *Studies in the Novel* 1 (1969): 323–33.

Cavell, Stanley. *Conditions Handsome and Unhandsome: The Constitution of Emersonian Perfectionism*. Chicago: University of Chicago Press, 1990.

Cavell, Stanley. *In Quest of the Ordinary: Lines of Skepticism and Romanticism*. 1998; Chicago: University of Chicago Press, 2004.

Chalmer, Alexander. *The Works of the English Poets: From Chaucer to Cowper*. 21 vols. London: J. Johnson, 1810.

Chavkin, Allan. 'Bellow and English Romanticism'. In *Saul Bellow in the 1980s: A Collection of Critical Essays*. Ed. Gloria L. Cronin and L. H. Goldman. East Lansing: Michigan State University Press, 1989, pp. 67–79.

Chavkin, Allan. '*Humboldt's Gift* and the Romantic Imagination'. *Philological Quarterly* 62 (1983): 1–19.

Chavkin, Allan. 'The Romantic Imagination of Saul Bellow'. In *English Romanticism and Modern Fiction*. Ed. Allan Chavkin. New York: AMS, 1993, pp. 113–38.

Chavkin, Allan. *The Secular Imagination: The Continuity of the Romantic Tradition in Wordsworth and Keats in Stevens, Faulkner, Roethke, and Bellow*. Dissertation. University of Illinois, Urbana-Champaign, 1977.

Cladis, Mark S. 'Radical Romanticism: Democracy, Religion, and the Environmental Imagination'. *Soundings: An Interdisciplinary Journal* 97.1 (2014): 21–49.

Clark, Timothy. *Cambridge Introduction to Literature and the Environment*. Cambridge: Cambridge University Press, 2011.

Cohen, Leah Hager. 'Point to Return'. Review of Toni Morrison. *Home*. *The New York Times*. 17 May 2012.

Coleridge, Samuel Taylor. *Biographia Literaria; or Biographical Sketches of my Life and Work*. 2 parts, vol 7. In *The Collected Works of Samuel Taylor Coleridge*. Ed. James Engell and Walter Jackson Bate. London: Routledge & Kegan Paul, 1983.

Coleridge, Samuel Taylor. *Coleridge's Poems*. 1912. 2 vols. Ed. E. H. Coleridge. Oxford: Oxford University Press, 2000.

Coleridge, Samuel Taylor, Percy Bysshe Shelley and John Keats. *The Poetical Works of Coleridge, Shelley, and Keats in One Volume*. Philadelphia: J. Grieg, 1832.

Cologne-Brookes, Gavin, Neil Sammells and David Trimms. Eds. *Writing and America*. London: Longman, 1996.

Critchley, Simon. *Things Merely Are: Philosophy in the Poetry of Wallace Stevens*. London: Routledge, 2005.

Curran, Stuart. *Poetic Form and British Romanticism*. New York: Oxford University Press, 1986.

D'Avanzo, Mario L. *A Cloud of Other Poets: Robert Frost and the Romantics*. Lanham: University Press of America, 1991.

Darling, Marsha. 'In the Realm of Responsibility: A Conversation with Toni Morrison'. *Women's Review of Books* 5 (1978): 5–6.

de Man, Paul. *The Rhetoric of Romanticism*. New York: Columbia University Press, 1984.

Derrida, Jacques. *Spectres of Marx: The State of the Debt, the Work of Mourning, and the New International*. Trans. Peggy Kamuf. Intro. Bernard Magnus and Stephen Cullenberg. New York: Routledge, 1994.

Dickinson, Emily. *Emily Dickinson: The Complete Poems*. 2nd edn. Ed. Thomas H. Johnson. London: Faber, 1975.

Dickinson, Emily. *The Letters of Emily Dickinson*. Ed. Thomas H. Johnson and Theodora W. Ward. Cambridge, MA: Belknap, 1958.

Dickstein, Morris. *A Mirror in the Roadway: Literature and the Real World*. Princeton: Princeton University Press, 2005.

Diehl, Joanne Feit. *Dickinson and the Romantic Imagination*. Princeton: Princeton University Press, 1981.

Donaldson, Scott. *Hemingway vs Fitzgerald: The Rise and Fall of a Literary Friendship*. London: Murray, 2000.

Emerson, Ralph Waldo. *The Collected Works of Ralph Waldo Emerson: Nature, Addresses, and Lectures*. Vol. 1. Ed. Alfred Riggs Ferguson, Joseph Slater and Joseph Ferguson Carr. Intro. Robert E. Spiller. Cambridge, MA: Belknap-Harvard, 1971.

Emerson, Ralph Waldo. *The Collected Works of Ralph Waldo Emerson: Society and Solitude.* Vol. 8. Ed. Douglas Emory Wilson. Intro. Ronald A. Bosco. Cambridge, MA: Harvard University Press, 2010.

Emerson, Ralph Waldo. *The Complete Prose Works of Ralph Waldo Emerson.* London: Ward, Lock, and Co., 1803.

Emerson, Ralph Waldo. *The Complete Works of Ralph Waldo Emerson: Essays First Series.* Vol. 2. Ed. Alfred R. Ferguson and Jean Ferguson Carr. Historical intro. Joseph Slater and textual intro. Jean Ferguson Carr. Cambridge, MA: Belknap Press, 1979.

Emerson, Ralph Waldo. *The Complete Works of Ralph Waldo Emerson: Essays Second Series.* Vol. 3. Ed. Alfred R. Ferguson and Jean Ferguson Carr. Historical intro. Joseph Slater and textual intro. Jean Ferguson Carr. Cambridge, MA: Belknap Press, 1983.

Emerson, Ralph Waldo. *The Portable Emerson.* Ed. Carl Bode and Malcolm Cowley. Harmondsworth: Viking-Penguin, 1981.

Emerson, Ralph Waldo. *The Topical Notebooks of Ralph Waldo Emerson.* Vol. 2. Ed. Ronald A. Bosco. Intro. Ralph H. Orth. Columbia: University of Missouri Press, 1993.

Faggen, Robert. *Robert Frost and the Challenge of Darwin.* Ann Arbor: University of Michigan Press, 2001.

Fargnoli, A. Nicholas, Michael Golay and W. Hamblin. *A Critical Companion to William Faulkner: A Literary Reference to his Life and Work.* New York: Infobase, 2008.

Faulkner, William. *Light in August.* 1932; London: Picador, 1991.

Faulkner, William. *The Portable William Faulkner.* Ed. Malcolm Cowley. 1948; London: Penguin-Viking, 1977.

Faulkner, William. *The Sound and the Fury.* 1929; London: Picador, 1993.

Faulkner Wells, Dean. *Ghosts of Rowan Oak: William Faulkner's Ghost Stories for Children.* Oxford, MS: Yoknapatawpha, 1980.

Ferguson, Rebecca Hope. *Rewriting Black Identities: Transition and Exchange in the Novels of Toni Morrison.* Brussels: Lang, 2007.

Fitzgerald, F. Scott. *The Beautiful and Damned.* Intro. Geoff Dyer. 1922; Harmondsworth: Penguin, 2004.

Fitzgerald, F. Scott. *The Collected Short Stories of F. Scott Fitzgerald.* Harmondsworth: Penguin, 1986.

Fitzgerald, F. Scott. *The Great Gatsby.* 1925; Harmondsworth: Penguin, 2006.

Fitzgerald, F. Scott. *The Letters of F. Scott Fitzgerald.* Ed. Andrew Turnbull. Harmondsworth: Penguin, 1968.

Fitzgerald, F. Scott. *The Stories of F. Scott Fitzgerald: The Crack-Up with Other Pieces and Stories.* Vol. 2. Harmondsworth: Penguin, 1965.

Fitzgerald, F. Scott. *Tender is the Night.* 1934; Harmondsworth: Penguin, 1986.

Fitzgerald, F. Scott. *This Side of Paradise*. Ed. and intro. Patrick O'Donnell. 1920; Harmondsworth: Penguin, 2000.

Fosso, Kurt. *Buried Communities: Wordsworth and the Bonds of Mourning*. Albany: State University of New York Press, 2004.

Fowler, Doreen. *Faulkner: The Return of the Repressed*. Charlottesville: University of Virginia Press, 2001.

Fredrickson, Michael. 'A Note on "The Idiot Boy" as a Possible Source for *The Sound and the Fury*'. *Minnesota Review* 6 (1966): 368–70.

Frost, Robert. *The Collected Poems of Robert Frost*. Ed. Edward Connery Lathem. London: Vintage, 2001.

Frost, Robert. *The Collected Prose of Robert Frost*. Ed. Mark Richardson. Cambridge, MA: Belknap-Harvard University Press, 2007.

Fry, Paul H. *Wordsworth and the Poetry of What We Are*. New Haven: Yale University Press, 2008.

Fuchs, Daniel. *Saul Bellow: Vision and Revision*. Madison: University of Wisconsin Press, 1974.

Fultz, Lucille P. *Toni Morrison: Playing with Difference*. Urbana: University of Illinois Press, 2003.

Garrard, Greg. *Ecocriticism*. London: Routledge, 2004.

Gifford, Terry. *Pastoral*. London: Routledge, 1999.

Gittings, Robert. *John Keats*. 1968; Harmondsworth: Penguin, 2001.

Gravil, Richard. *Romantic Dialogues: Anglo-American Continuities, 1776–1862*. New York: St. Martin's, 2000.

Greenham, David. *Emerson's Transatlantic Romanticism*. London: Palgrave Macmillan, 2012.

Grube, John. '*Tender is the Night*: Keats and Scott Fitzgerald'. *Dalhousie Review* 45 (1964): 433–40.

Gwynn, Frederick Landis and Joseph Leo Blotner. Eds. *Faulkner in the University*. Charlottesville: University of Virginia Press, 1959.

Halliwell, Martin. *Images of Idiocy: The Figure of the Idiot in Modern Fiction and Film*. London: Routledge, 2016.

Harper, Gordon Lloyd. 'The Art of Fiction: Saul Bellow'. *Paris Review* 9 (1966): 49–73.

Hartman, Geoffrey H. *The Unremarkable Wordsworth*. Foreword D. G. Marshall. Minneapolis: University of Minnesota Press, 1987.

Heinze, Denise. *The Dilemma of 'Double-Consciousness': Toni Morrison's Novels*. Athens: University of Georgia Press, 1993.

Hemingway, Andrew and Allan Wallach. Eds. *Transatlantic Romanticism: British and American Art and Literature, 1790–1860*. Amherst: University of Massachusetts Press, 2015.

Hertz, David Michael. *Angels of Reality: Emersonian Unfoldings in Wright, Stevens, and Ives*. Carbondale: Southern Illinois University Press, 1993.

Hollander, John. *The Figure of Echo: A Mode of Allusion in Milton and After*. Berkeley: University of California Press, 1981.

Hook, Andrew. *F. Scott Fitzgerald: A Literary Life*. London: Palgrave Macmillan, 2002.

Housman, A. E. *A Shropshire Lad and Other Poems*. Ed. Archie Burnett. Intro. Nick Laird. Afterword Jack Sparrow. Harmondsworth: Penguin, 2014.

Hyland, Peter. *Saul Bellow*. Macmillan Modern Novelists Series. London: Macmillan, 1992.

Jacobus, Mary. *Romantic Things: A Tree, a Rock, a Cloud*. Chicago: University of Chicago Press, 2012.

Kawash, Samira. 'Haunted Houses, Sinking Ships: Race, Architecture, and Identity in *Beloved* and *Middle Passage*'. *The New Centennial Review* 1.3 (2001): 67–87.

Keane, Patrick J. *Emerson, Romanticism, and Intuitive Reason: The Transatlantic 'Light of All Our Day'*. Columbia: University of Missouri Press, 2005.

Keats, John. *The Letters of John Keats 1814–1821*. 2 vols. Ed. Hyder Rollins. Cambridge, MA: Harvard University Press, 1958.

Keats, John. *The Poems of John Keats*. Ed. Jack Stillinger. 1978; Cambridge, MA: Harvard University Press, 1979.

Kerridge, Richard. 'Environmentalism and Ecocriticism'. In *Literary Theory and Criticism: An Oxford Guide*. Ed. Patricia Waugh. Oxford: Oxford University Press, 2006, pp. 530–43.

Kolodny, Annette. *The Lay of the Land: Metaphor as History and Experience in American Life and Letters*. Chapel Hill: University of North Carolina Press, 1975.

Kuehl, John. *F. Scott Fitzgerald: A Study of the Short Fiction*. Twayne's Studies in Short Fiction. Series 22. Boston: Hall, 1991.

Leader, Zachary. *The Life of Saul Bellow: Love and Strife 1965–2005*. London: Cape, 2019.

Leavis, F. R. *Revaluation: Tradition and Development in English Poetry*. 1936; Harmondsworth: Penguin, 1964.

Leggett, Bobby Joe. *Early Stevens: The Nietzschean Intertext*. Durham, NC: Duke University Press, 1993.

Lehan, Richard D. *F. Scott Fitzgerald and the Craft of Fiction*. Carbondale: Southern Illinois University Press, 1966.

Lika, Foteini. *Roidis and the Borrowed Muse: British Historiography, Fiction and Satire in Pope Joan*. Newcastle: Cambridge Scholars, 2018.

Loftus, Margaret Frances. 'John Keats in the Works of F. Scott Fitzgerald'. *KIYO: Studies in English Literature* 7 (1972): 17–26.

Macall, Dan. '"The Self-Same Song that Found a Path": Keats and *The Great Gatsby*'. *American Literature* 42 (1971): 521–30.

McGowan, Philip. 'Reading Fitzgerald Reading Keats'. In *Twenty-First-Century Readings of 'Tender is the Night'*. Ed. William Blazek and Laura Rattray. Liverpool: Liverpool University Press, 2007, pp. 204–20.

Mack, Michael. *Disappointment: From Spinoza to Contemporary Literature*. London: Bloomsbury, 2020.

McKusick, James C. *Green Writing: Romanticism and Ecology*. New York: St. Martin's, 2000.

McSweeney, Kerry. *The Language of the Senses: Sensory-Perceptual Dynamics in Wordsworth, Coleridge, Thoreau, Whitman, and Dickinson*. Liverpool: Liverpool University Press, 1998.

Majdiak, David. 'The Romantic Self and *Henderson the Rain King*'. *Bucknell Review* 19 (1971): 125–46.

Manning, Susan. *Poetics of Character: Transatlantic Encounters 1700–1900*. Cambridge: Cambridge University Press, 2013.

Mantel, Hilary. 'How Sorrow Became Complete'. Review of Toni Morrison. *A Mercy*. *The Guardian*. 8 November 2008.

Marvell, Andrew. *The Complete Poems: Andrew Marvell*. Ed. Elizabeth Story Donno. Harmondsworth: Penguin, 1987.

Meehan, Sean Ross. 'Ecology and Imagination: Emerson, Thoreau, and the Nature Metonymy'. *Criticism* 55.2 (2013): 299–329.

Meindl, Dieter. 'Romantic Idealism and *The Wild Palms*'. In *William Faulkner and Idealism*. Ed. Michael Gresset and S. J. Patrick Samway. Jackson: University Press of Mississippi, 1983, pp. 86–94.

Millgate, Michael. *The Achievement of William Faulkner*. London: Random, 1966.

Minter, David L. Ed. *Twentieth-Century Interpretations of 'Light in August'*. Englewood Cliffs, NJ: Prentice Hall, 1969.

Monckton Milnes, Richard. Ed. *Life, Letters, and Literary Remains of John Keats*. London: Moxon, 1848.

Monterio, George. 'James Gatz and John Keats'. *Fitzgerald/Hemingway Annual* (1972): 291–4.

Moores, D. J. *Mystical Discourse: A Transatlantic Bridge*. Leuven: Peeters, 2006.

Morrison, Toni. *Beloved*. London: Picador-Pan, 1988.

Morrison, Toni. *Home*. London: Vintage, 2012.

Morrison, Toni. 'Memory, Creation, and Writing'. *Thought* 59.235 (1984): 385–90.

Morrison, Toni. *A Mercy*. London: Chatto, 2008.

Morrison, Toni. *The Origin of Others*. The Charles Eliot Norton Lecture. 2016. Foreword Ta-Neshisi Coates. Cambridge, MA: Harvard University Press, 2017.

Morrison, Toni. *Playing in the Dark: Whiteness and the Literary Imagination*. Cambridge, MA: Harvard University Press, 1992.

Morton, Timothy. 'Beauty Is Death'. In *The Persistence of Beauty: Victorians to the Moderns*. Ed. Michael O'Neill, Mark Sandy and Sarah Wootton. London: Chatto, 2015, pp. 151–62.

Morton, Timothy. *The Ecological Thought*. Cambridge, MA: Harvard University Press, 2010.

Morton, Timothy. *Ecology without Nature: Rethinking Environmental Aesthetics*. Cambridge, MA: Harvard University Press, 2007.

Nicol, Kathryn and Jennifer Terry. Eds. *MELUS* 36.2 (2011). Special Issue on Toni Morrison: New Directions.

Nietzsche, Friedrich. *Beyond Good and Evil*. Trans. R. J. Hollingdale. Harmondsworth: Penguin, 1990.

Nietzsche, Friedrich. *The Gay Science*. Trans. and intro. Walter Kaufmann. New York: Vintage-Random, 1974.

Nietzsche, Friedrich. *Human All-Too Human: A Book for Free Spirits*. Trans. R. J. Hollingdale. Intro. Richard Schacht. Cambridge: Cambridge University Press, 1996.

Nietzsche, Friedrich. *Twilight of the Idols/The Anti-Christ*. Trans. R. J. Hollingdale. Intro. Michael Tanner. 1968; Harmondsworth: Penguin, 1990.

Nietzsche, Friedrich. *The Will to Power*. Trans. Walter Kaufmann and R. J. Hollingdale. 3 vols. New York: Vintage, 1968.

Nilsen, Helge N. 'Saul Bellow and Transcendentalism: From "The Victim" to "Herzog"'. *College Language Association* 30.3 (1987): 307–27.

Nowlin, Michael. 'Toni Morrison's *Jazz* and Racial Dreams of the American Writer'. *American Literature* 71.1 (1999): 151–74.

O'Neill, Michael. *The All-Sustaining Air: Romantic Legacies and Renewals in British, American, and Irish Poetry since 1900*. Oxford: Oxford University Press, 2007.

O'Neill, Michael. Ed. *Keats in Context*. Cambridge: Cambridge University Press, 2017.

O'Neill, Michael. *Shelleyan Reimaginings and Influence: New Relations*. Oxford: Oxford University Press, 2019.

O'Neill, Michael and Anthony Howe, eds, with the assistance of Madeleine Callaghan. *The Oxford Handbook of Percy Bysshe Shelley*. Oxford: Oxford University Press, 2013.

Page, Philip. 'Circularity in Toni Morrison's *Beloved*'. Women Writers Issue of *African American Review* 26.1 (1992): 31–9.

Pauly, Thomas H. 'Gatsby as Gangster'. *Journal of American Fiction* 21.2 (1993): 225–36.

Plath, Sylvia. *Collected Poems*. London: Faber, 1981.

Poetzsch, Markus. *Visionary Dreariness: Readings in Romanticism's Quotidian Sublime*. New York: Routledge, 2006.

Pollak, Vivian R. *The Erotic Whitman*. Berkeley: University of California Press, 2000.

Priddy, Ann. *Bloom's How to Write about William Faulkner*. Intro. Harold Bloom. New York: Infobase, 2010.

Putzel, Max. *Genius of Place: William Faulkner's Triumphant Beginnings*. Baton Rouge: Louisiana State University Press, 1985.

Quayum, M. A. *Saul Bellow and American Transcendentalism*. New York: Lang, 2004.

Quinney, Laura. *The Poetics of Disappointment: Wordsworth to Ashbery*. Charlottesville: University of Virginia Press, 1999.

Rajan, Tilottama. 'Displacing Post-Structuralism: Romanticism after Paul de Man'. *Studies in Romanticism* 24.4 (1991): 451–74.

Ravinthiran, Vidyan. 'Race, Style, and the Soul of Saul Bellow's Prose'. *Essays in Criticism* 16.4 (2016): 488–517.

Reeves, Gareth. 'Songs of the Self: Berryman's Whitman'. *Romanticism* 14.1 (2008): 47–56.

Rio-Jelliffe, Rebecca. *Obscurity's Myriad Components: The Theory and Practice of William Faulkner*. Lewisburg: Bucknell University Press, 2001.

Robinson, David. *Natural Life: Thoreau's Worldly Transcendentalism*. Ithaca: Cornell University Press, 2004.

Rohbach, Emily. *Modernity's Mist: British Romanticism and the Poetics of Anticipation*. Lit Z Series. New York: Fordham University Press, 2016.

Rosenzweig, Saul. *Freud, Jung, and Hall the King-maker: The Historic Expedition to America (1909), with G. Stanley Hall as host and William James as guest*. St. Louis, MS: Hogrefe & Huber, 1992.

Roulston, Robert and Helen H. '*The Great Gatsby*: Fitzgerald's Opulent Synthesis (1925)'. In *Critical Interpretations*. Ed. Morris Dickstein. Pasadena: Salem, 2009, pp. 124–43.

Rovit, Earl. Ed. *Saul Bellow: A Collection of Critical Essays*. Englewood Cliffs, NJ: Prentice Hall, 1975.

Ruppersburg, Hugh M. 'Byron Bunch and Percy Grimm: Strange Twins of *Light in August*'. *The Mississippi Quarterly* 30.3 (1970): 441–3. Special Issue on William Faulkner.

Salomon, Willis. 'Saul Bellow on the Soul: Character and the Spirit of Culture in *Humboldt's Gift* and *Ravelstein*'. *Partial Answers: Journals of Literature and the History of Ideas* 14.1 (2016): 127–40.

Sandy, Mark. Ed. *Romantic Presences in the Twentieth Century*. Farnham: Ashgate, 2012.

Sandy, Mark. *Romanticism, Memory, and Mourning*. Farnham: Ashgate, 2013.

Sattlemeyer, Robert. *Thoreau's Reading: An Intellectual Life with Bibliographical Catalogue*. Princeton: Princeton University Press, 1988.

Scherr, Barry J. 'Lawrence, Keats, and *Tender is the Night*: Loss of Self and "Love Battler" Motifs'. *Recovering Literature: A Journal of Contextualist Criticism* 14 (1986): 7–17.

Schoenwald, R. L. 'F. Scott Fitzgerald as Keats'. *Boston University Studies in English* 3 (1957): 12–21.

Schraepen, Edmond. Ed. *Saul Bellow and his Work*. Brussels: Centrum voor Tall-en Literatuurwetenschap, 1978.

Schulz, Max F. *Radical Sophistication: Studies in Contemporary Jewish-American Novelists*. Athens: Ohio University Press, 1969.

Shakespeare, William. *Hamlet*. Ed. Ann Thompson and Neil Taylor. London: Bloomsbury, 2018.

Shakespeare, William. *Macbeth*. Ed. Kenneth Muir. Arden Shakespeare. London: Routledge, 1988.

Shapiro, Stephen. *The Culture and Commerce of the Early American Novel: Reading the Trans-Atlantic World System*. Chicago: University of Chicago Press, 2008.

Shelley, Percy Bysshe. *Letters from Abroad, Translations, and Fragments*. 2 vols. Ed. Mary Shelley. London: Moxon, 1840.

Shelley, Percy Bysshe. *Shelley: The Poetic Works*. Philadelphia: Grissy and Markley, 1853.

Shelley, Percy Bysshe. *Shelley's Poetry and Prose*. Ed. Donald H. Reiman and Neil Fraistat. 1977; New York: Norton, 2002.

Simpson, David. *Wordsworth, Commodification and Social Concern*. Cambridge: Cambridge University Press, 2009.

Slabey, Robert M. 'The "Romanticism" of *The Sound and the Fury*'. *The Mississippi Quarterly* 16.3 (1963): 146–59.

Smith, Lorrie. '"Walking" from England to America: Re-Viewing Thoreau's Romanticism'. *The New England Quarterly* 58 (1985): 221–41.

Sowder, William J. *Existential-Phenomenological Readings of Faulkner*. Conway: UCA, 1991.

Steinman, Lisa M. 'Introduction to Romanticism and Contemporary Poetry and Poetics'. July 2003. <https://romantic-circles.org/praxis/poetics/steinman/steinman.html> (date of access: 20 May 2020).

Steinman, Lisa M. *Masters of Repetition: Poetry, Culture, and Work in Thomson, Wordsworth, Shelley, and Emerson*. New York: St. Martin's, 1998.

Stern, Milton R. *The Golden Moment: The Novels of F. Scott Fitzgerald*. 1970; Chicago: University of Illinois Press, 1971.

Stevens, Wallace. *Letters of Wallace Stevens*. Ed. Holly Stevens. Foreword Richard Howard. 1966; Berkeley: University of California Press, 1989.

Stevens, Wallace. *The Necessary Angel: Essays on Reality and Imagination.* New York: Knopf, 1951.

Stevens, Wallace. *Wallace Stevens: Collected Poems.* London: Faber, 1984.

Sukkbir, Singh. *The Survivor in Contemporary American Fiction: Saul Bellow, Bernard Malamud, John Updike, and Kurt Vonnegut.* Delhi: BR Publishing, 1991.

Swann, Charles. 'A Fitzgerald Debt to Keats? From "Isabella" into *Tender is the Night*'. *Notes and Queries* 37 (1990): 437–8.

Tanner, Tony. 'Notes for a Comparison between American and European Romanticism'. *Journal of American Studies* 2.1 (1968): 83–103.

Tanner, Tony. *Saul Bellow.* London and Edinburgh: Boyd, 1965.

Tanner, Tony. *Scenes of Nature, Signs of Men.* Cambridge: Cambridge University Press, 1987.

Terry, Jennifer. *Shuttles in the Rocking Loom: Mapping the Black Diaspora in African American and Caribbean Fiction.* Liverpool: Liverpool University Press, 2013.

Thoreau, Henry David. *Autumnal Tints.* Bedford, MA: Applewood, 1996.

Thoreau, Henry David. *Notes on Birds of New England.* Ed. Francis H. Allen. Illus. John James Audubon. New York: Dover, 2019.

Thoreau, Henry David. *The Portable Thoreau.* Ed. Carl Bode. 1965; Harmondsworth: Viking-Penguin, 1987.

Thoreau, Henry David. *The Writings of Henry D. Thoreau: Journal.* 8 vols. Gen. ed. Robert Sattlemeyer. Princeton: Princeton University Press, 1981–2002.

Tovey, Paige. *The Transatlantic Eco-Romanticism of Gary Snyder.* London: Palgrave Macmillan, 2013.

Towner, Theresa M. *The Cambridge Introduction to William Faulkner.* Cambridge: Cambridge University Press, 2008.

Tuttleton, James W. *Vital Signs: Essays on American Literature and Criticism.* Chicago: Dee, 1996.

Tuttleton, James W. 'Vitality and Vampirism in *Tender is the Night*'. In *Critical Essays on F. Scott Fitzgerald's 'Tender is the Night'.* Ed. Milton R. Stern. Boston: Hall, 1986, pp. 238–46.

Ulmer, William A. *Shelleyan Eros: The Rhetoric of Romantic Love.* Princeton: Princeton University Press, 1990.

Updike, John. 'Dreamy Wilderness: Unmastered Women in Colonial Virginia'. Review of Toni Morrison. *A Mercy. The New Yorker.* 3 November 2008.

Urgo, Joseph R. and Ann J. Abadie. Eds. *Faulkner's Inheritance: Faulkner and Yoknapatawpha.* Jackson: University Press of Mississippi, 2005.

Vendler, Helen. *On Extended Wings: Wallace Stevens' Longer Poems.* Cambridge, MA: Harvard University Press, 1969.

Wadlington, Warwick. *Reading Faulknerian Tragedy*. Ithaca: Cornell University Press, 1987.

Walcott, Derek. *Derek Walcott: Collected Poems, 1948–1984*. New York: Farrar, 1986.

Wallace, Kathleen R. and Karla Armbruster. 'The Novels of Toni Morrison: "Wild Wilderness Where There Was None"'. In *Beyond Nature Writing: Expanding the Boundaries of Ecocriticism*. Ed. Kathleen R. Wallace and Karla Armbruster. Charlottesville: University of Virginia Press, 2001, pp. 211–30.

Weinstein, Arnold. *Nobody's Home: Speech, Self, and Place in American Fiction: From Hawthorne to DeLillo*. Oxford: Oxford University Press, 1993.

Whitman, Walt. *Leaves of Grass*. 1855. Ed. and intro. Malcolm Cowley. 1976; Harmondsworth: Penguin, 1985.

Whitman, Walt. *Walt Whitman: The Complete Poems*. Ed. Francis Murphy. Harmondsworth: Penguin, 1996.

Wilson, Jonathan. *On Bellow's Planet: Readings from the Dark Side*. London: Fairleigh Dickinson University Press, 1985.

Wolfson, Susan. *Romantic Shades and Shadows*. Baltimore: Johns Hopkins University Press, 2018.

Woodland, Malcolm. *Wallace Stevens and the Apocalyptic Mode*. Iowa City: University of Iowa Press, 2009.

Wootton, Sarah. Ed. *Romanticism* 22.3 (2016). Special Issue on 'Light in Literature'.

Wordsworth, William. *The Excursion*. Ed. Sally Bushell, James A. Butler and Michael C. Jaye. Ithaca: Cornell University Press, 2007.

Wordsworth, William. *The Prelude: The Four Texts (1795, 1799, 1805, 1850)*. Ed. Jonathan Wordsworth. Harmondsworth: Penguin, 1995.

Wordsworth, William. *The Prelude: A Parallel Text*. Ed. James C. Maxwell. Harmondsworth: Penguin, 1982.

Wordsworth, William. *The Waggoner*. In *Poetical Works of William Wordsworth*. Vol. 1. London: Moxon, 1886.

Wordsworth, William. *The White Doe of Rylstone*. In *The Poems of William Wordsworth: Collected Readings from the Cornell Edition*. Ed. Jared Curtis. Grasmere: Humanities-Ebooks, 2011.

Wordsworth, William. *William Wordsworth: The Major Works*. Ed. Stephen Gill. Oxford: Oxford University Press, 2008.

Wordsworth, William and Samuel Taylor Coleridge. *Lyrical Ballads*. 1798. Ed. R. L. Brett and A. R. Jones. London: Methuen, 1963.

Yeats. W. B. *W. B. Yeats: The Major Works*. Ed. Edward Larrissy. 1997; Oxford: Oxford University Press, 2001.

Zweig, Paul. *Walt Whitman: The Making of the Poet*. New York: Basic, 1984.

Index

Printed and bound by CPI Group (UK) Ltd, Croydon, CR0 4YY

28/01/2025

01827094-0002